HEAD
GAMES

THE GRAPHIC NOVEL

HEAD GAMES

THE GRAPHIC NOVEL

CRAIG McDONALD AND KEVIN SINGLES

with Les McClaine

:01

First Second
New York

Travels with Hector

By Craig McDonald

Welcome aboard. In the following pages, you'll be riding shotgun in a 'fifty-seven ragtop Bel Air with Hector Lassiter, pulp novelist, screenwriter, and adventurer.

Hector is also known as "the man who lives what he writes and writes what he lives."

He's the protagonist of a finite arc of ten novels—the last, *Three Chords & The Truth*, a *Head Games* sequel and circle-closer, appeared in 2016—as well as a collection of short stories.

With this volume, he's at last made the leap to graphic novels.

If any label best describes the Hector Lassiter series, it's probably "historical thrillers"—the books combine myth and history.

The Lassiter novels spin around secret histories and unexplored or underexplored aspects of real events. They're set in real places, and use not just history to drive their plots, but also incorporate real people.

As a career journalist, I'm often frustrated by the impossibility of nailing down people or events definitively. Read five biographies of the same man, say, of Ernest Hemingway, and you'll feel like you've read about five different people.

So I've concluded defining fact as it relates to history is as elusive a goal as stroking smoke or tapping a bullet in flight.

History, it's been said, is a lie agreed to. But maybe in fiction we can find if not fact, something bordering on truth. With that possibility in mind, I explore what I can make of accepted history through the eyes of one man.

The "hero" of this series, your guide through these books, is Hector Mason Lassiter, a shades-of-gray guy who is a charmer, a rogue, a bit of a rake, and, himself, a crime novelist.

Some others in the novels say he bears a passing resemblance to the actor William Holden. Hector smokes and drinks and eats red meat. He lives his life on a large canvas. He's wily, but often impulsive; he's honorable, but mercurial.

He often doesn't understand his own drives. That is to say, he's a man. He's a man's man and a lady's man. He's a romantic, but mostly unlucky in love. Yet his life's largely shaped by the women passing through it.

Hec was born in Galveston, Texas, on January 1, 1900. He came in with the twentieth century, and it was my aim that his arc of novels span that century—essentially, through each successive novel, giving us a kind of under-history or secret history of the twentieth century.

Tall and wise beyond his years, as a boy Hector lied about his age and enlisted in the military. He accompanied Black Jack Pershing in his hunt down into Mexico to chase the Mexican revolutionary Pancho Villa who attacked and murdered many American civilians in the town of Columbus, New Mexico. Villa's was the first and only successful terrorist assault on the United States homeland prior to the events of September 11, 2001.

Much of that part of Hector's life figures into *Head Games*: you'll catch glimpses in the pages that follow.

Head Games, set largely in 1957, was the first published Hector Lassiter novel and a finalist for the Edgar and Anthony awards, along with similar honors overseas. Its follow-up in original publication sequence, *Toros & Torsos*, opens in 1935 and features Ernest Hemingway as a kind of sidekick. Subsequent books about Hector similarly hopscotched back and forth through the decades.

The recent Betimes Books releases of the Hector Lassiter series presents the novels in roughly chronological order—at least in terms of where each story starts as it opens.

The Lassiter novels were written back to back, and the series was mostly shaped and in place before *Head Games* was officially published as a novel in 2007. It's very unusual in that sense: a series of discrete novels that are tightly linked and when taken together stand as a single, larger story.

My approach as a writer has always been to try and share the movie I see in my head.

It's simply stunning to me how artists Kevin Singles and Les McClaine perfectly capture the images that were running through my mind more than a decade ago when I was trying to write about this wild road trip across Lost America.

Welcome to the world of Hector Lassiter.

HEAD GAMES

THE GRAPHIC NOVEL

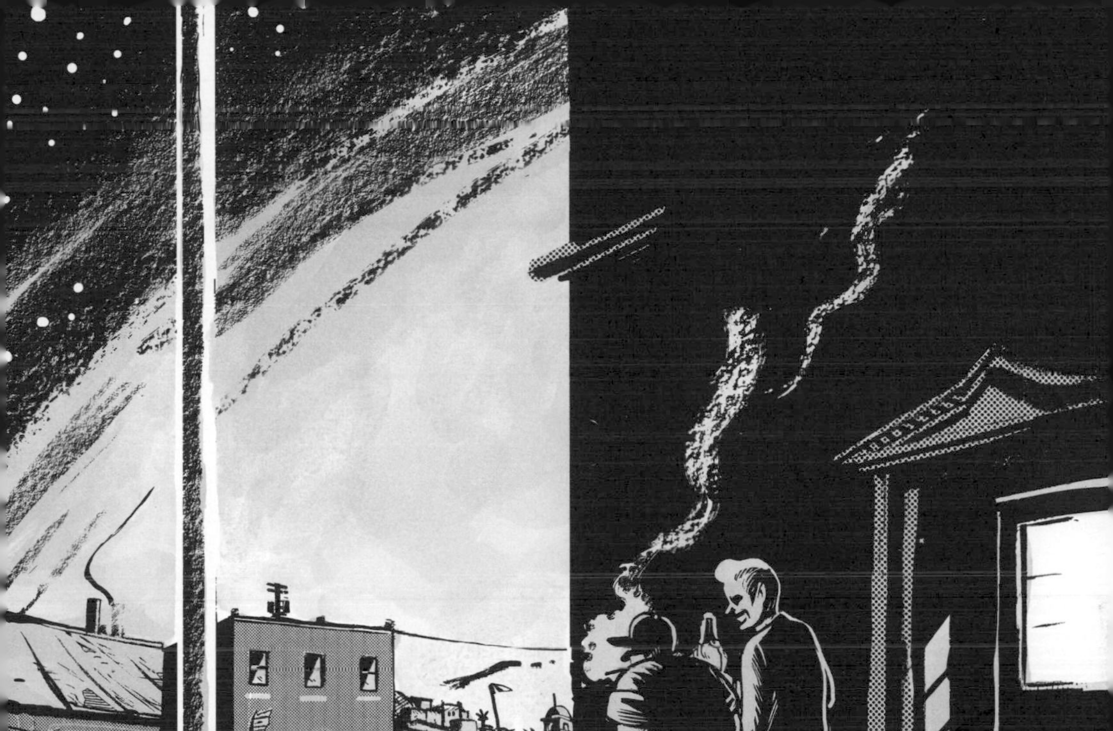

Part I: 1957—The Land of Hope and Dreams

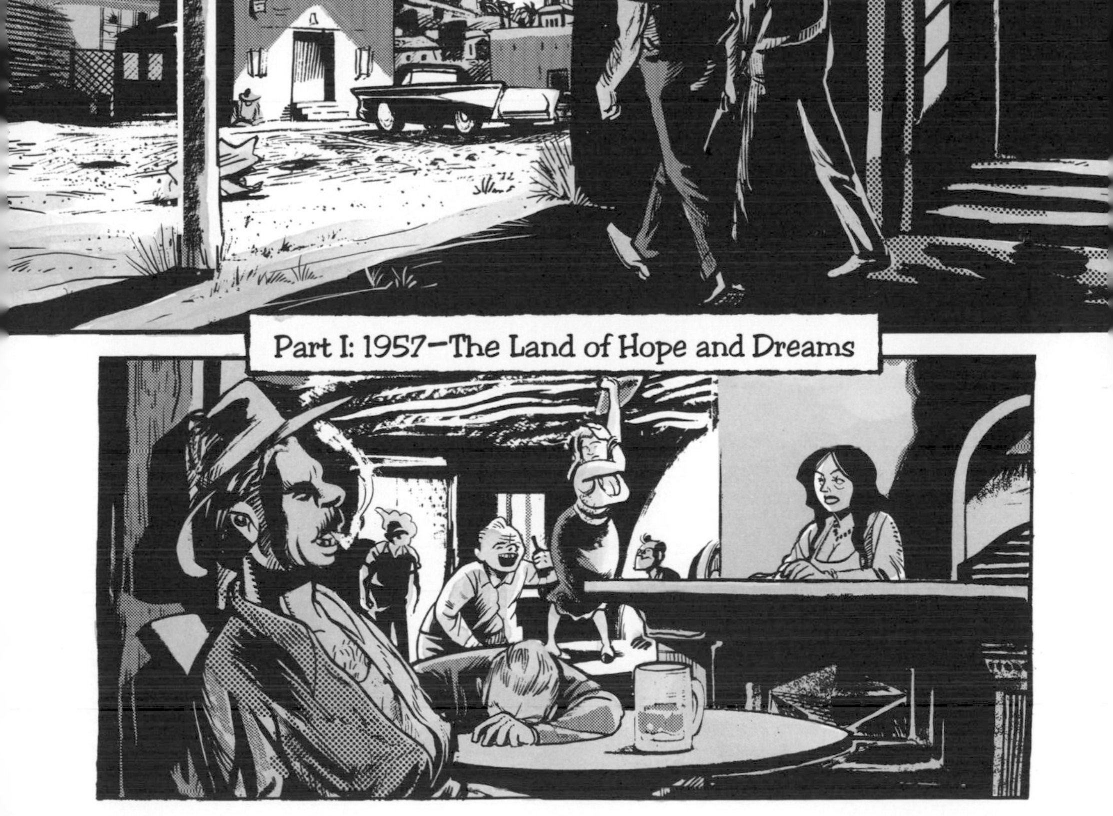

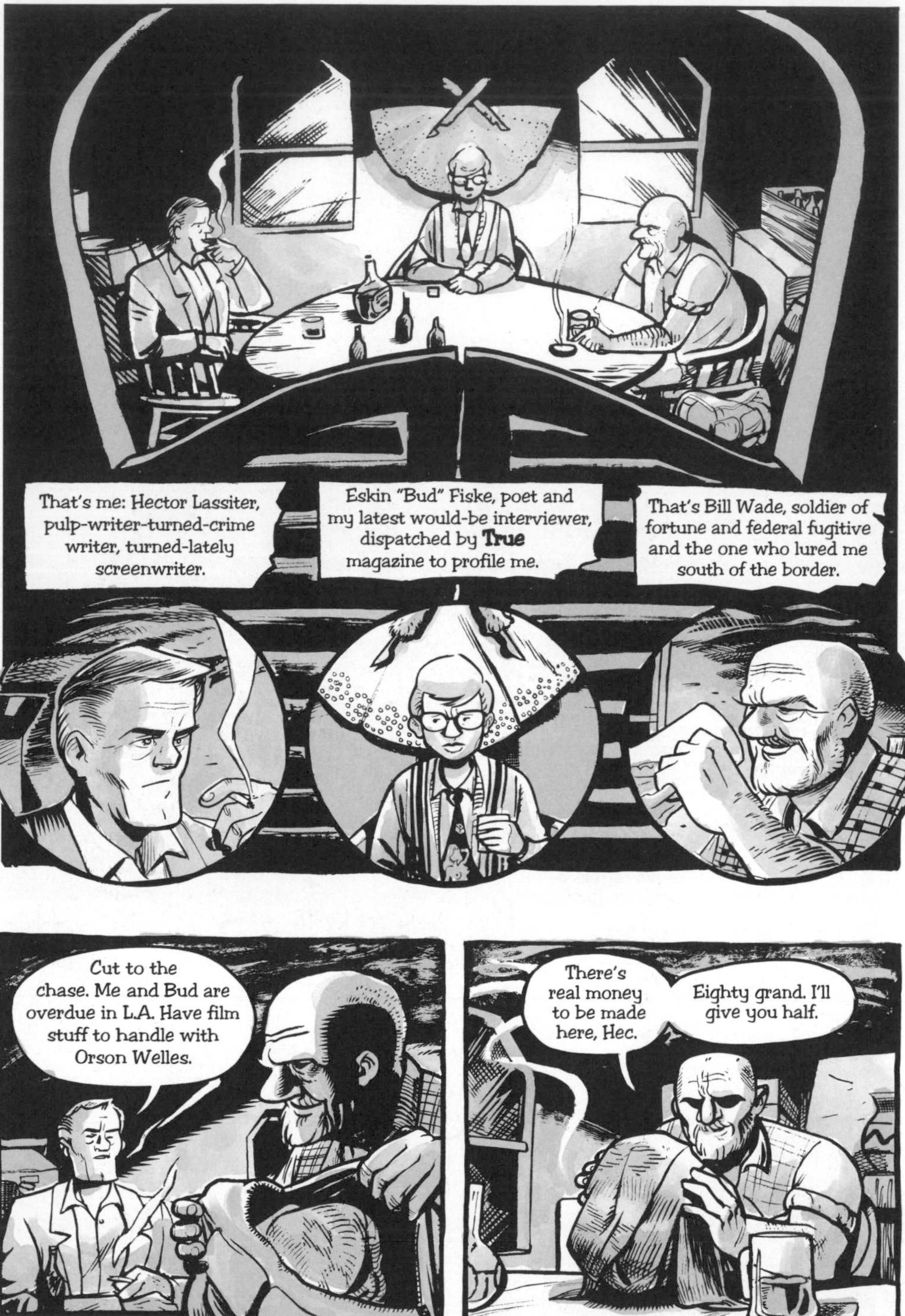
That's me: Hector Lassiter, pulp-writer-turned-crime writer, turned-lately screenwriter.
Eskin "Bud" Fiske, poet and my latest would-be interviewer, dispatched by True magazine to profile me.
That's Bill Wade, soldier of fortune and federal fugitive and the one who lured me south of the border.
Cut to the chase. Me and Bud are overdue in L.A. Have film stuff to handle with Orson Welles.
There's real money to be made here, Hec.
Eighty grand. I'll give you half.

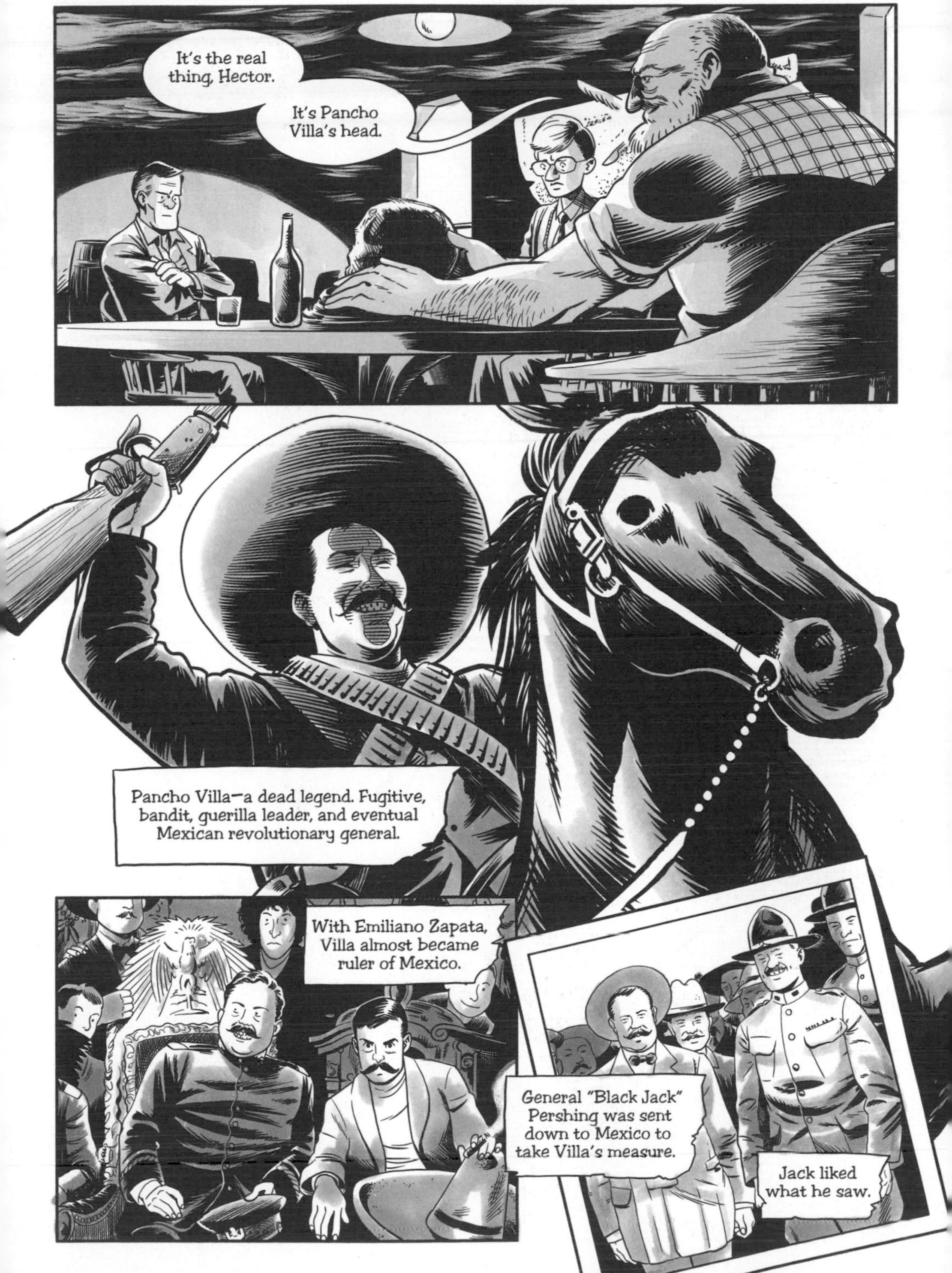
It's the real thing, Hector.
It's Pancho Villa's head.
Pancho Villa—a dead legend. Fugitive, bandit, guerilla leader, and eventual Mexican revolutionary general.
With Emiliano Zapata, Villa almost became ruler of Mexico.
General "Black Jack" Pershing was sent down to Mexico to take Villa's measure.
Jack liked what he saw.

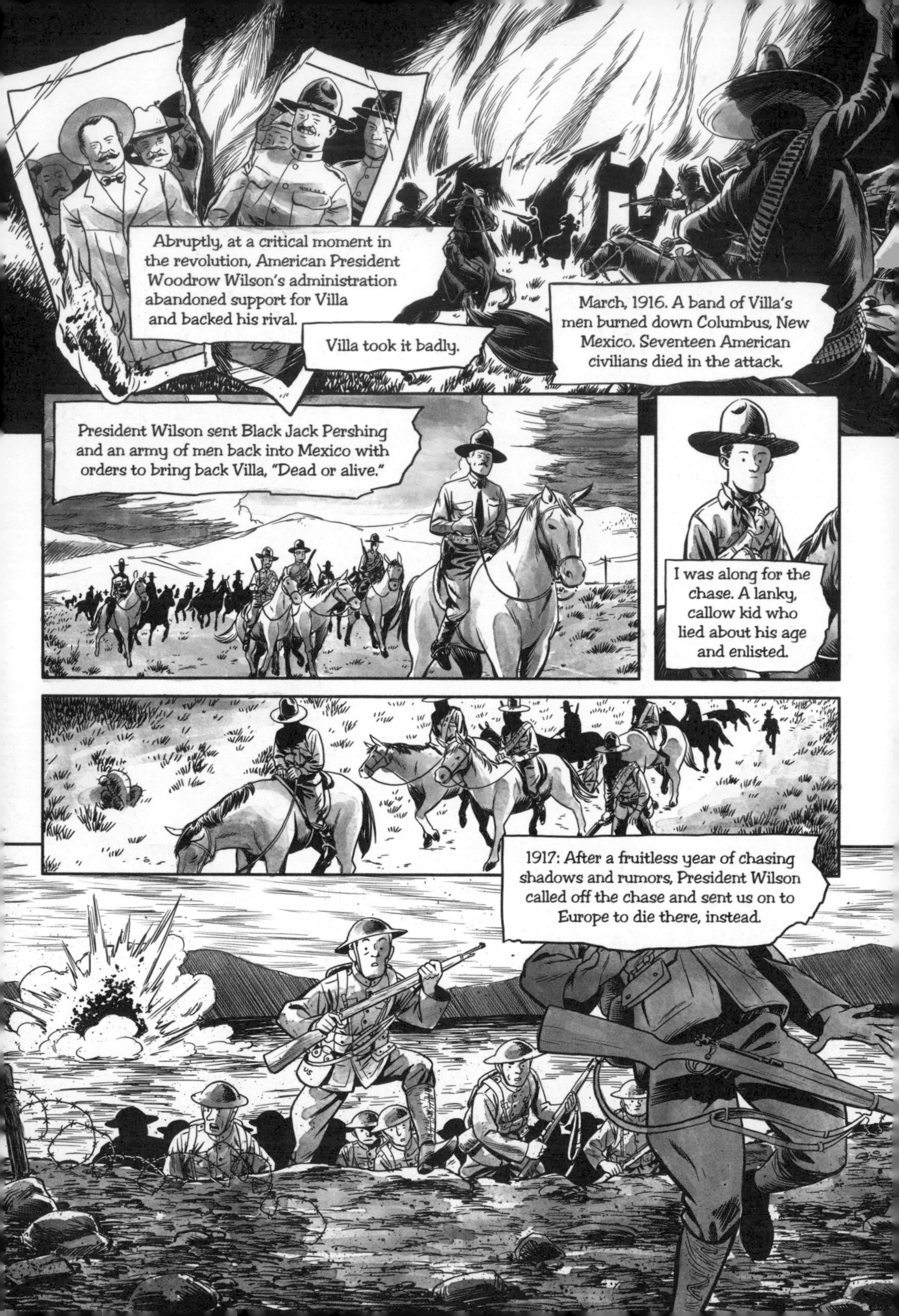
Abruptly, at a critical moment in the revolution, American President Woodrow Wilson's administration abandoned support for Villa and backed his rival.
Villa took it badly.
March, 1916. A band of Villa's men burned down Columbus, New Mexico. Seventeen American civilians died in the attack.
President Wilson sent Black Jack Pershing and an army of men back into Mexico with orders to bring back Villa, "Dead or alive."
I was along for the chase. A lanky, callow kid who lied about his age and enlisted.
1917: After a fruitless year of chasing shadows and rumors, President Wilson called off the chase and sent us on to Europe to die there, instead.

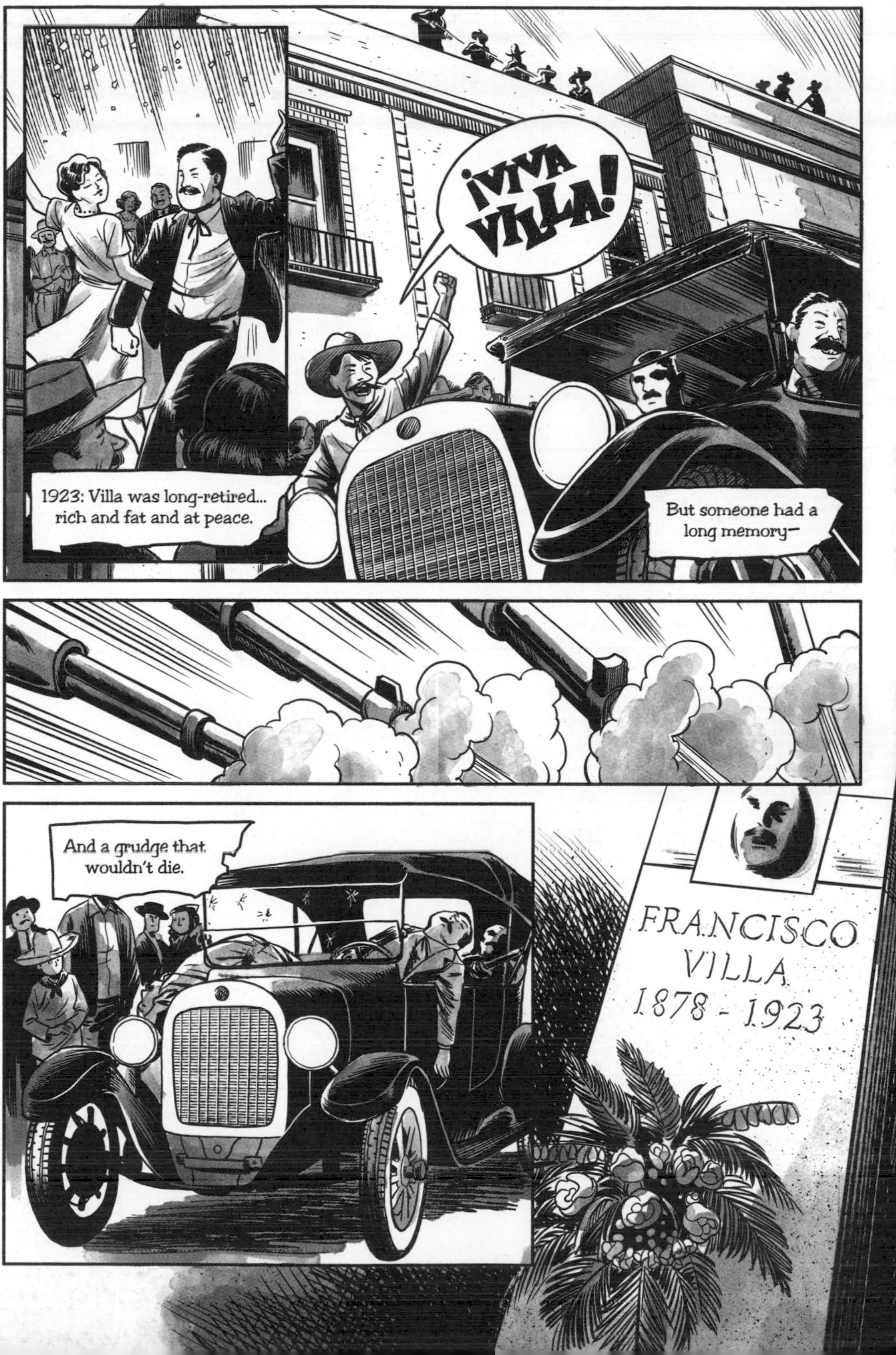

1923: Villa was long-retired... rich and fat and at peace.
¡VIVA VILLA!
But someone had a long memory–
And a grudge that wouldn't die.
FRANCISCO VILLA 1878 - 1923

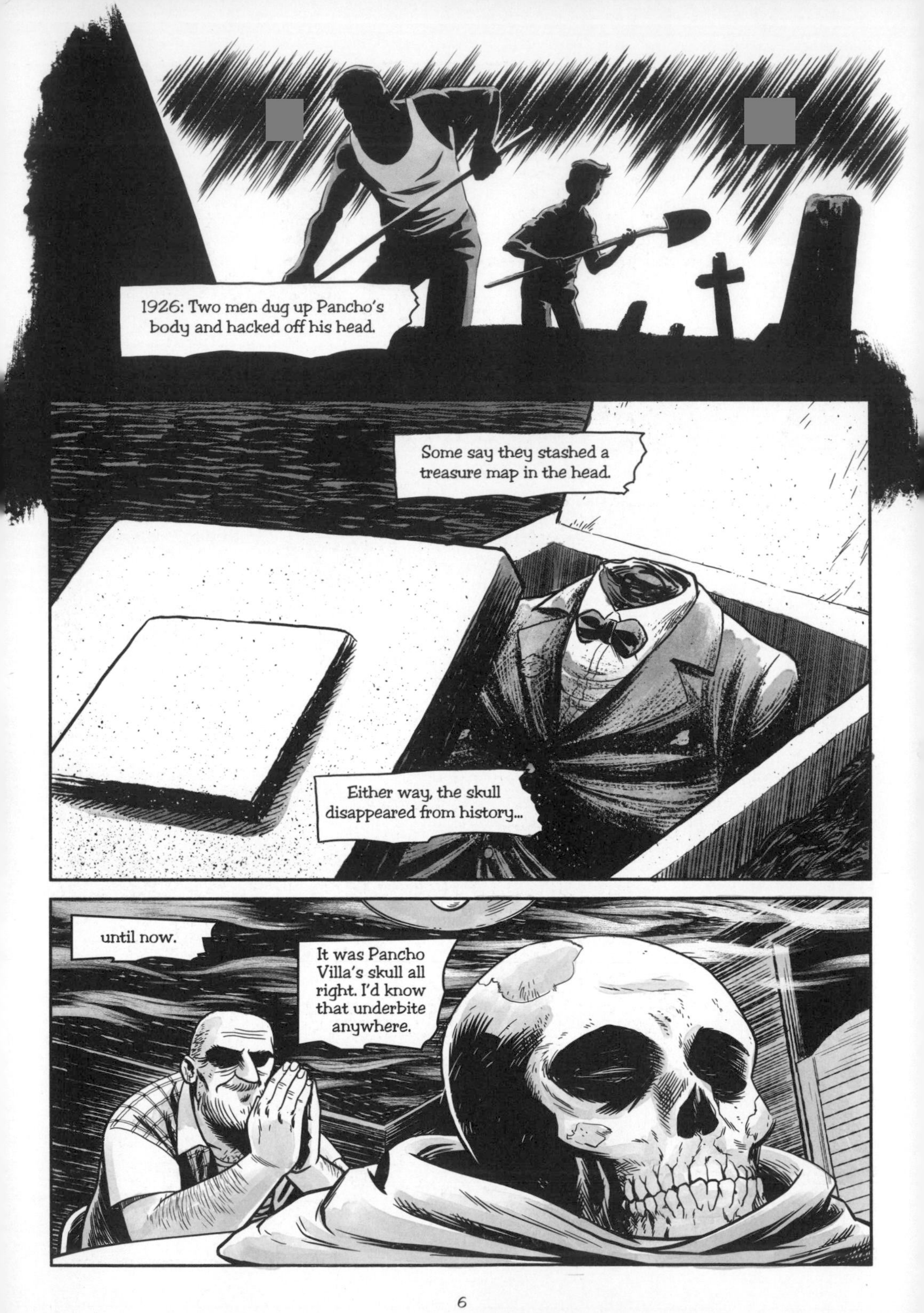
1926: Two men dug up Pancho's body and hacked off his head.
Some say they stashed a treasure map in the head.
Either way, the skull disappeared from history...
until now.
It was Pancho Villa's skull all right. I'd know that underbite anywhere.

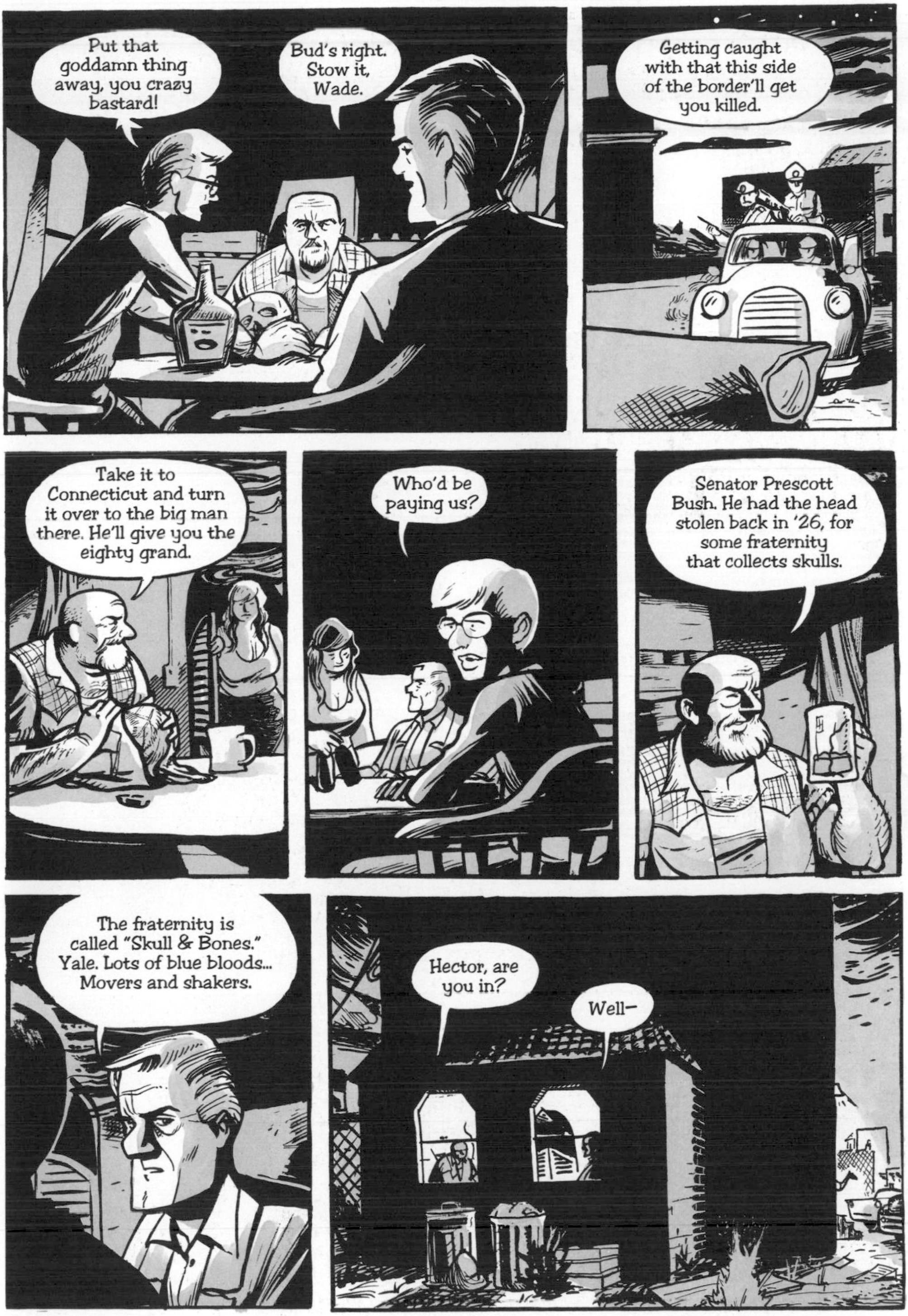
Put that goddamn thing away, you crazy bastard!
Bud's right. Stow it, Wade.
Getting caught with that this side of the border'll get you killed.
Take it to Connecticut and turn it over to the big man there. He'll give you the eighty grand.
Who'd be paying us?
Senator Prescott Bush. He had the head stolen back in '26, for some fraternity that collects skulls.
The fraternity is called "Skull & Bones." Yale. Lots of blue bloods... Movers and shakers.
Hector, are you in?
Well-

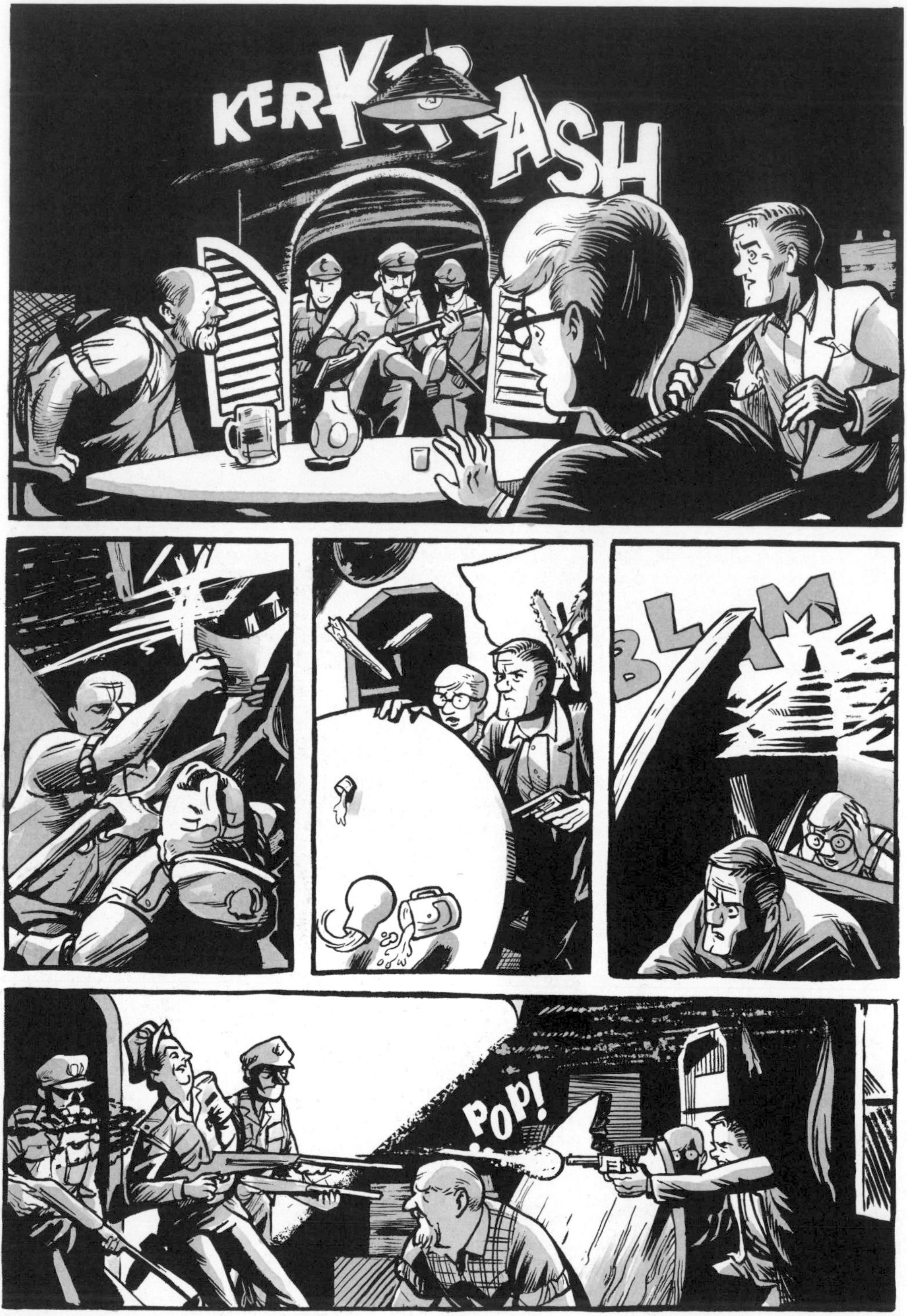
KER-KRASH
BLAM
POP!

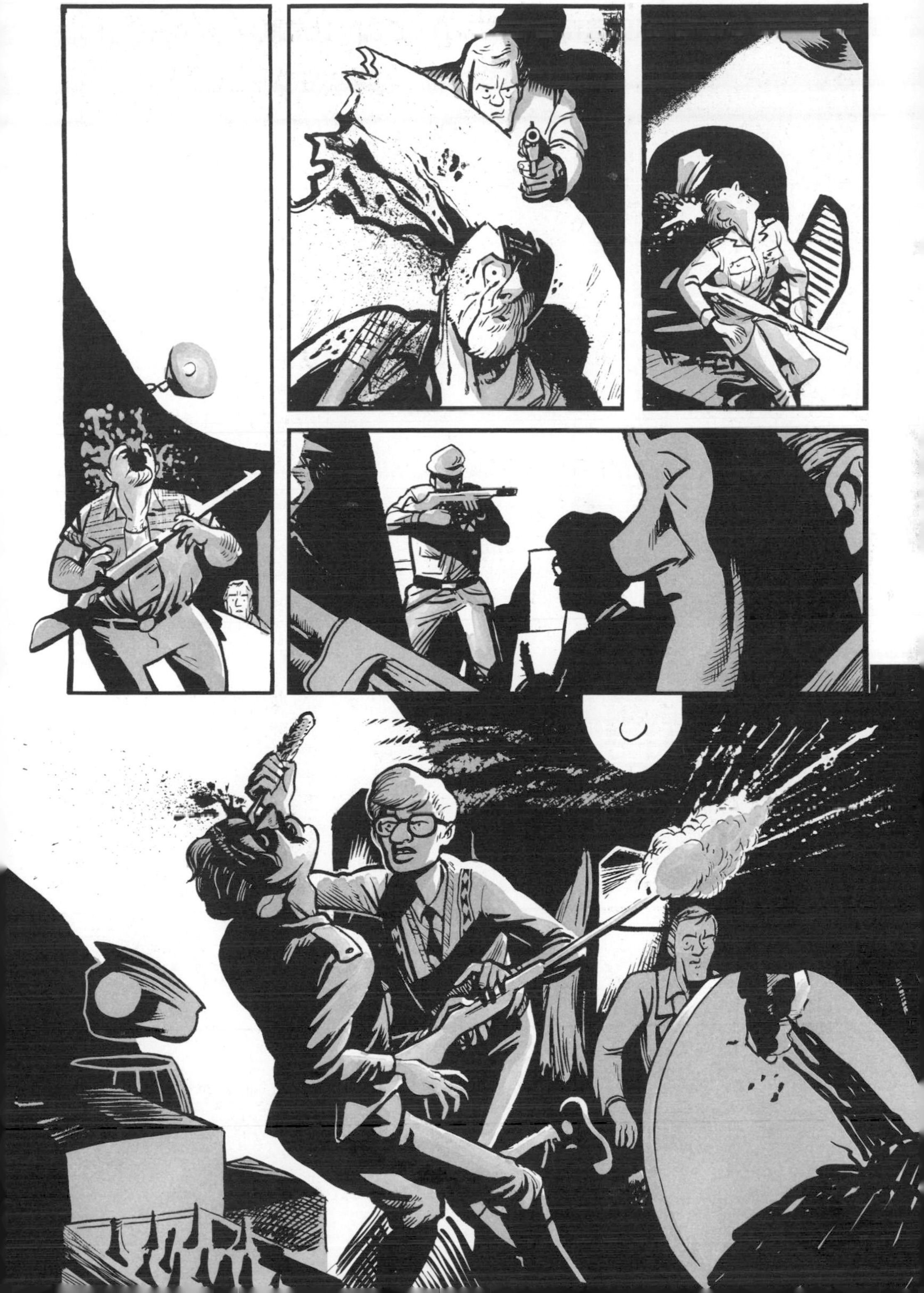

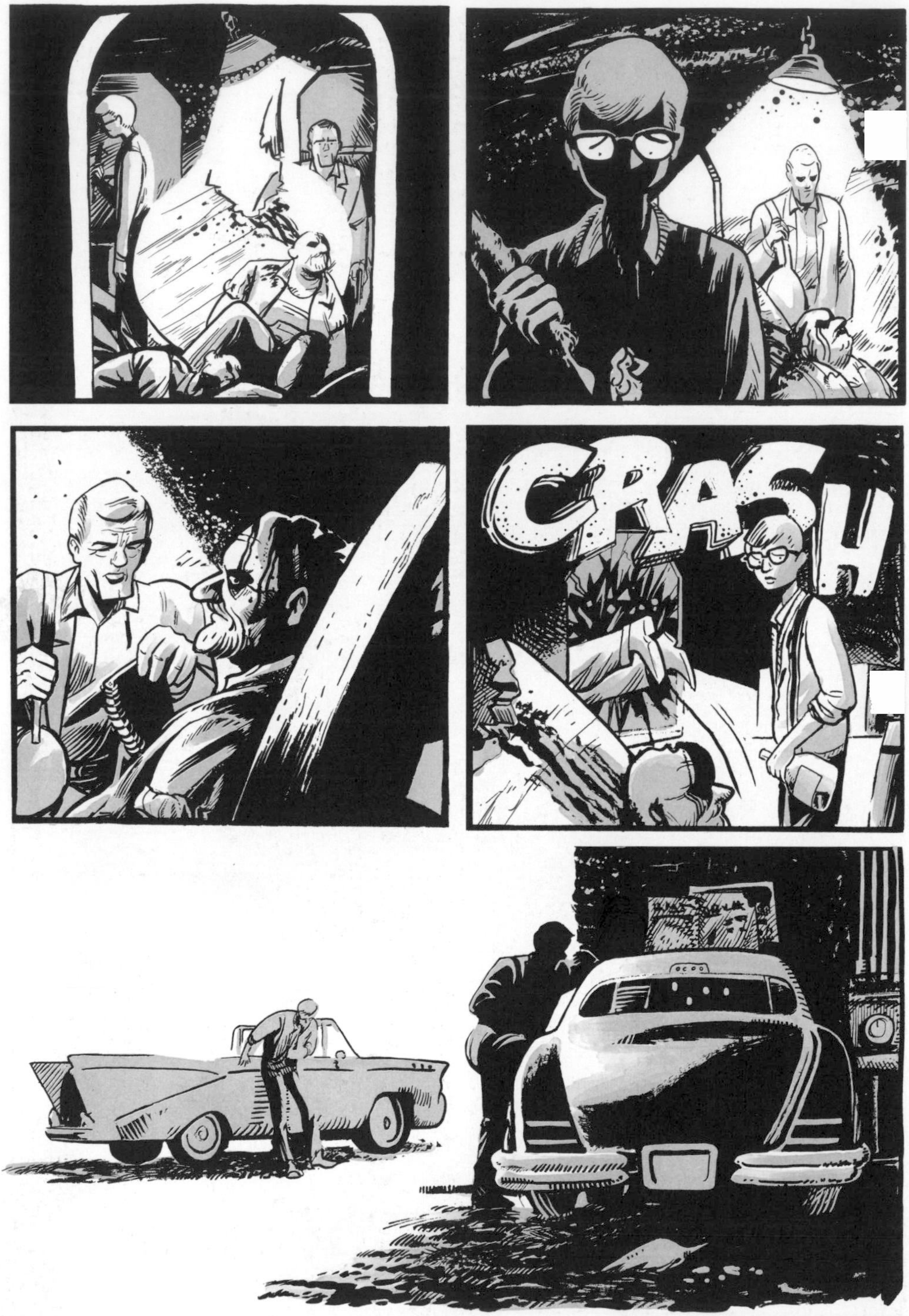
CRASH

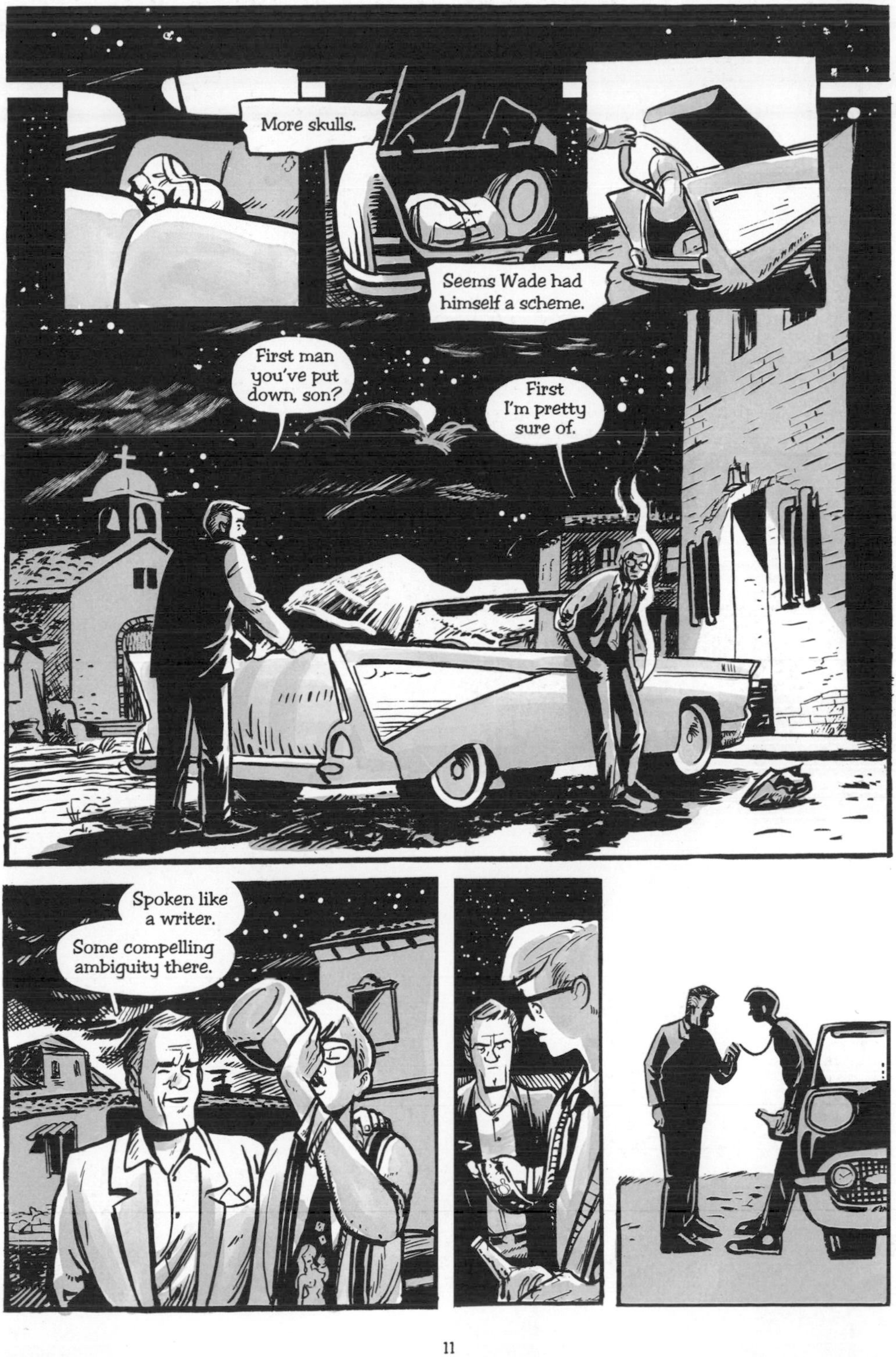
More skulls.
Seems Wade had himself a scheme.
First man you've put down, son?
First I'm pretty sure of.
Spoken like a writer.
Some compelling ambiguity there.

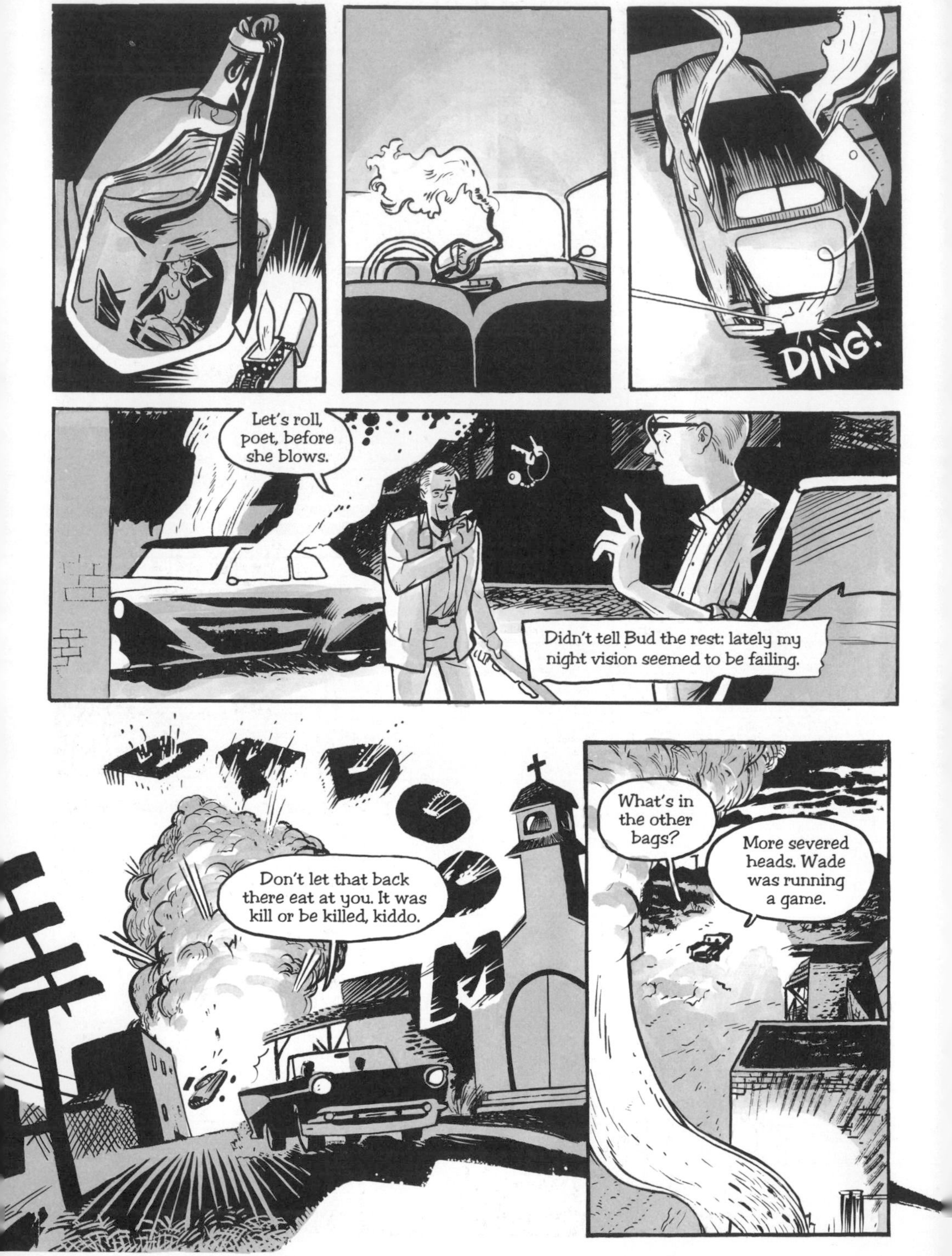
DING!
Let's roll, poet, before she blows.
Didn't tell Bud the rest: lately my night vision seemed to be failing.
Don't let that back there eat at you. It was kill or be killed, kiddo.
What's in the other bags?
More severed heads. Wade was running a game.

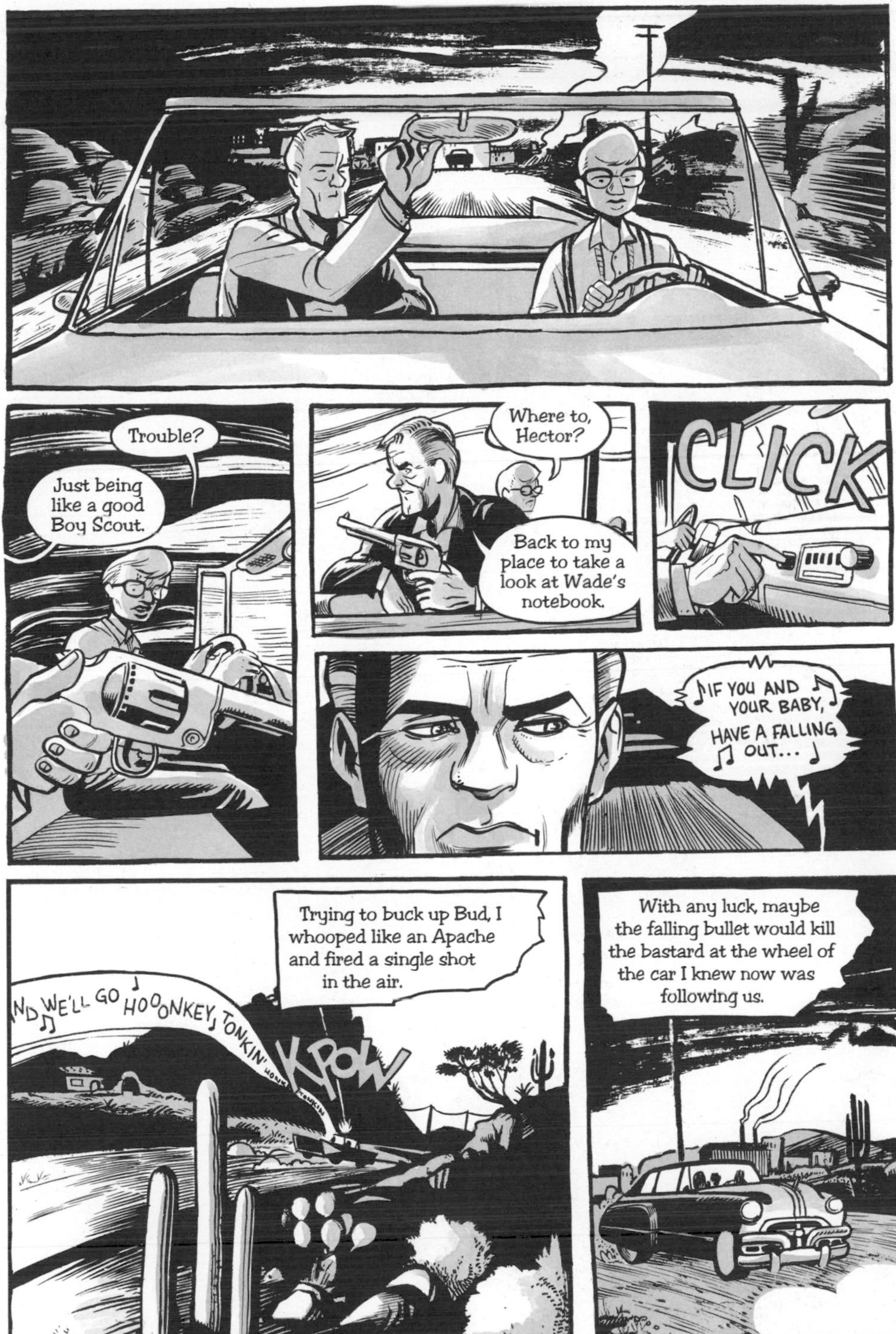
Trouble?
Just being like a good Boy Scout.
Where to, Hector?
Back to my place to take a look at Wade's notebook.
CLICK
IF YOU AND YOUR BABY, HAVE A FALLING OUT...
Trying to buck up Bud, I whooped like an Apache and fired a single shot in the air.
ND WE'LL GO HOOONKEY, TONKIN'
KPOW
With any luck, maybe the falling bullet would kill the bastard at the wheel of the car I knew now was following us.

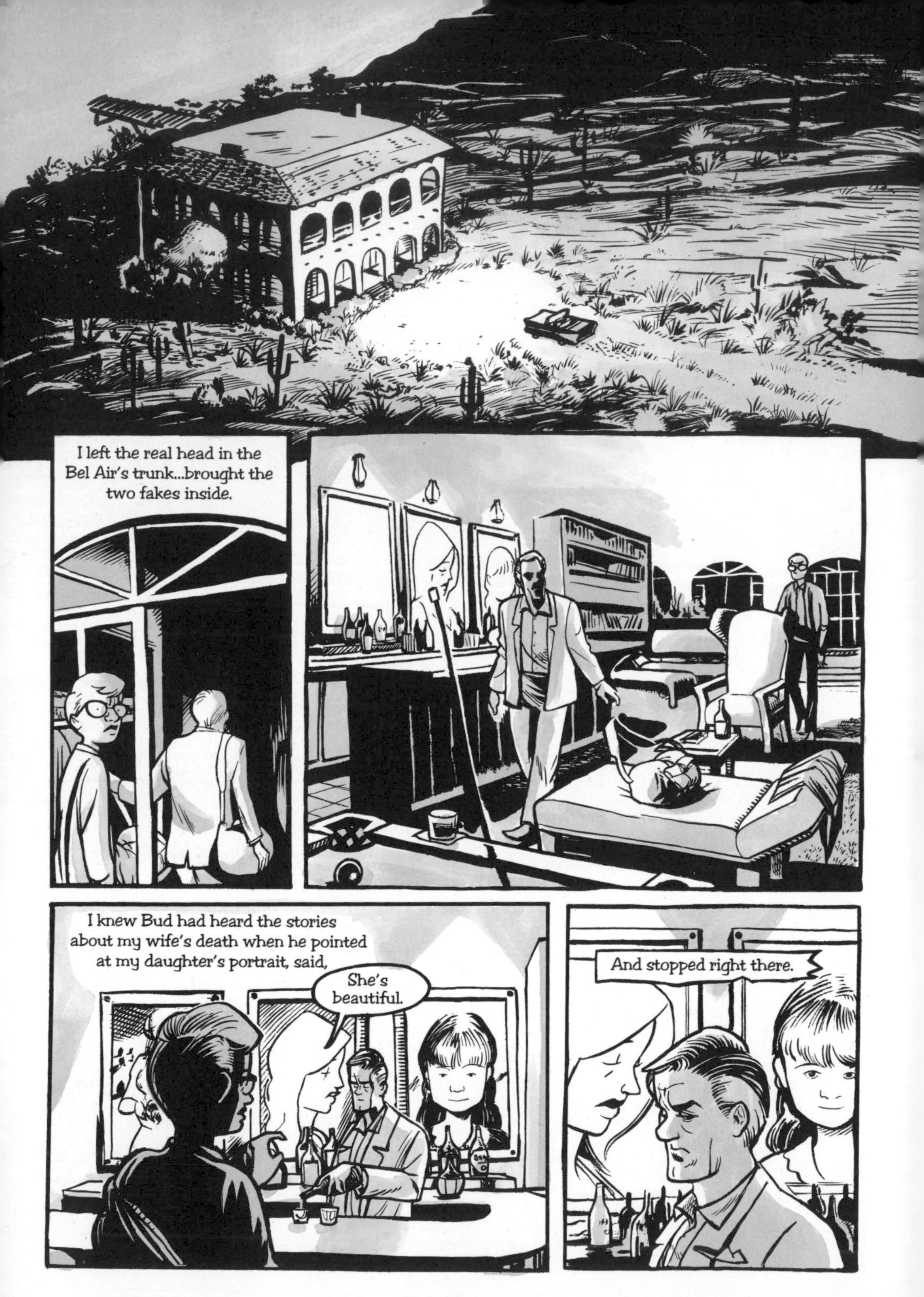

I left the real head in the Bel Air's trunk...brought the two fakes inside.
I knew Bud had heard the stories about my wife's death when he pointed at my daughter's portrait, said,
She's beautiful.
And stopped right there.

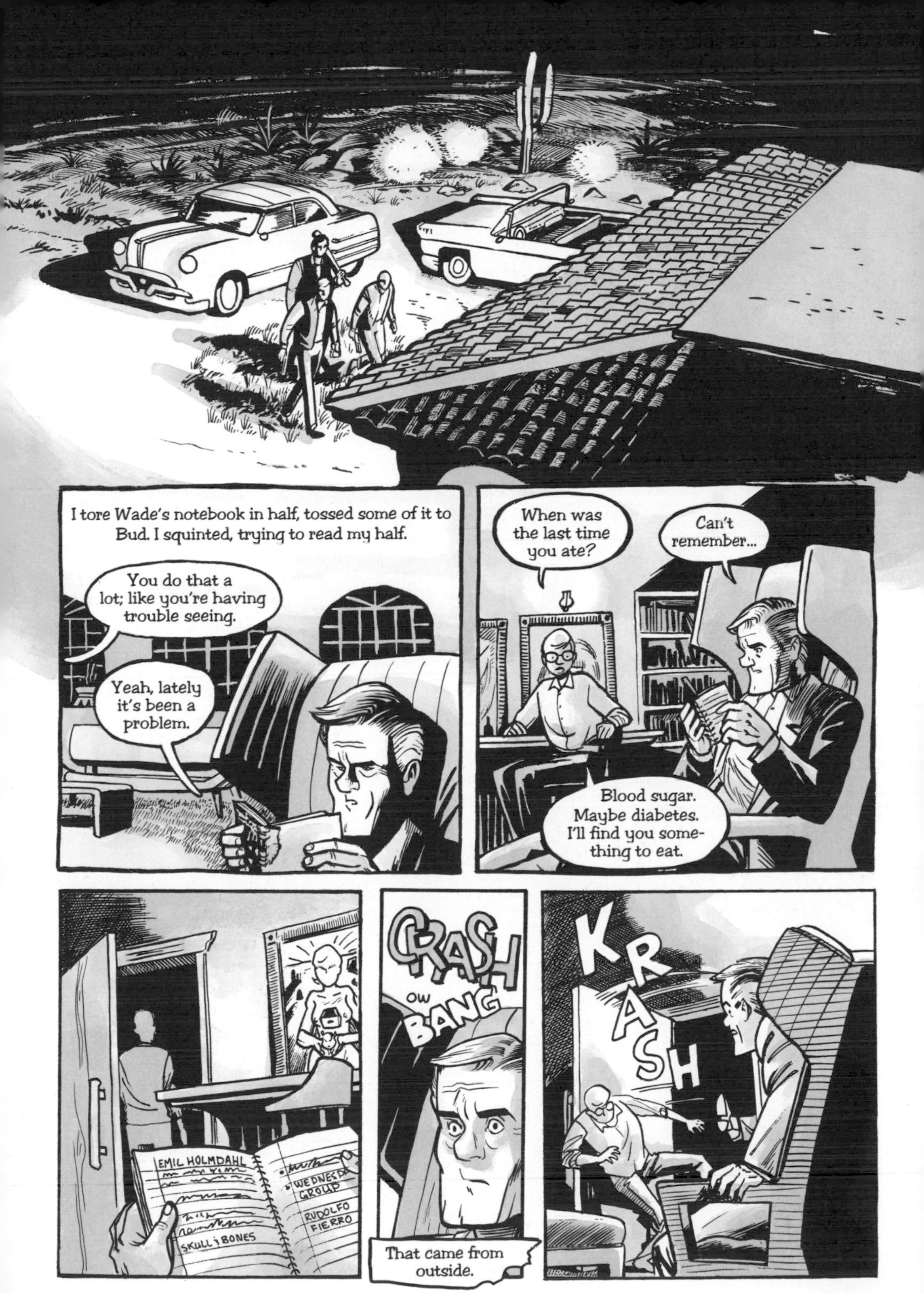
I tore Wade's notebook in half, tossed some of it to Bud. I squinted, trying to read my half.
You do that a lot; like you're having trouble seeing.
Yeah, lately it's been a problem.
When was the last time you ate?
Can't remember...
Blood sugar. Maybe diabetes. I'll find you something to eat.
EMIL HOLMDAHL
WEDNESDAY GROUP
RUDOLFO FIERRO
SKULL & BONES
CRASH
OW
BANG
That came from outside.
KRASH

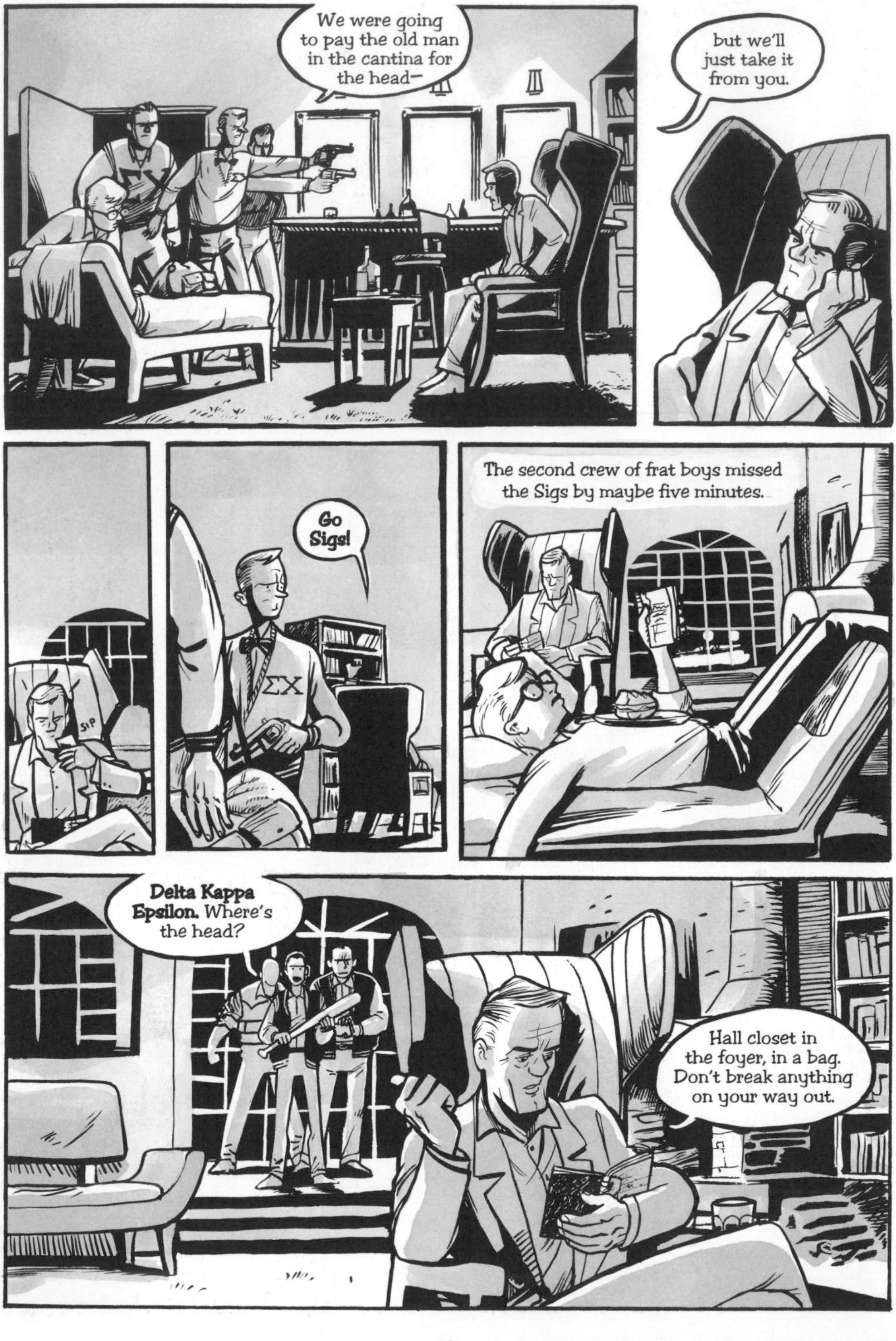
We were going to pay the old man in the cantina for the head—
but we'll just take it from you.
Go Sigs!
SIP
The second crew of frat boys missed the Sigs by maybe five minutes.
Delta Kappa Epsilon. Where's the head?
Hall closet in the foyer, in a bag. Don't break anything on your way out.

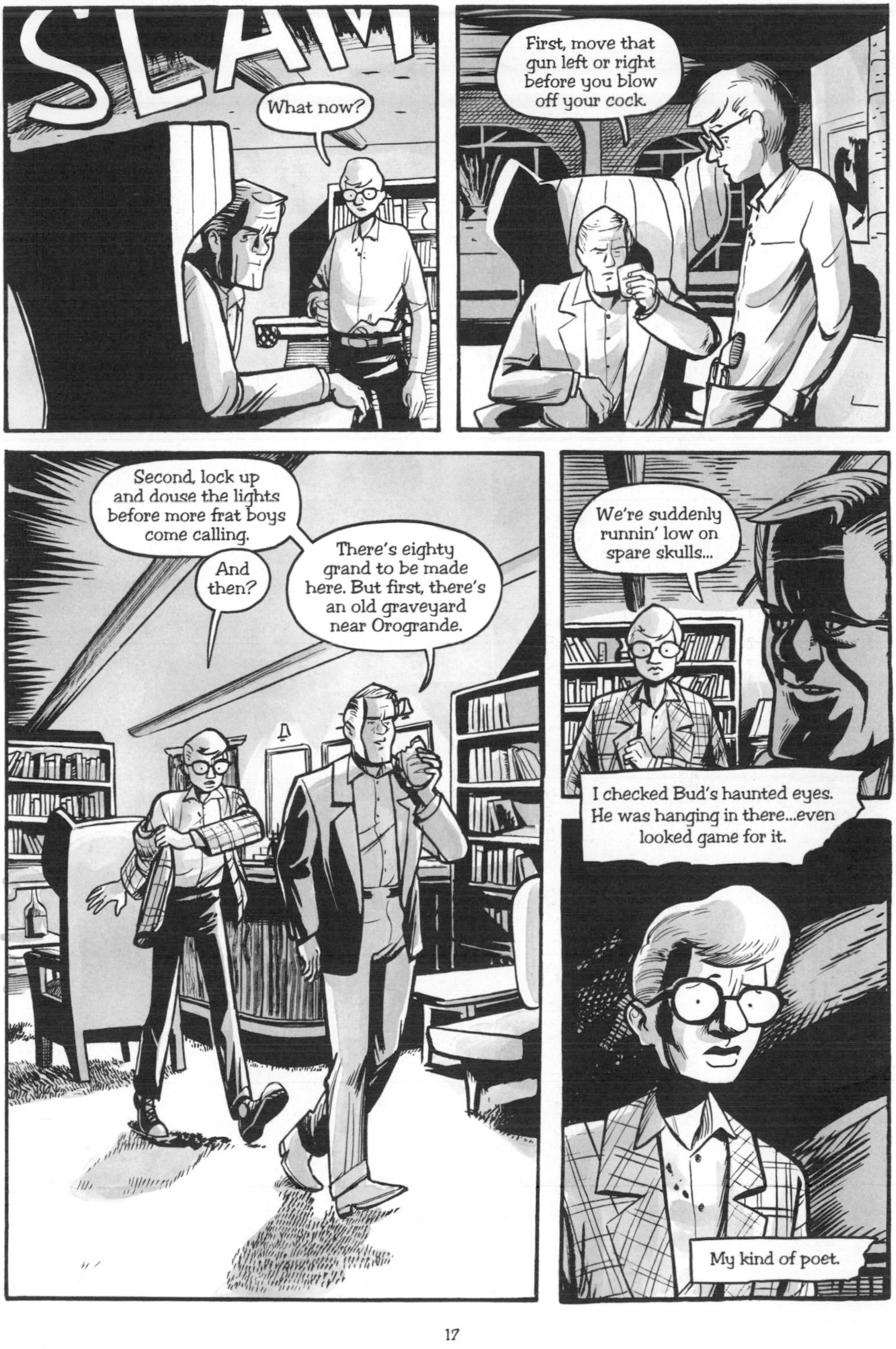
SLAM
What now?
First, move that gun left or right before you blow off your cock.
Second, lock up and douse the lights before more frat boys come calling.
And then?
There's eighty grand to be made here. But first, there's an old graveyard near Orogrande.
We're suddenly runnin' low on spare skulls...
I checked Bud's haunted eyes. He was hanging in there...even looked game for it.
My kind of poet.

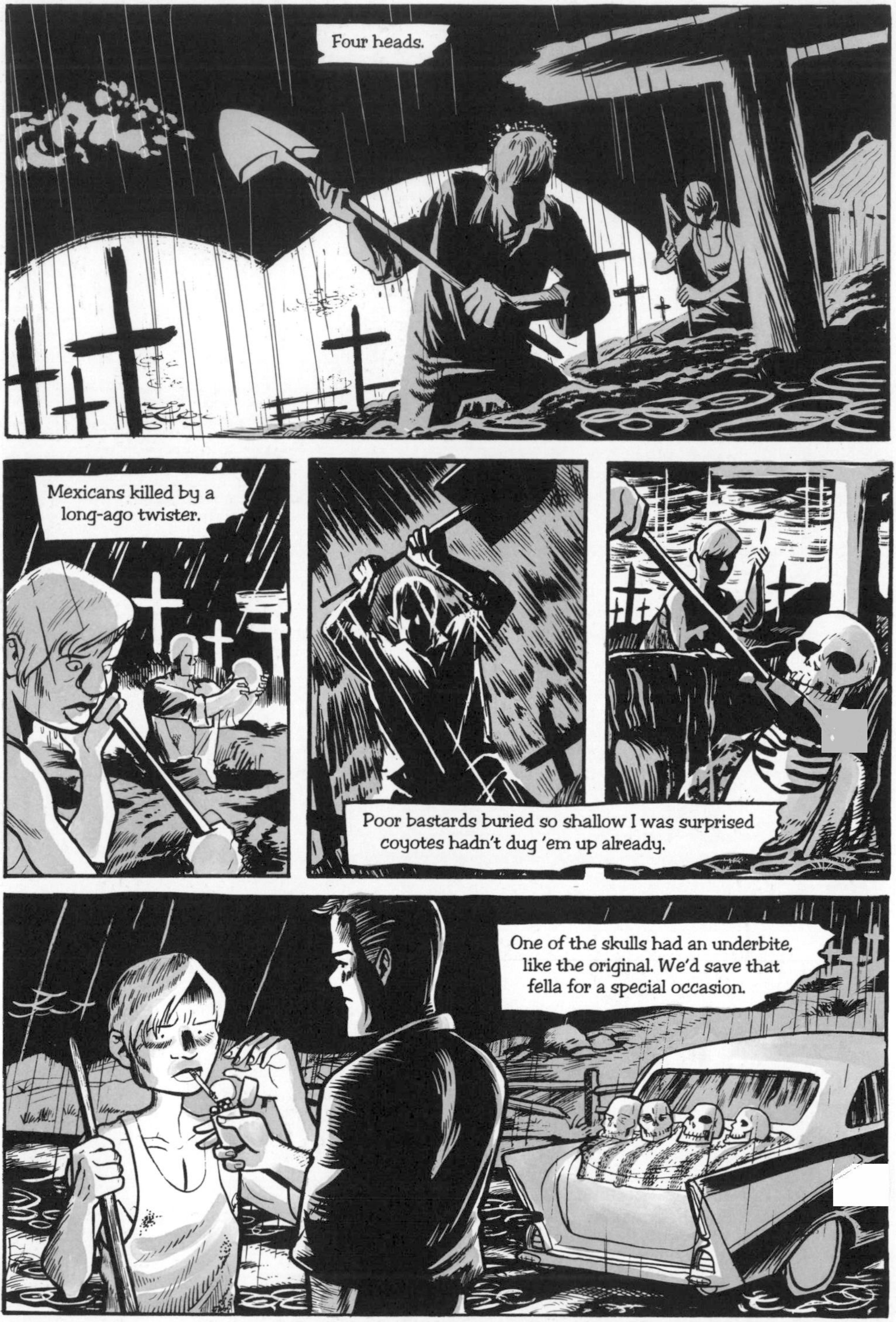
Four heads.
Mexicans killed by a long-ago twister.
Poor bastards buried so shallow I was surprised coyotes hadn't dug 'em up already.
One of the skulls had an underbite, like the original. We'd save that fella for a special occasion.

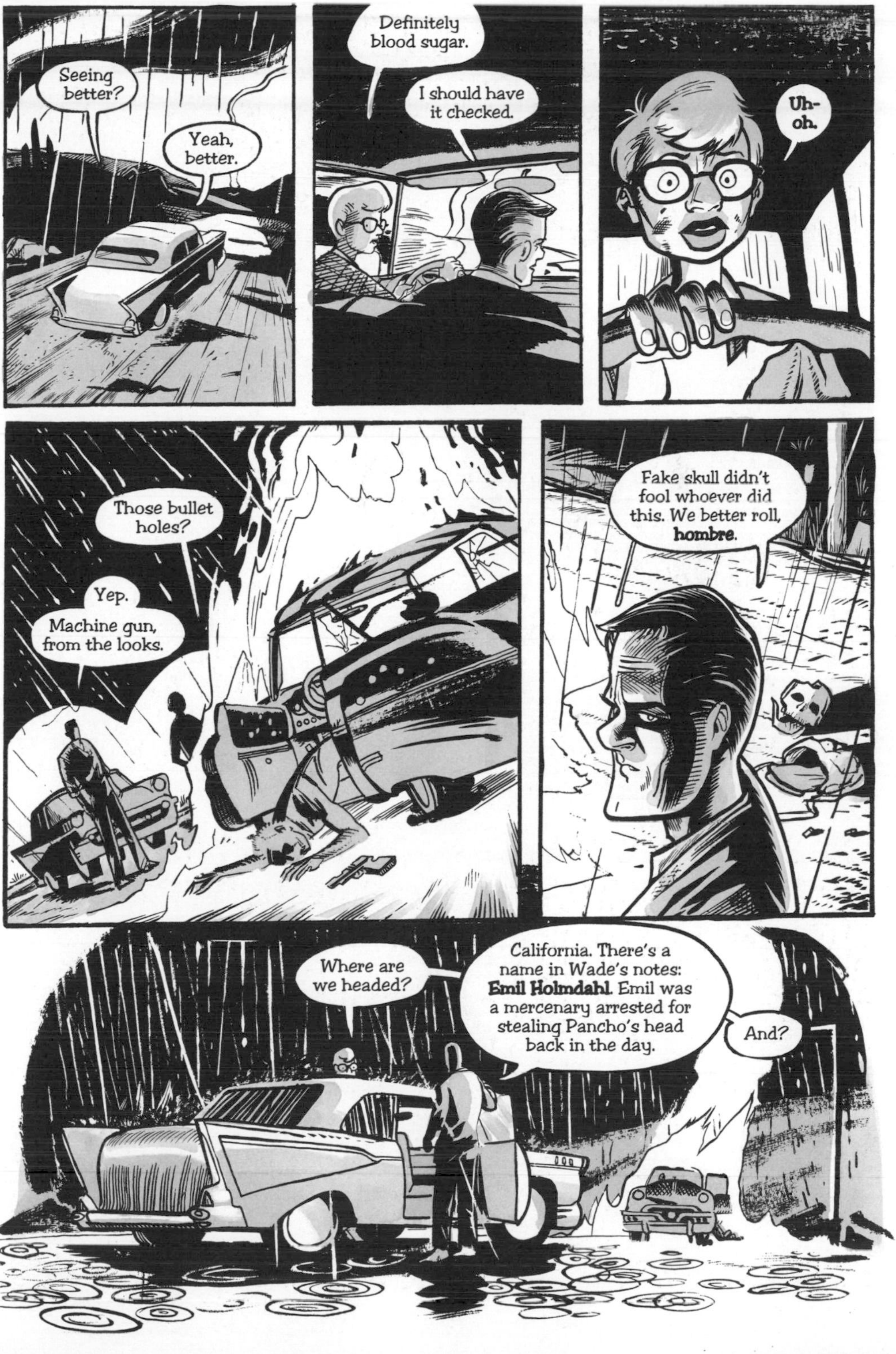
Seeing better?
Yeah, better.
Definitely blood sugar.
I should have it checked.
Uh-oh.
Those bullet holes?
Yep.
Machine gun, from the looks.
Fake skull didn't fool whoever did this. We better roll, **hombre**.
Where are we headed?
California. There's a name in Wade's notes: **Emil Holmdahl**. Emil was a mercenary arrested for stealing Pancho's head back in the day.
And?

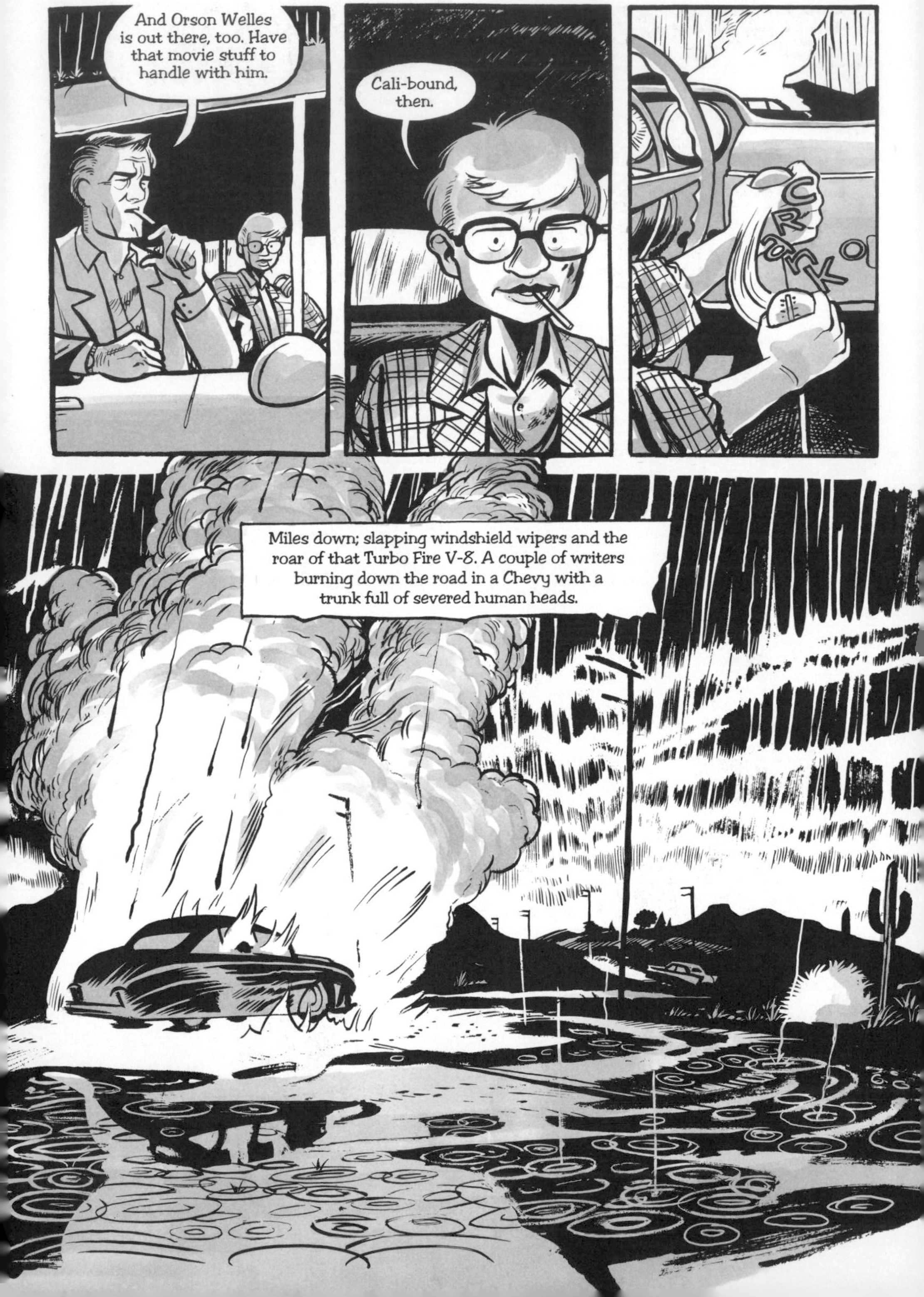

And Orson Welles is out there, too. Have that movie stuff to handle with him.
Cali-bound, then.
Miles down; slapping windshield wipers and the roar of that Turbo Fire V-8. A couple of writers burning down the road in a Chevy with a trunk full of severed human heads.

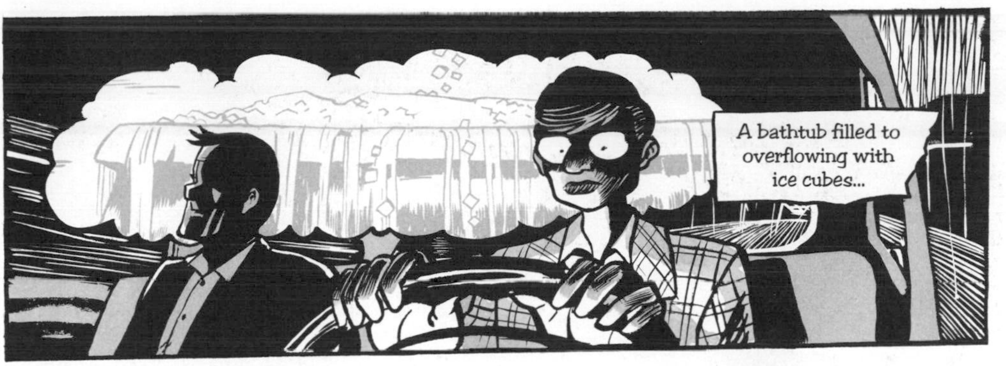
A bathtub filled to overflowing with ice cubes...

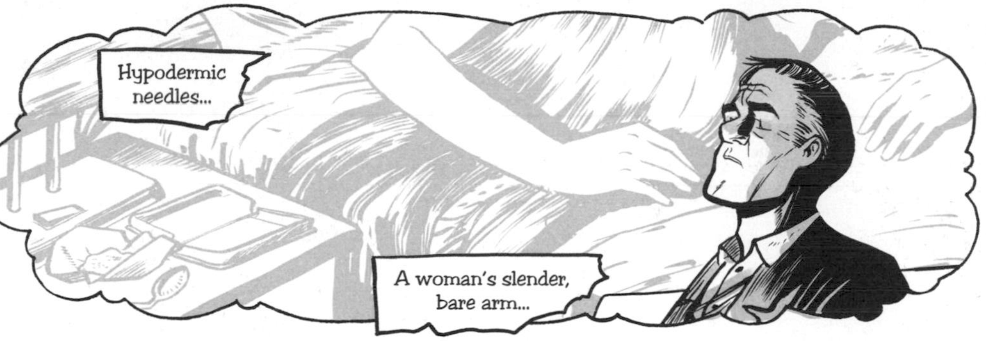
Hypodermic needles...
A woman's slender, bare arm...

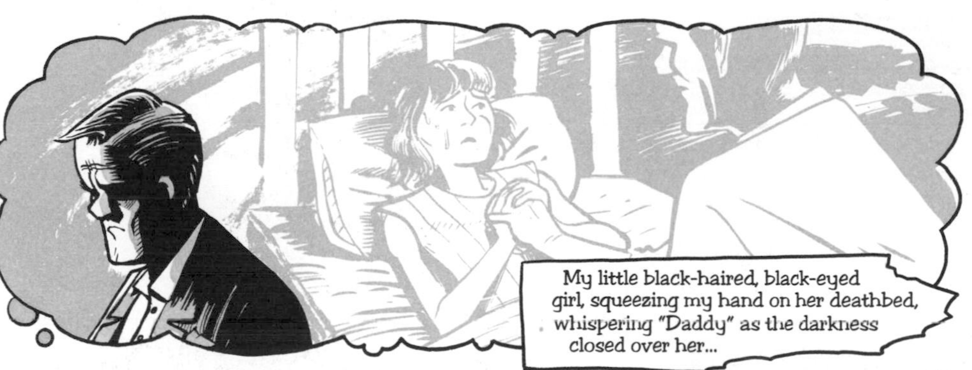
My little black-haired, black-eyed girl, squeezing my hand on her deathbed, whispering "Daddy" as the darkness closed over her...

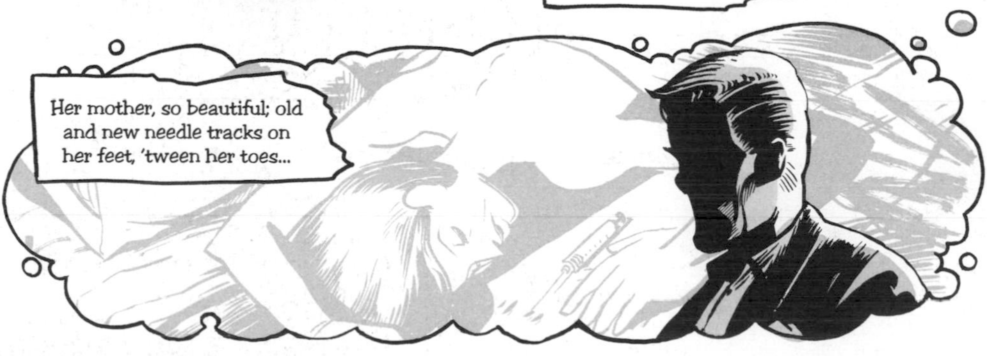
Her mother, so beautiful; old and new needle tracks on her feet, 'tween her toes...

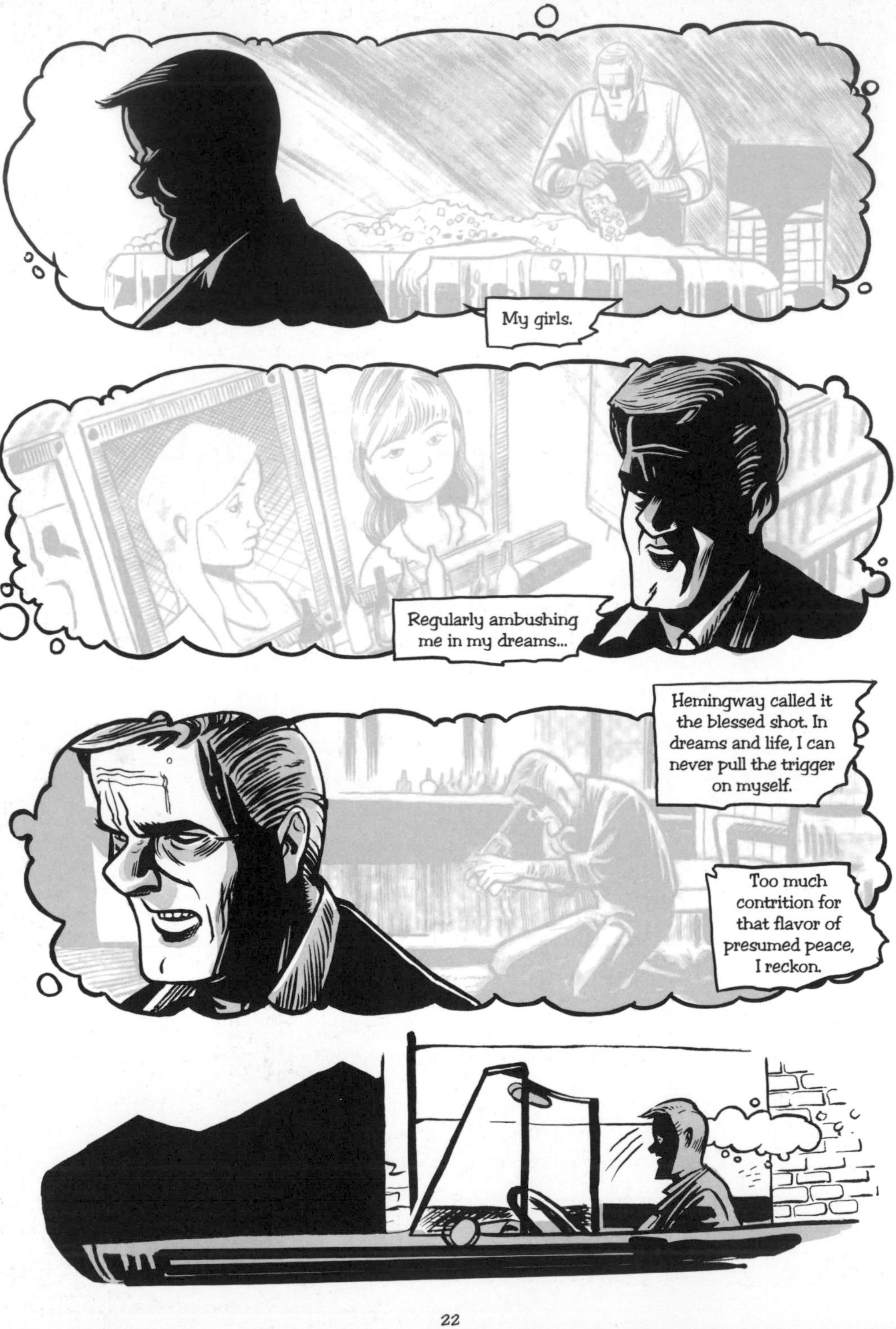
My girls.
Regularly ambushing me in my dreams...
Hemingway called it the blessed shot. In dreams and life, I can never pull the trigger on myself.
Too much contrition for that flavor of presumed peace, I reckon.

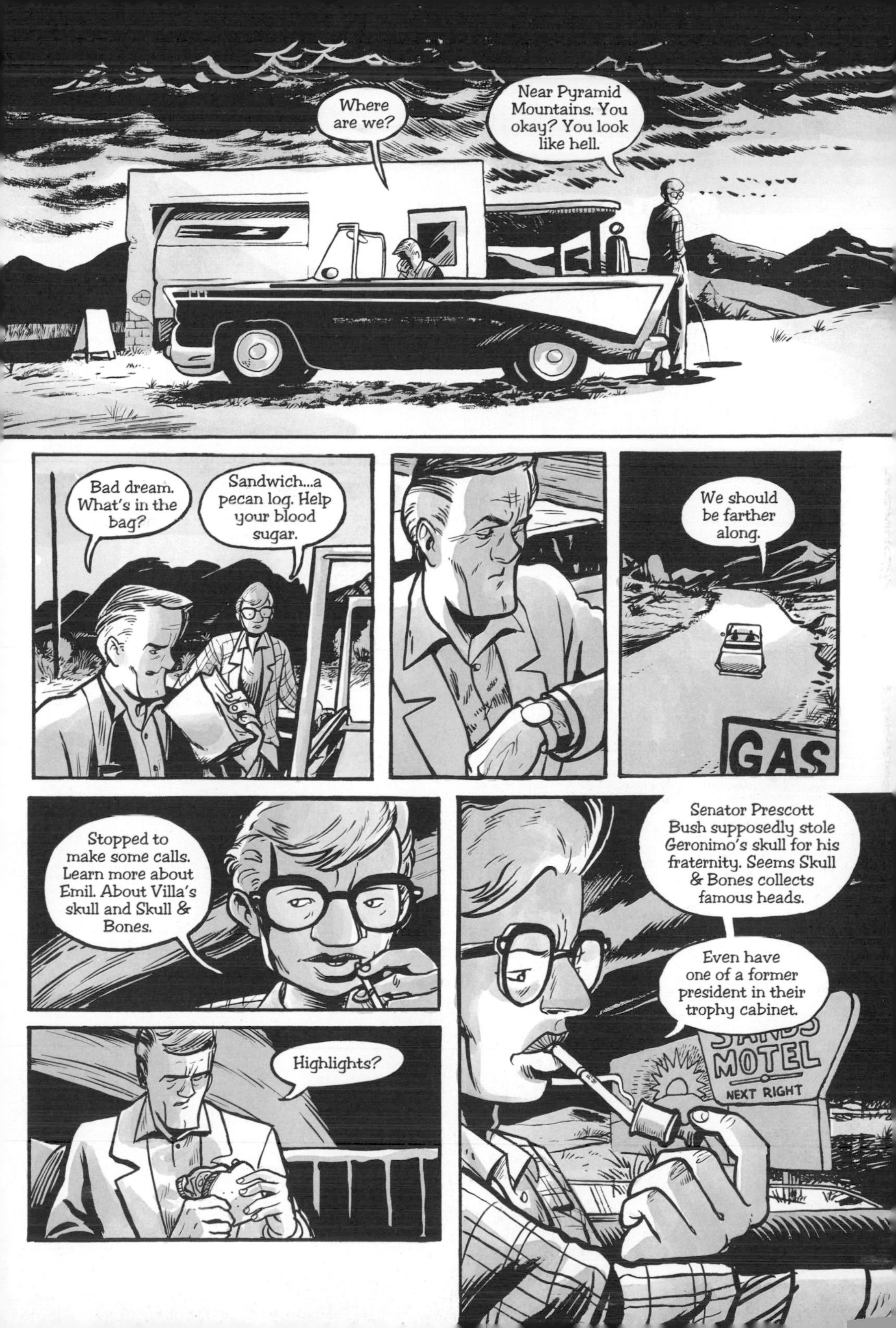
Where are we?
Near Pyramid Mountains. You okay? You look like hell.
Bad dream. What's in the bag?
Sandwich...a pecan log. Help your blood sugar.
We should be farther along.
GAS
Stopped to make some calls. Learn more about Emil. About Villa's skull and Skull & Bones.
Highlights?
Senator Prescott Bush supposedly stole Geronimo's skull for his fraternity. Seems Skull & Bones collects famous heads.
Even have one of a former president in their trophy cabinet.
MOTEL
NEXT RIGHT

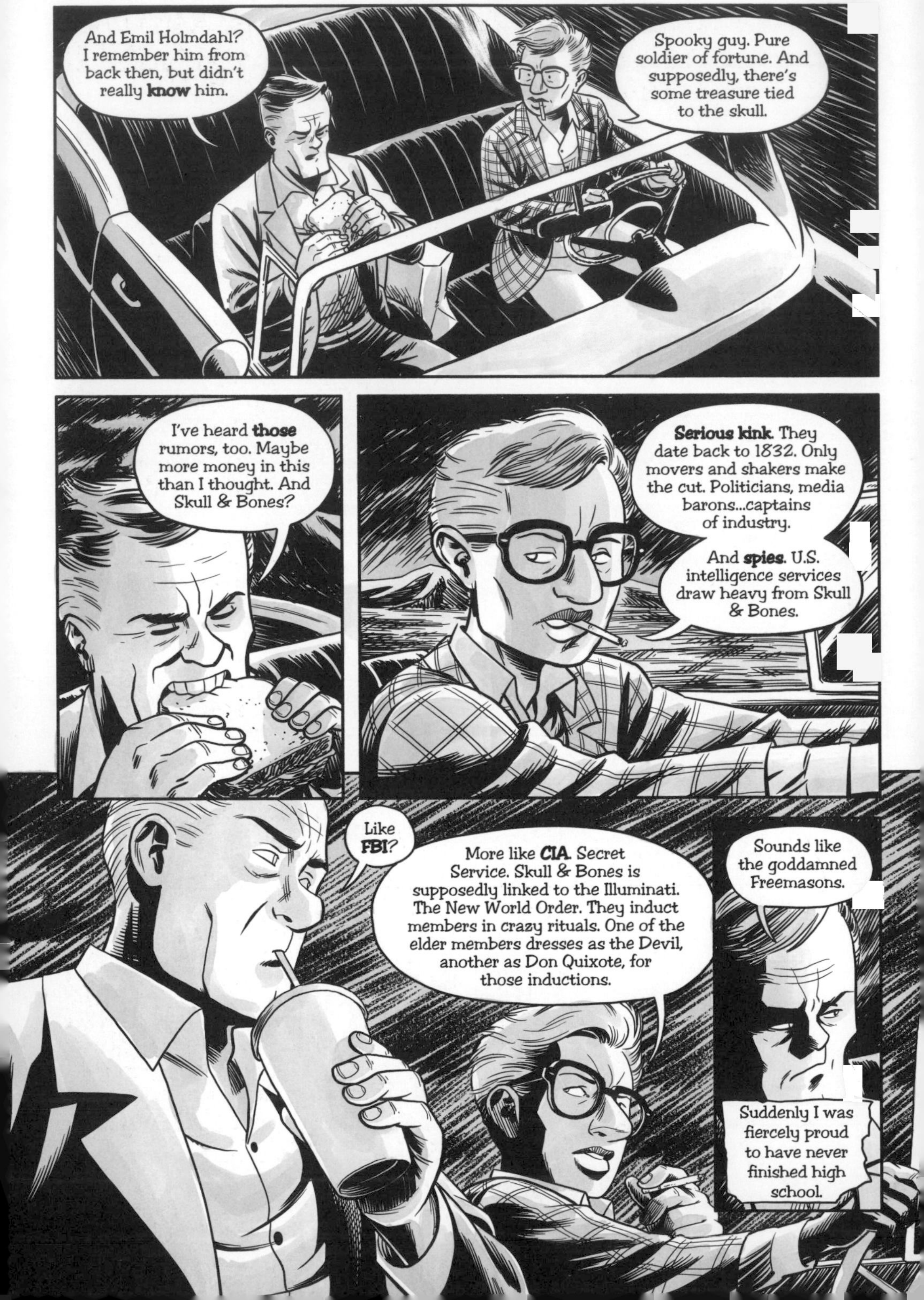
And Emil Holmdahl? I remember him from back then, but didn't really **know** him.
Spooky guy. Pure soldier of fortune. And supposedly, there's some treasure tied to the skull.
I've heard **those** rumors, too. Maybe more money in this than I thought. And Skull & Bones?
Serious kink. They date back to 1832. Only movers and shakers make the cut. Politicians, media barons...captains of industry.
And **spies**. U.S. intelligence services draw heavy from Skull & Bones.
Like **FBI**?
More like **CIA**. Secret Service. Skull & Bones is supposedly linked to the Illuminati. The New World Order. They induct members in crazy rituals. One of the elder members dresses as the Devil, another as Don Quixote, for those inductions.
Sounds like the goddamned Freemasons.
Suddenly I was fiercely proud to have never finished high school.

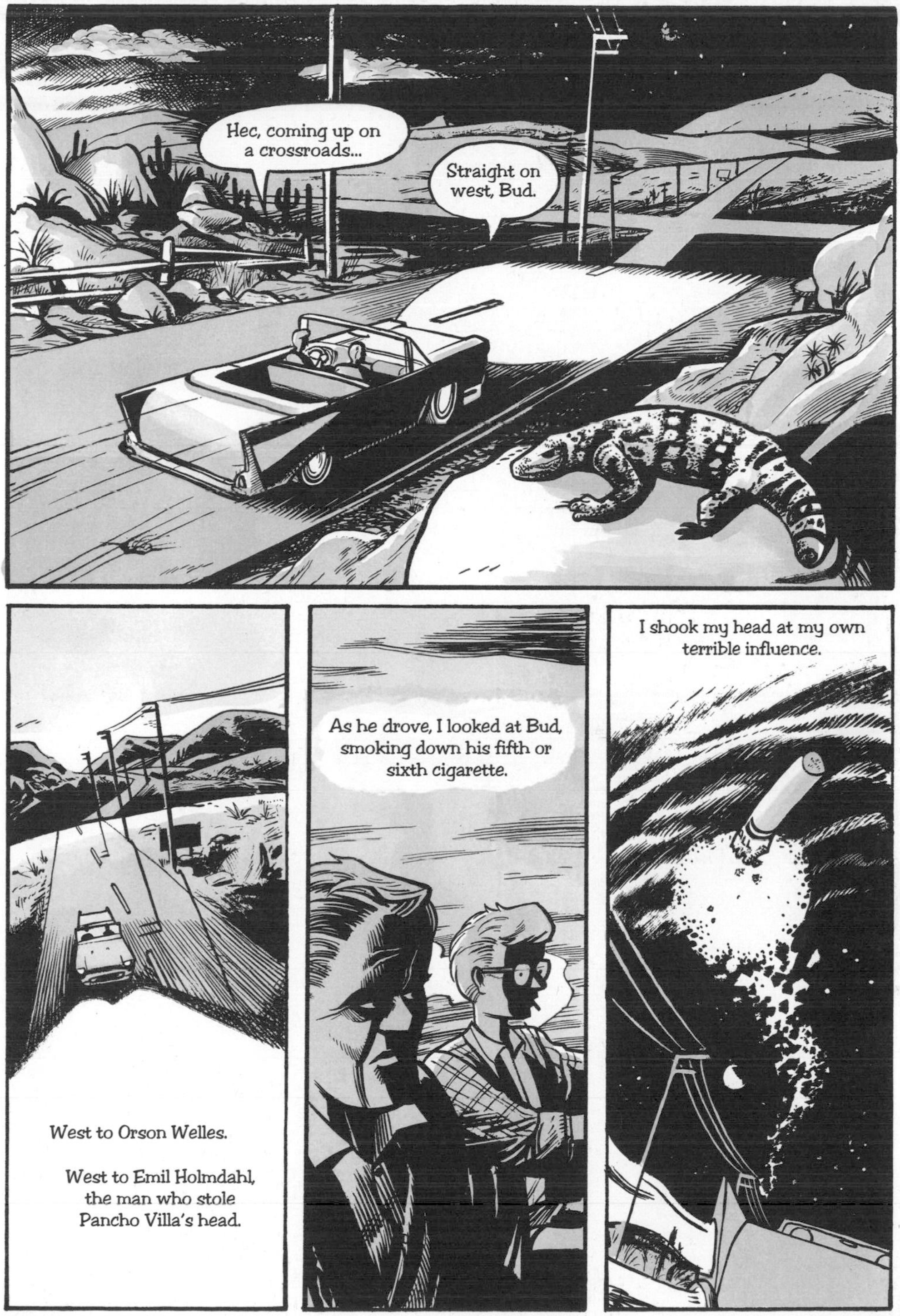
Hec, coming up on a crossroads...
Straight on west, Bud.
West to Orson Welles.
West to Emil Holmdahl, the man who stole Pancho Villa's head.
As he drove, I looked at Bud, smoking down his fifth or sixth cigarette.
I shook my head at my own terrible influence.

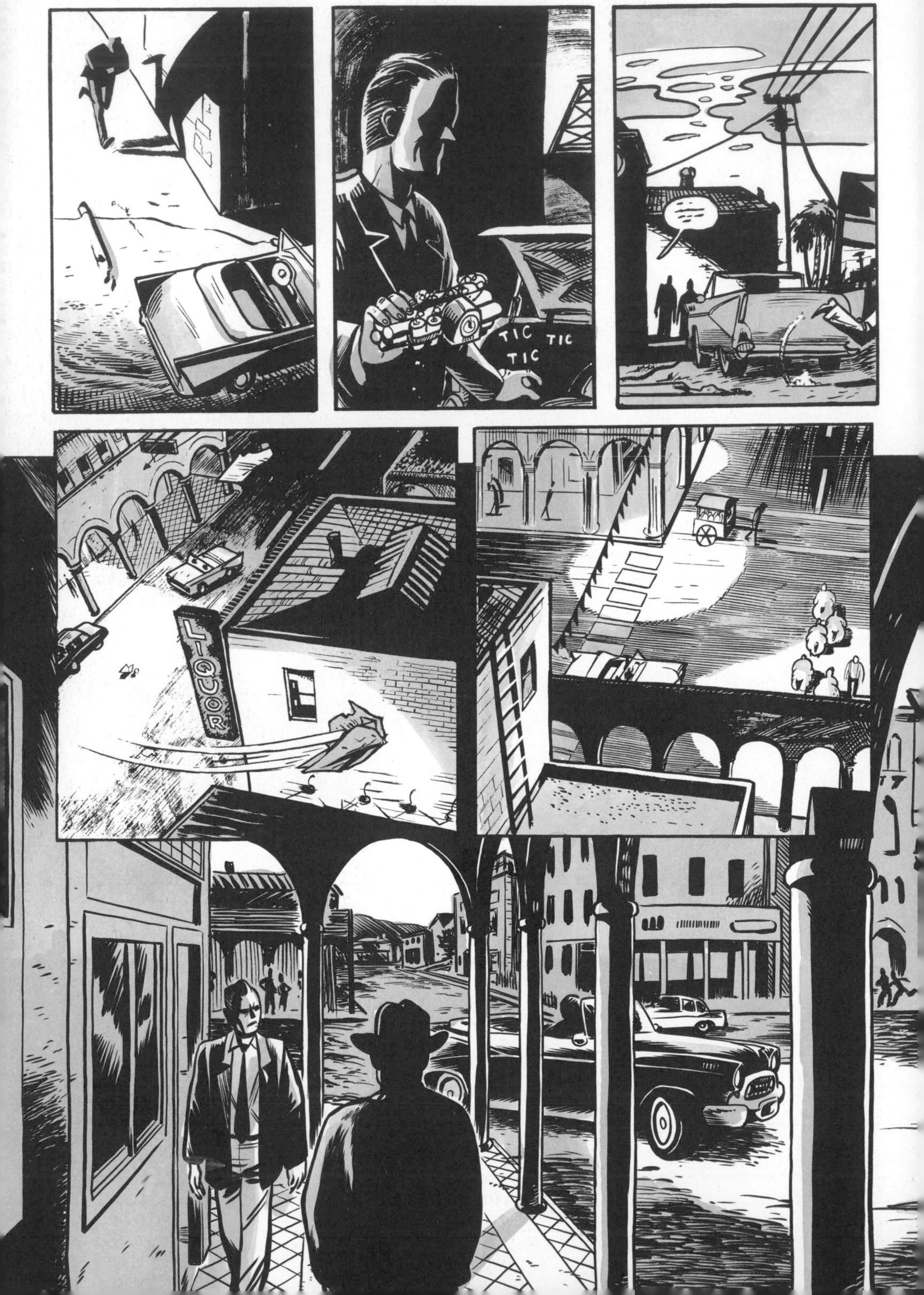
TIC TIC
TIC
LIQUOR

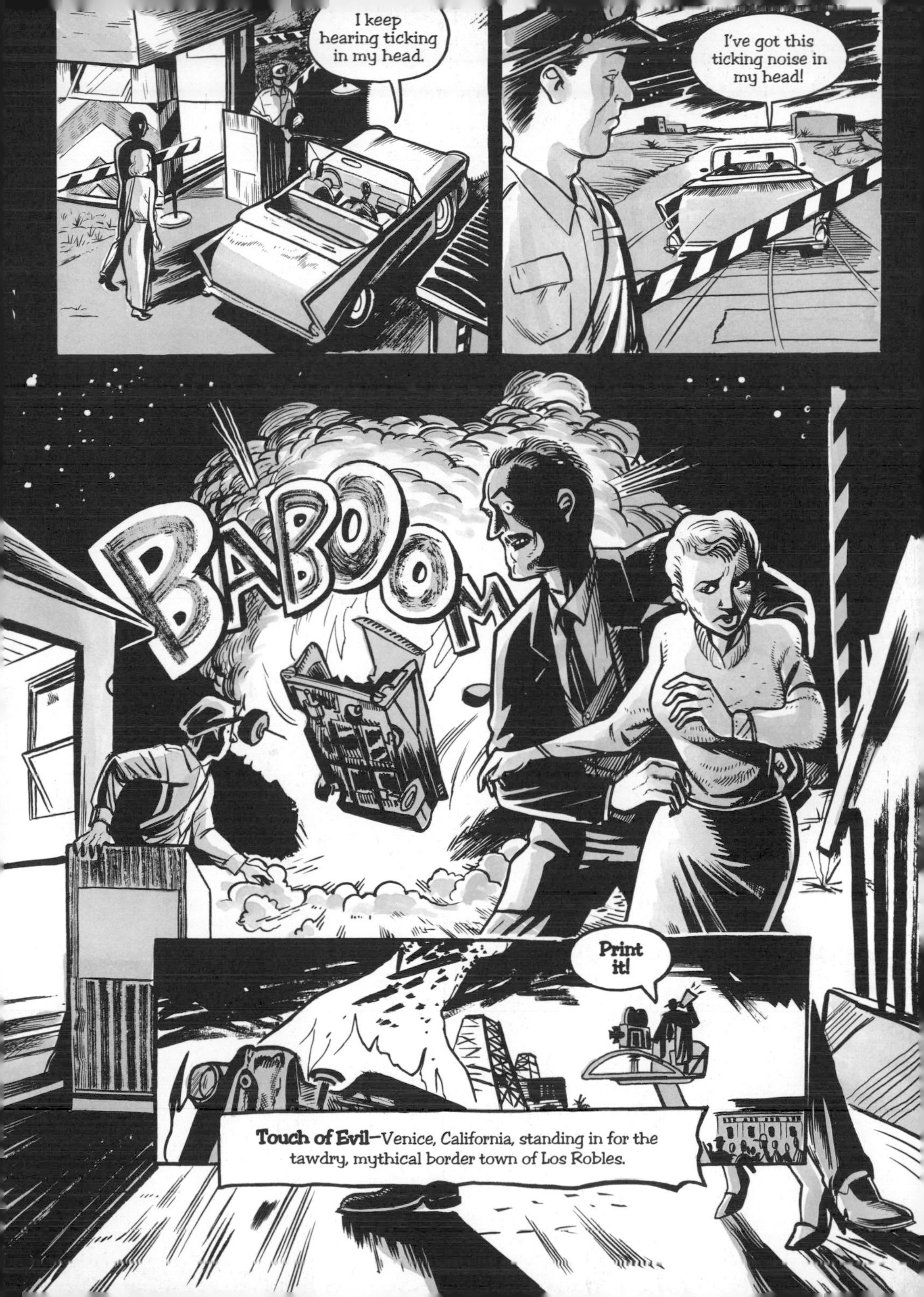
I keep hearing ticking in my head.
I've got this ticking noise in my head!
BABOOM
Print it!
Touch of Evil—Venice, California, standing in for the tawdry, mythical border town of Los Robles.

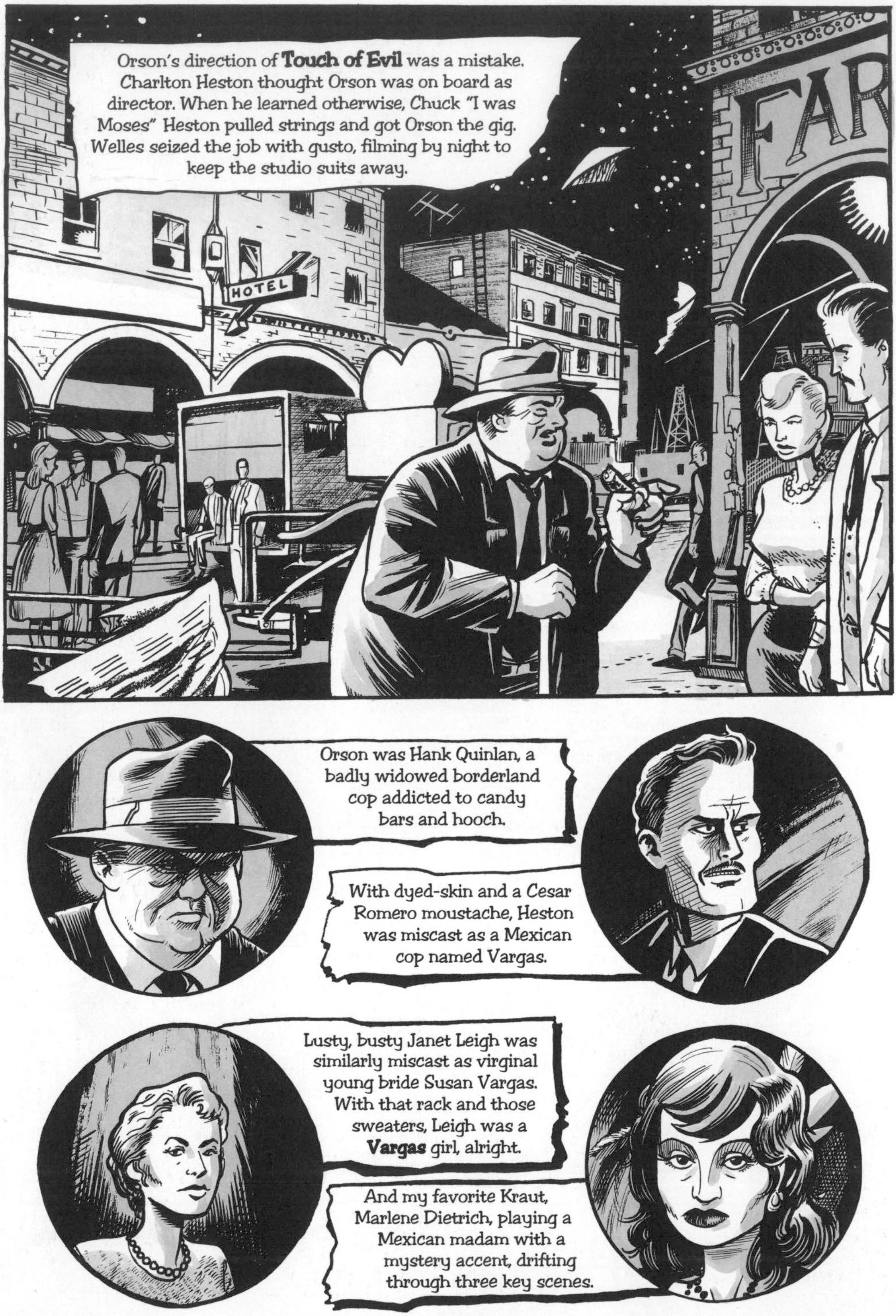
Orson's direction of **Touch of Evil** was a mistake. Charlton Heston thought Orson was on board as director. When he learned otherwise, Chuck "I was Moses" Heston pulled strings and got Orson the gig. Welles seized the job with gusto, filming by night to keep the studio suits away.
HOTEL
Orson was Hank Quinlan, a badly widowed borderland cop addicted to candy bars and hooch.
With dyed-skin and a Cesar Romero moustache, Heston was miscast as a Mexican cop named Vargas.
Lusty, busty Janet Leigh was similarly miscast as virginal young bride Susan Vargas. With that rack and those sweaters, Leigh was a **Vargas** girl, alright.
And my favorite Kraut, Marlene Dietrich, playing a Mexican madam with a mystery accent, drifting through three key scenes.

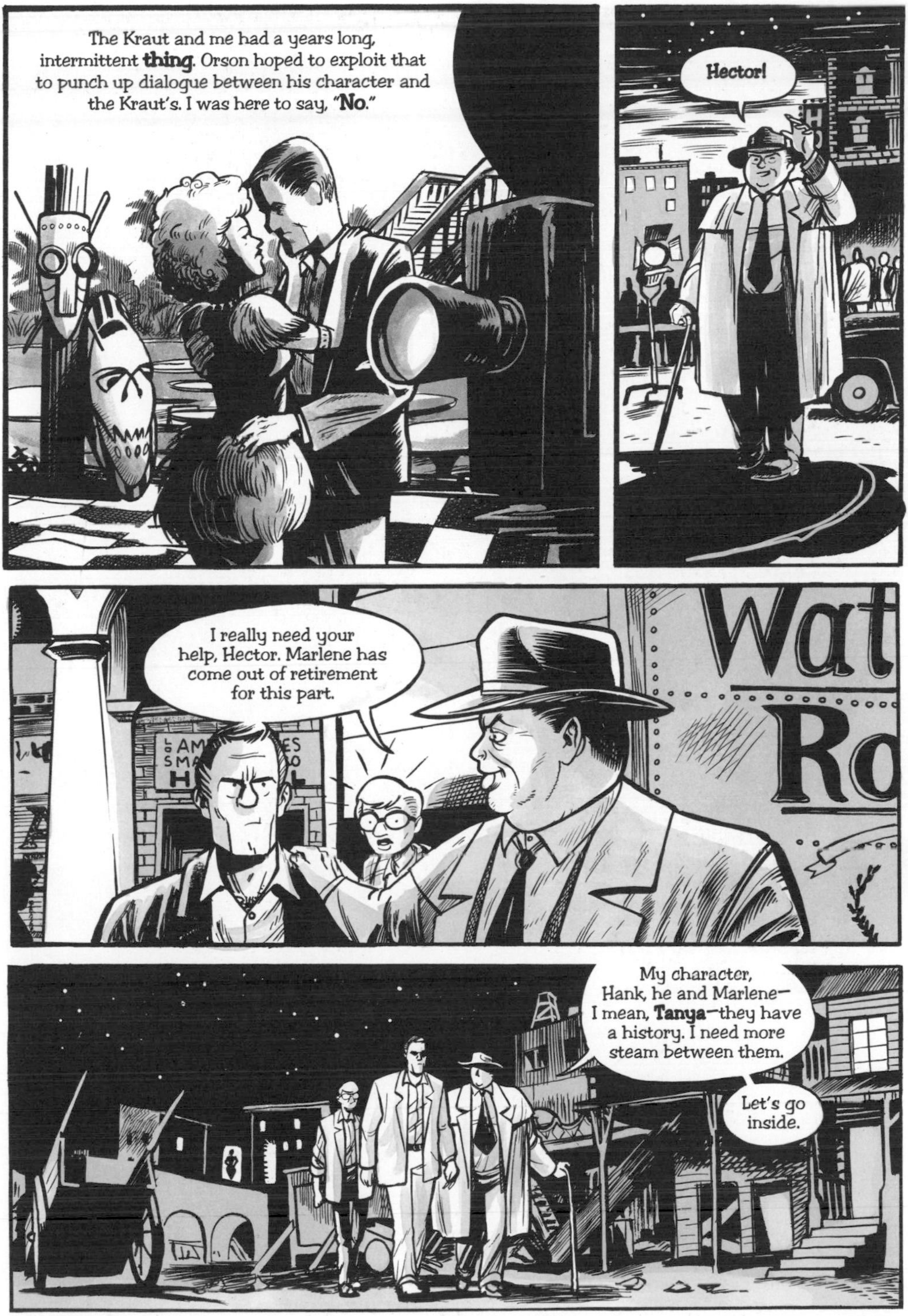
The Kraut and me had a years long, intermittent **thing**. Orson hoped to exploit that to punch up dialogue between his character and the Kraut's. I was here to say, "**No.**"
Hector!
I really need your help, Hector. Marlene has come out of retirement for this part.
My character, Hank, he and Marlene— I mean, **Tanya**—they have a history. I need more steam between them.
Let's go inside.

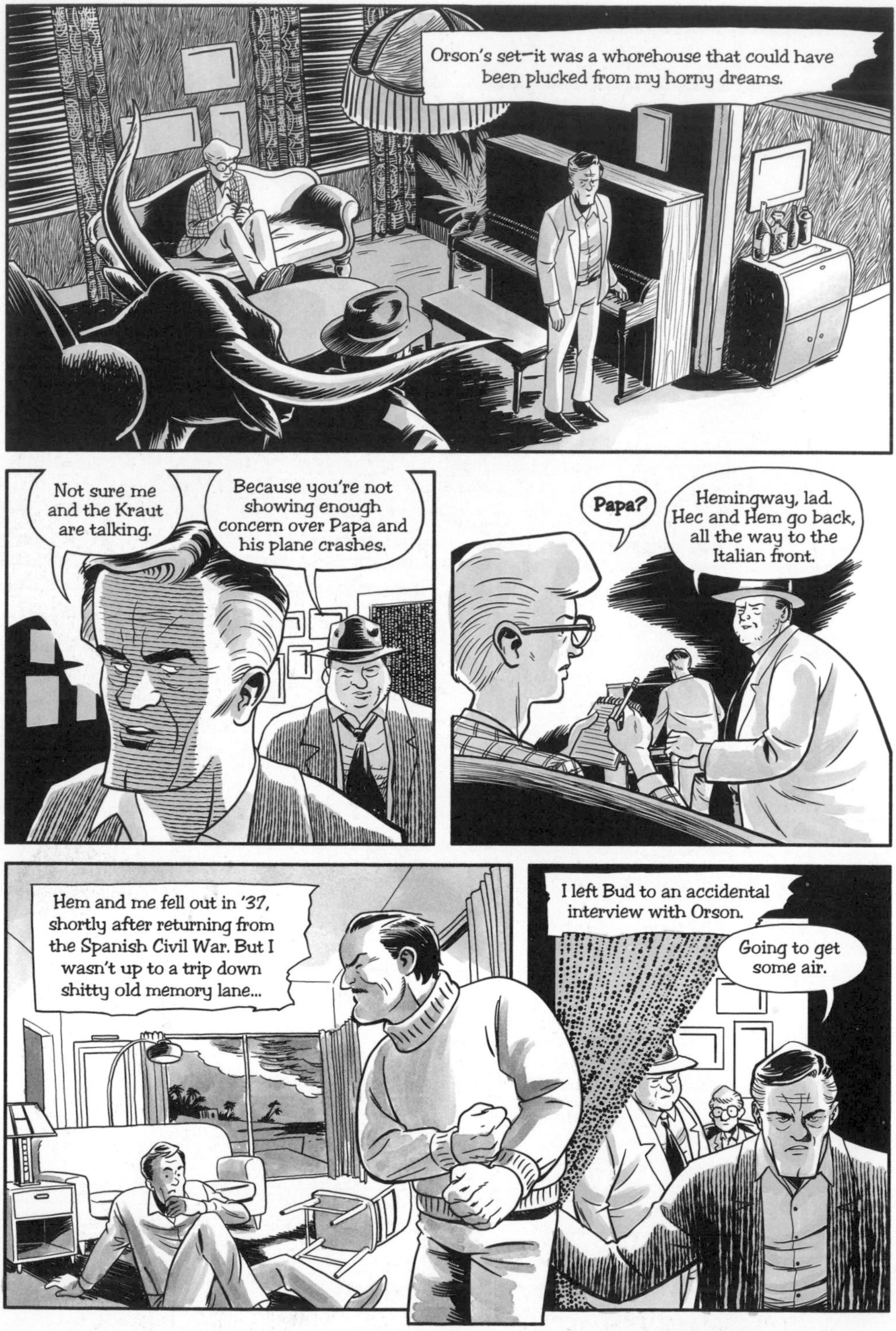
Orson's set—it was a whorehouse that could have been plucked from my horny dreams.
Not sure me and the Kraut are talking.
Because you're not showing enough concern over Papa and his plane crashes.
Papa?
Hemingway, lad. Hec and Hem go back, all the way to the Italian front.
Hem and me fell out in '37, shortly after returning from the Spanish Civil War. But I wasn't up to a trip down shitty old memory lane...
I left Bud to an accidental interview with Orson.
Going to get some air.

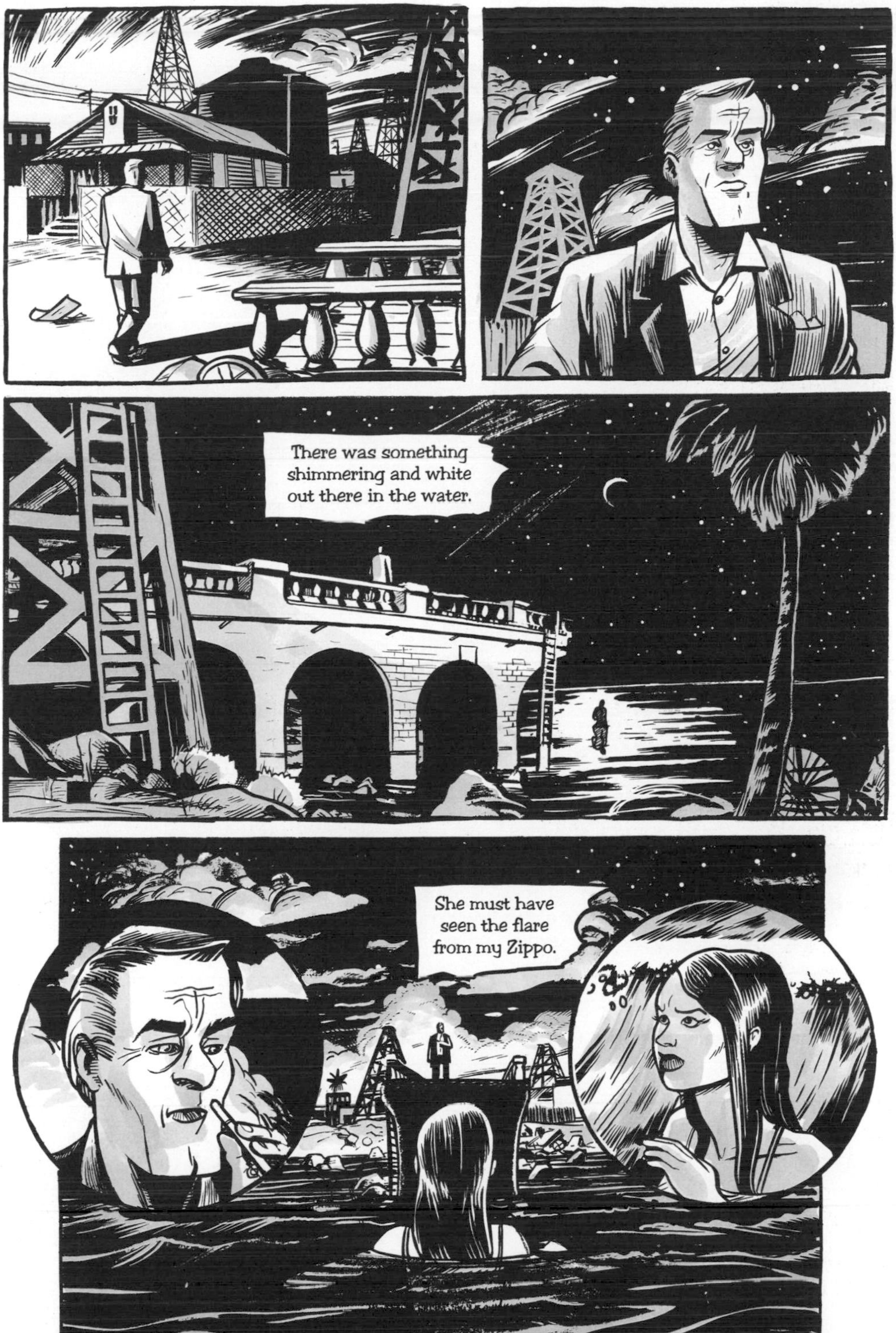
There was something shimmering and white out there in the water.
She must have seen the flare from my Zippo.

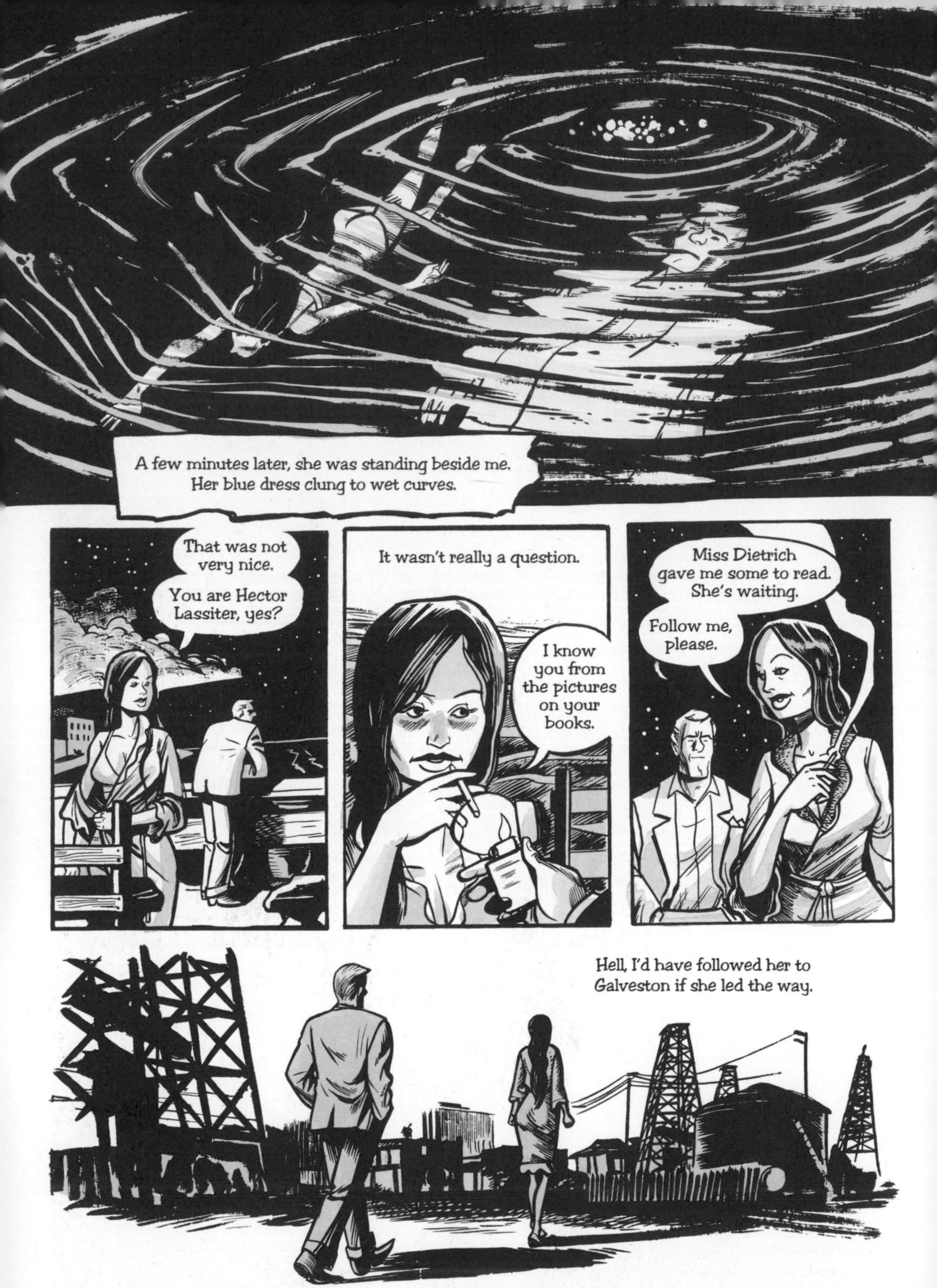
A few minutes later, she was standing beside me. Her blue dress clung to wet curves.
That was not very nice.
You are Hector Lassiter, yes?
It wasn't really a question.
I know you from the pictures on your books.
Miss Dietrich gave me some to read. She's waiting.
Follow me, please.
Hell, I'd have followed her to Galveston if she led the way.

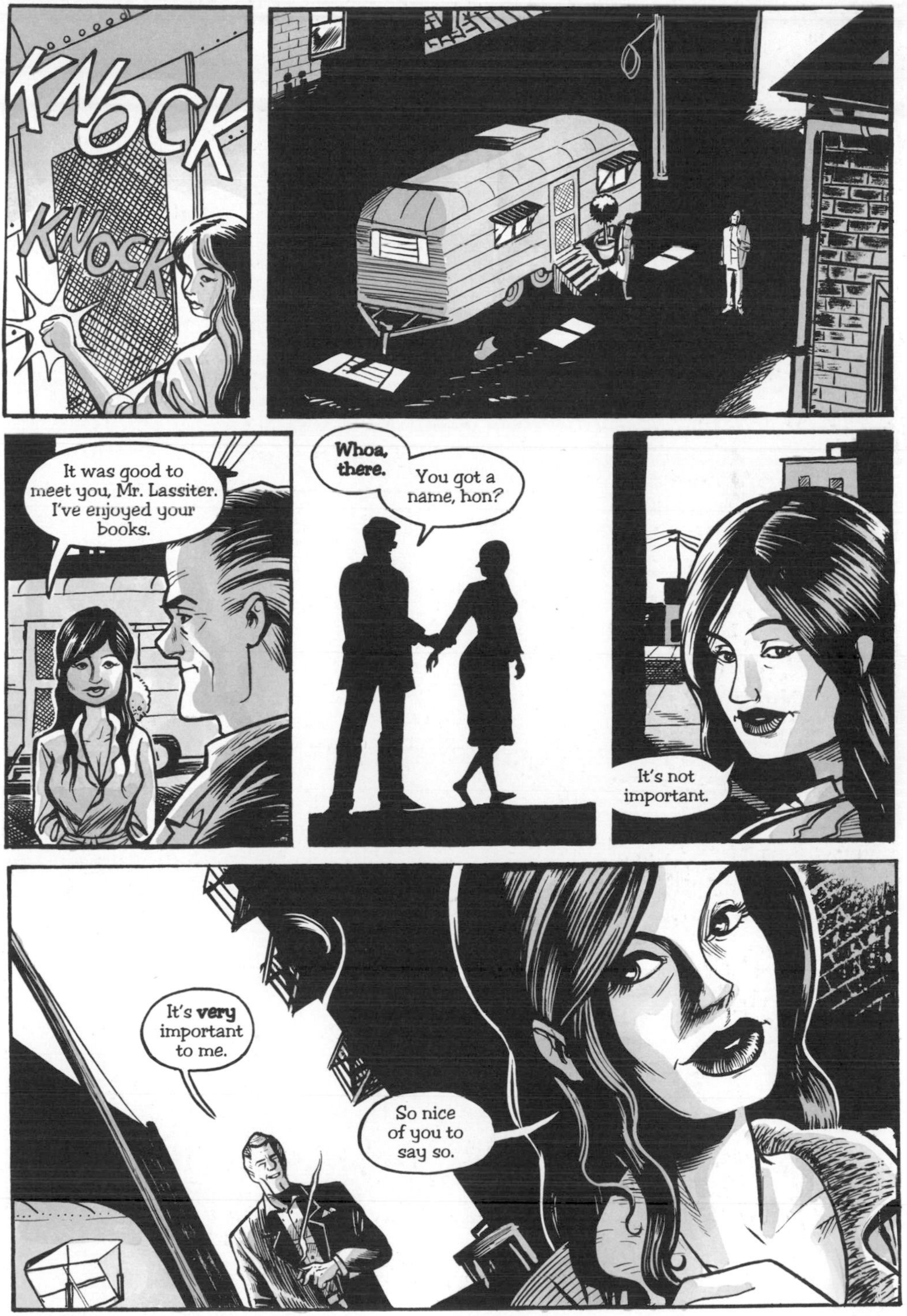
KNOCK
KNOCK
It was good to meet you, Mr. Lassiter. I've enjoyed your books.
Whoa, there.
You got a name, hon?
It's not important.
It's very important to me.
So nice of you to say so.

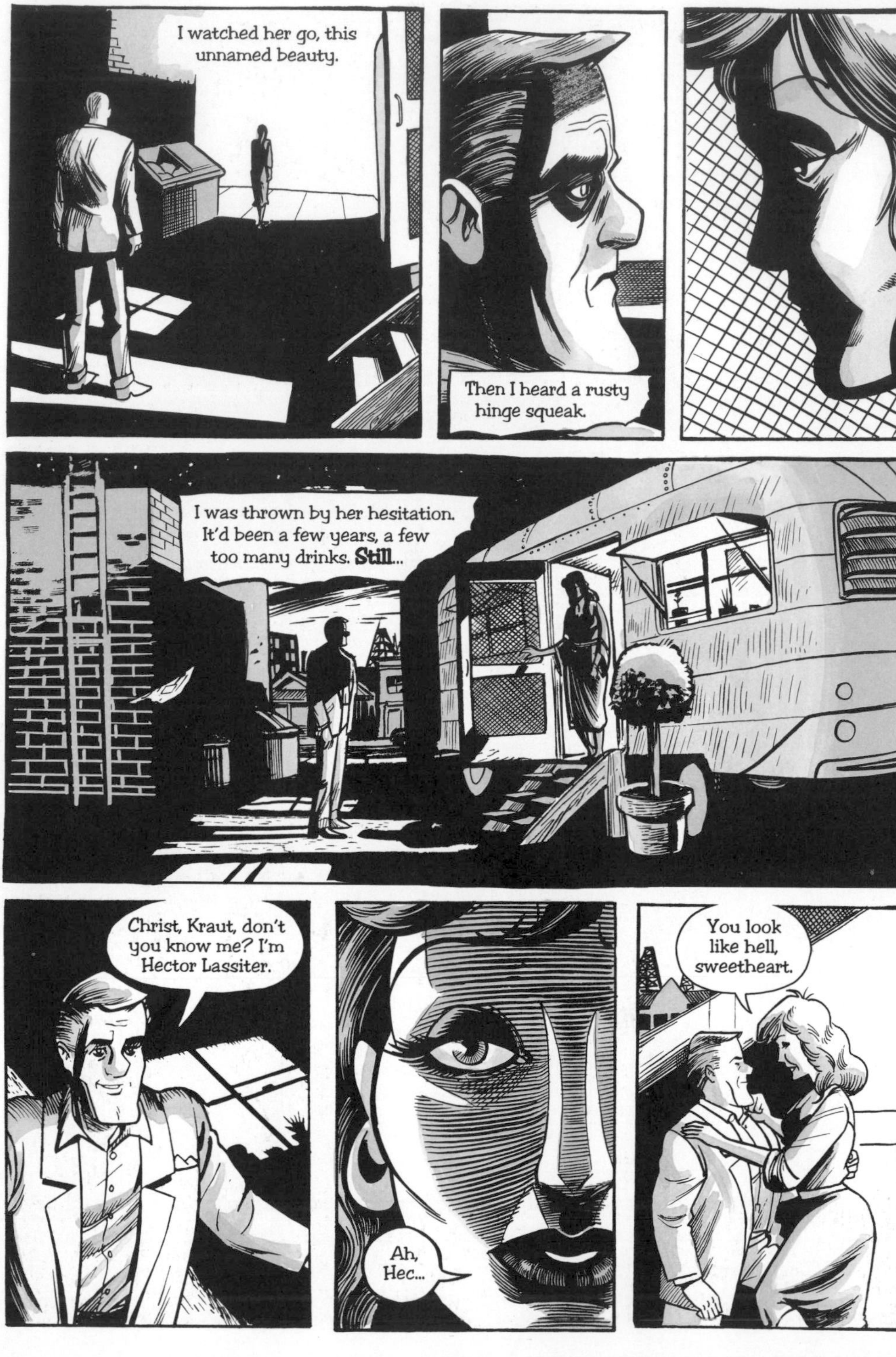
I watched her go, this unnamed beauty.
Then I heard a rusty hinge squeak.
I was thrown by her hesitation. It'd been a few years, a few too many drinks. **Still**...
Christ, Kraut, don't you know me? I'm Hector Lassiter.
Ah, Hec...
You look like hell, sweetheart.

You've had a wicked year. I know what Dolores meant to you. How are you really, Hec?

Surviving. Writing. Drinking. Too much of the last. You embrace what keeps you in the game, I guess.

You sound like Papa:

"First one must endure."

I knew it was her preamble to a twenty-year refrain: **Patch it up with Hem, please.**

Hem's going to have to call me. He owes **me** the apology.

You two are like warring brothers. And about equally star-crossed.

Wanna read my fortune, Kraut? Tell me my future?

Welles' script made it clear: Marlene's character was a fortune-teller when she wasn't running women.

I'm not sure how much future you have left.

I think maybe you've already spent your future, my love.

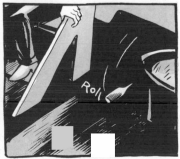

CLINK

Roll

35

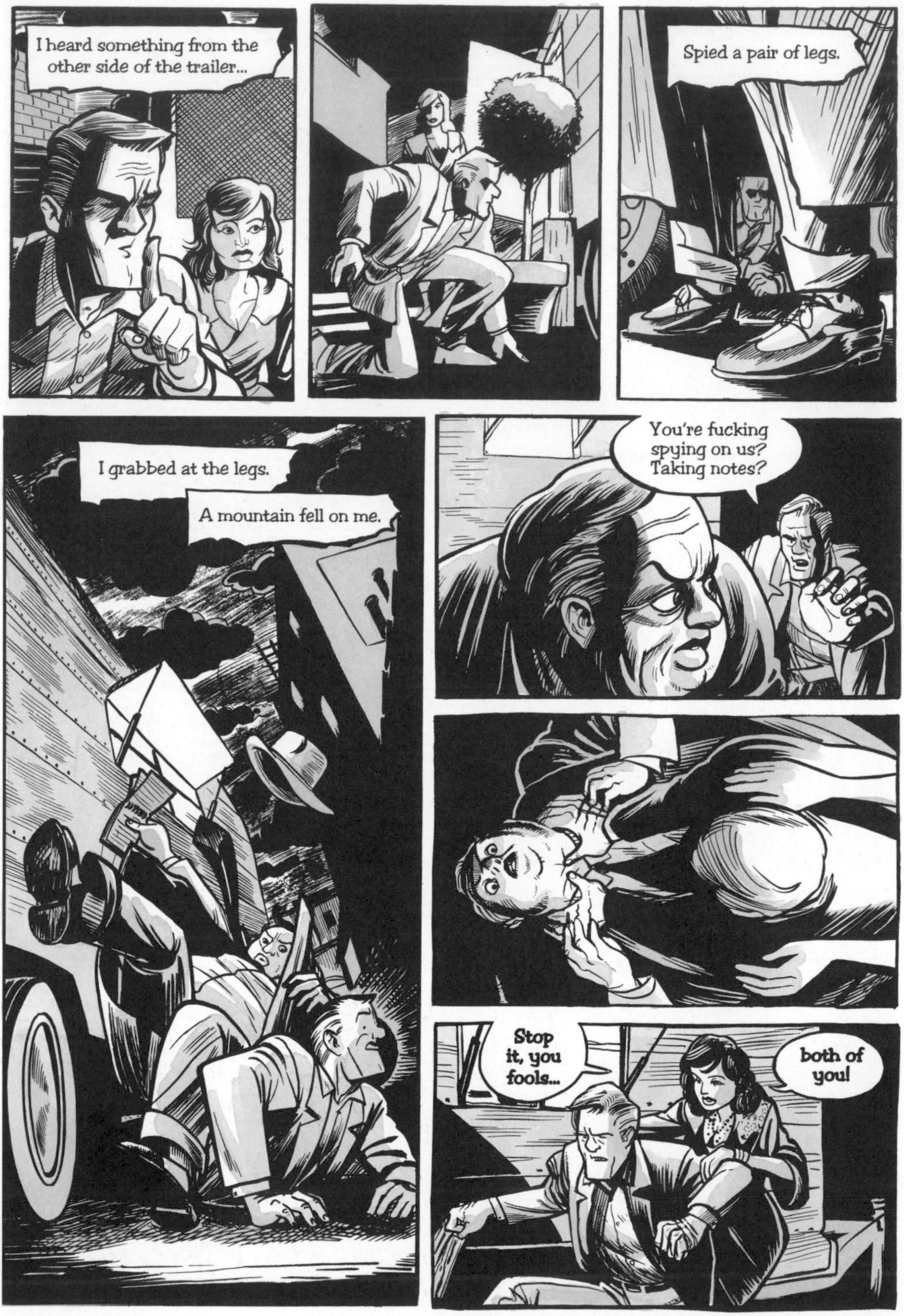
I heard something from the other side of the trailer...
Spied a pair of legs.
I grabbed at the legs.
A mountain fell on me.
You're fucking spying on us? Taking notes?
Stop it, you fools...
both of you!

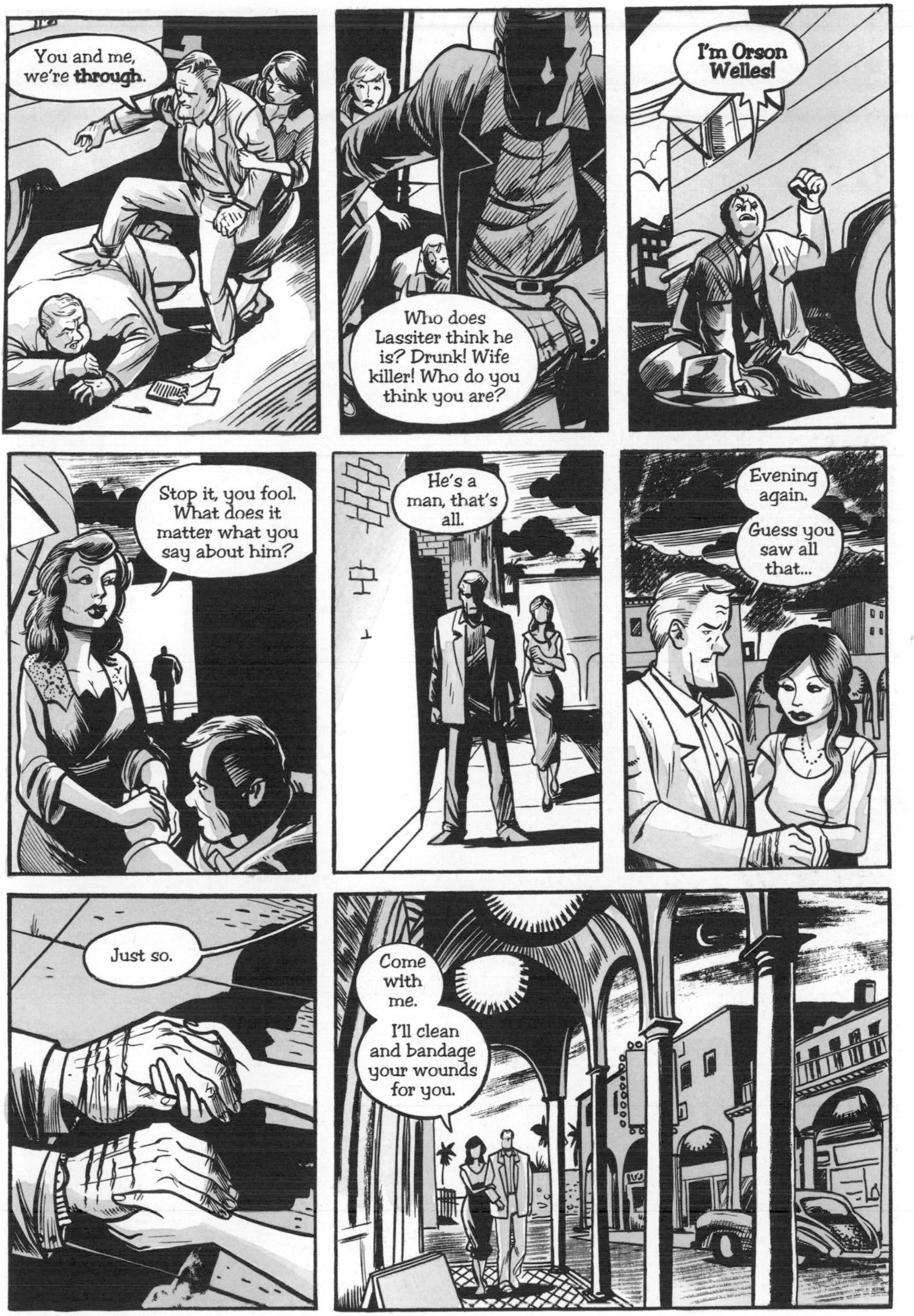
You and me, we're **through**.
Who does Lassiter think he is? Drunk! Wife killer! Who do you think you are?
I'm Orson Welles!
Stop it, you fool. What does it matter what you say about him?
He's a man, that's all.
Evening again.
Guess you saw all that...
Just so.
Come with me.
I'll clean and bandage your wounds for you.

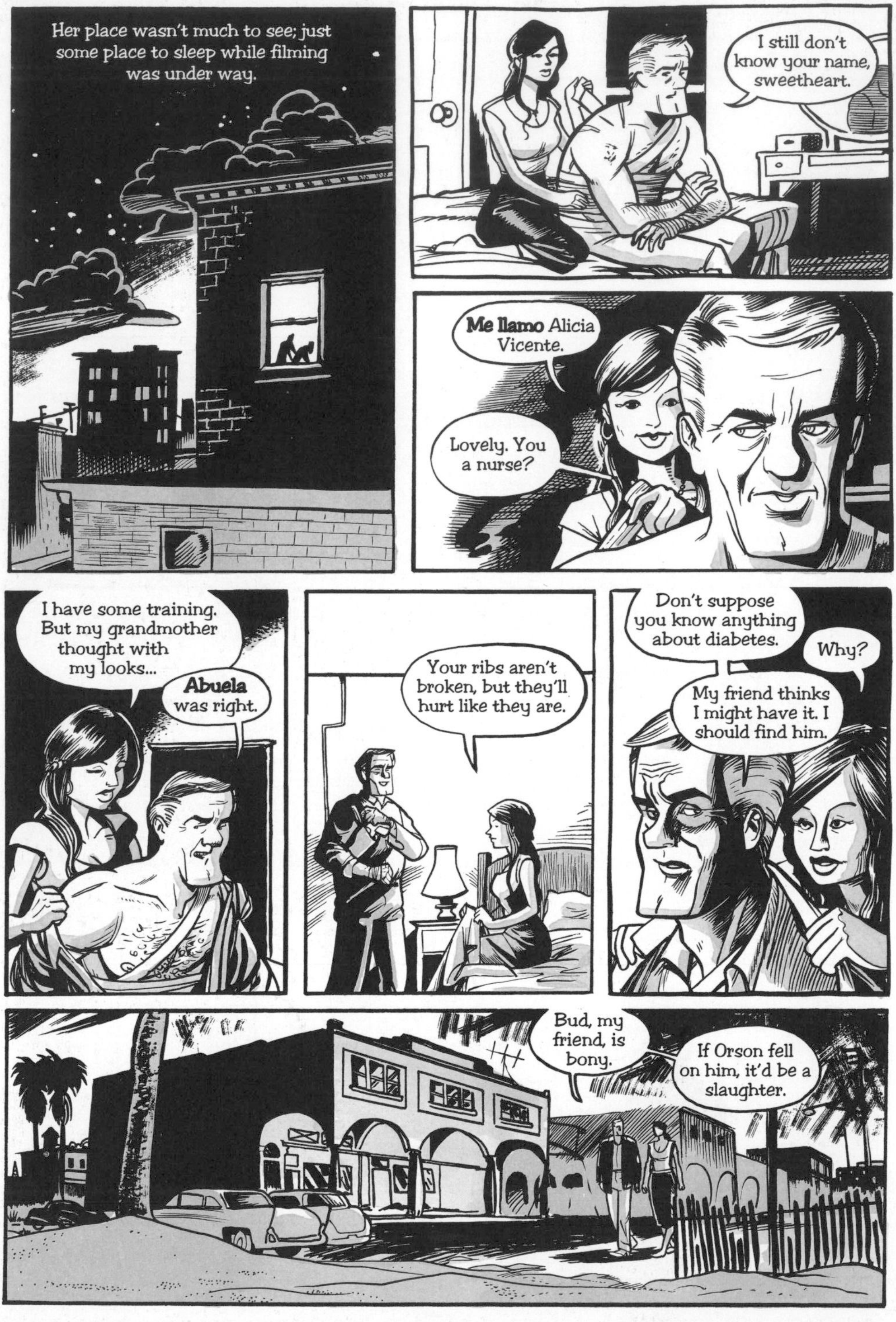
Her place wasn't much to see; just some place to sleep while filming was under way.
I still don't know your name, sweetheart.
Me llamo Alicia Vicente.
Lovely. You a nurse?
I have some training. But my grandmother thought with my looks...
Abuela was right.
Your ribs aren't broken, but they'll hurt like they are.
Don't suppose you know anything about diabetes.
Why?
My friend thinks I might have it. I should find him.
Bud, my friend, is bony.
If Orson fell on him, it'd be a slaughter.

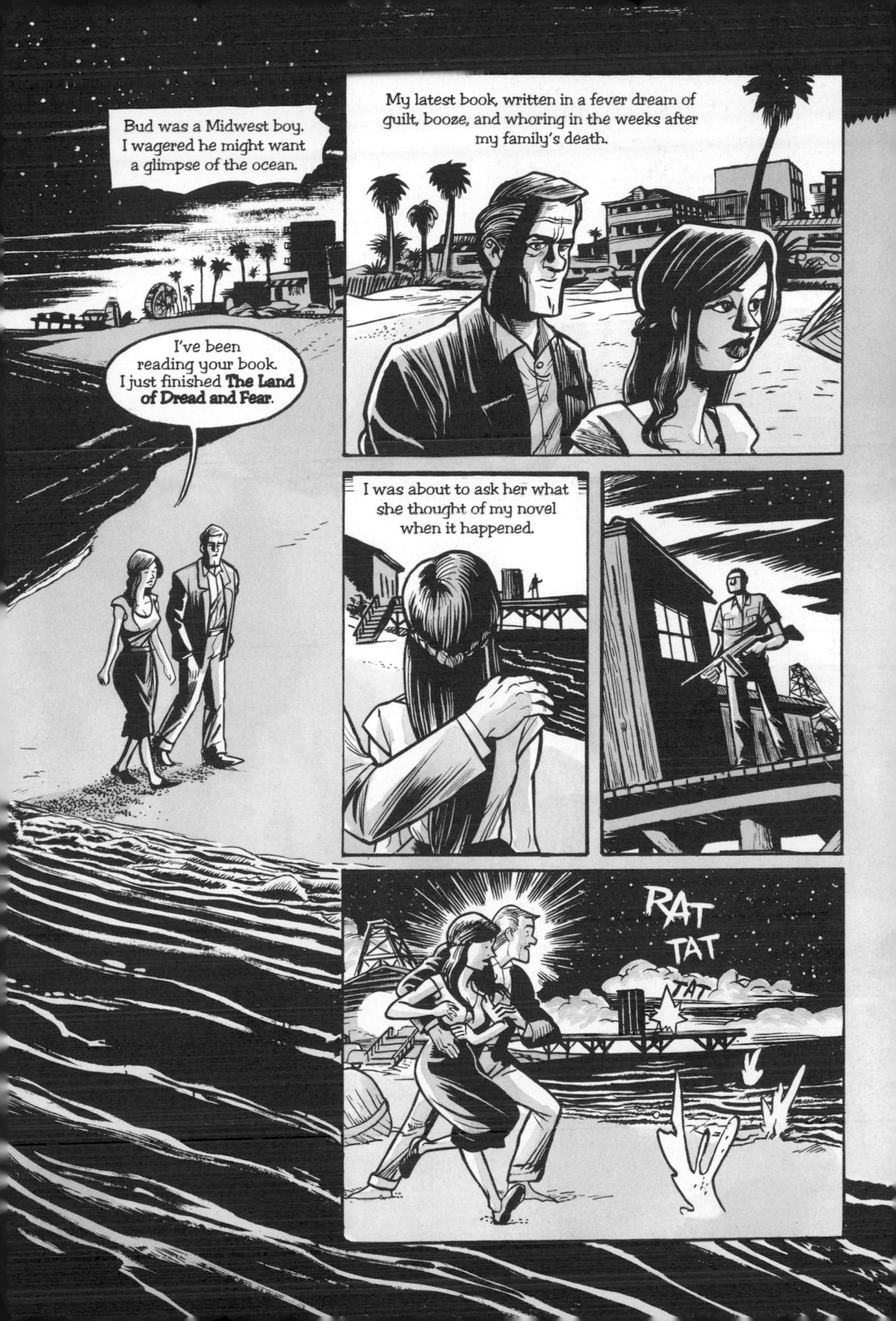
Bud was a Midwest boy. I wagered he might want a glimpse of the ocean.
I've been reading your book. I just finished **The Land of Dread and Fear**.
My latest book, written in a fever dream of guilt, booze, and whoring in the weeks after my family's death.
I was about to ask her what she thought of my novel when it happened.
RAT
TAT
TAT

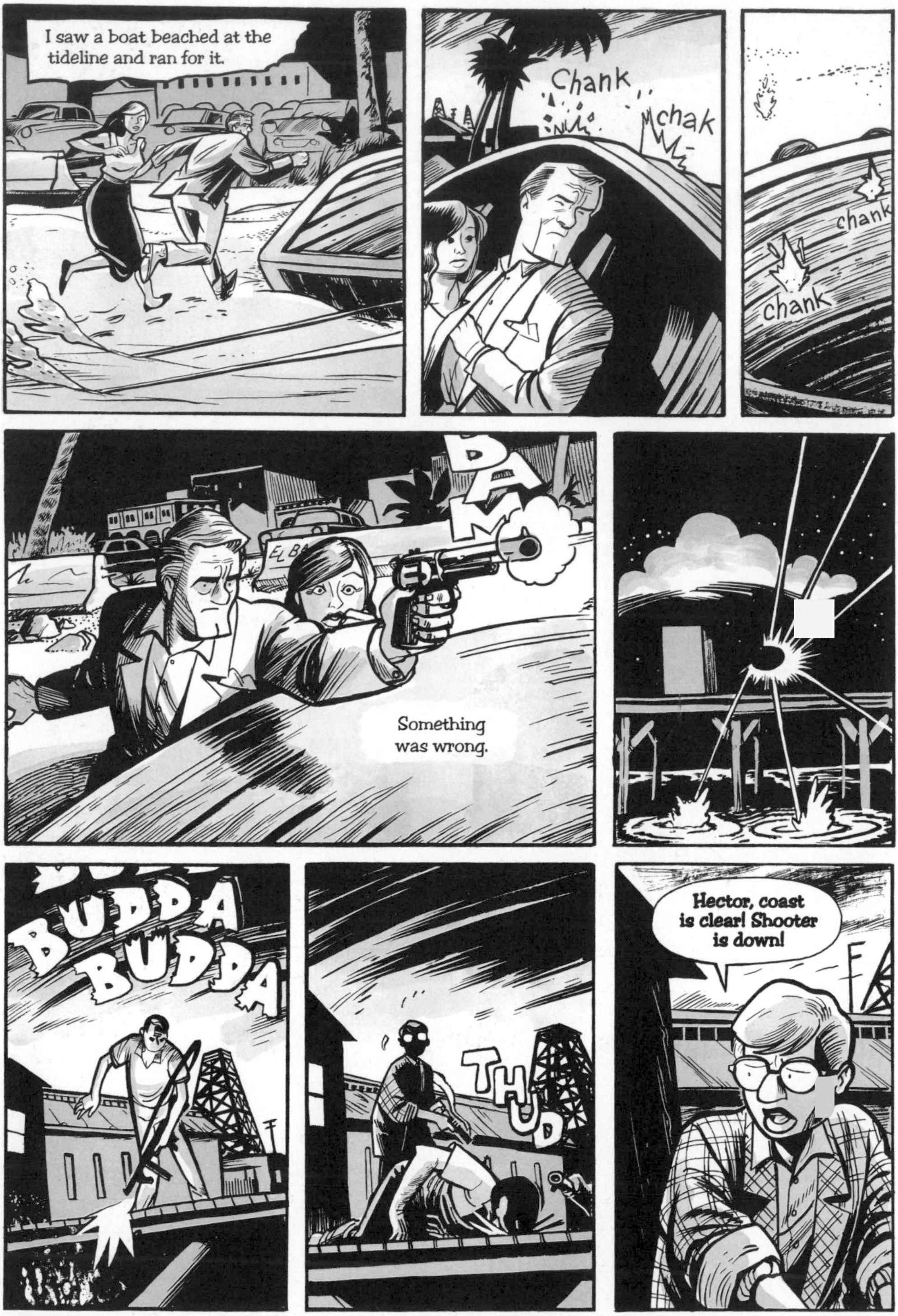
I saw a boat beached at the tideline and ran for it.
Chank
chak
chank
chank
BAM
Something was wrong.
BUDDA BUDDA
THUD
Hector, coast is clear! Shooter is down!

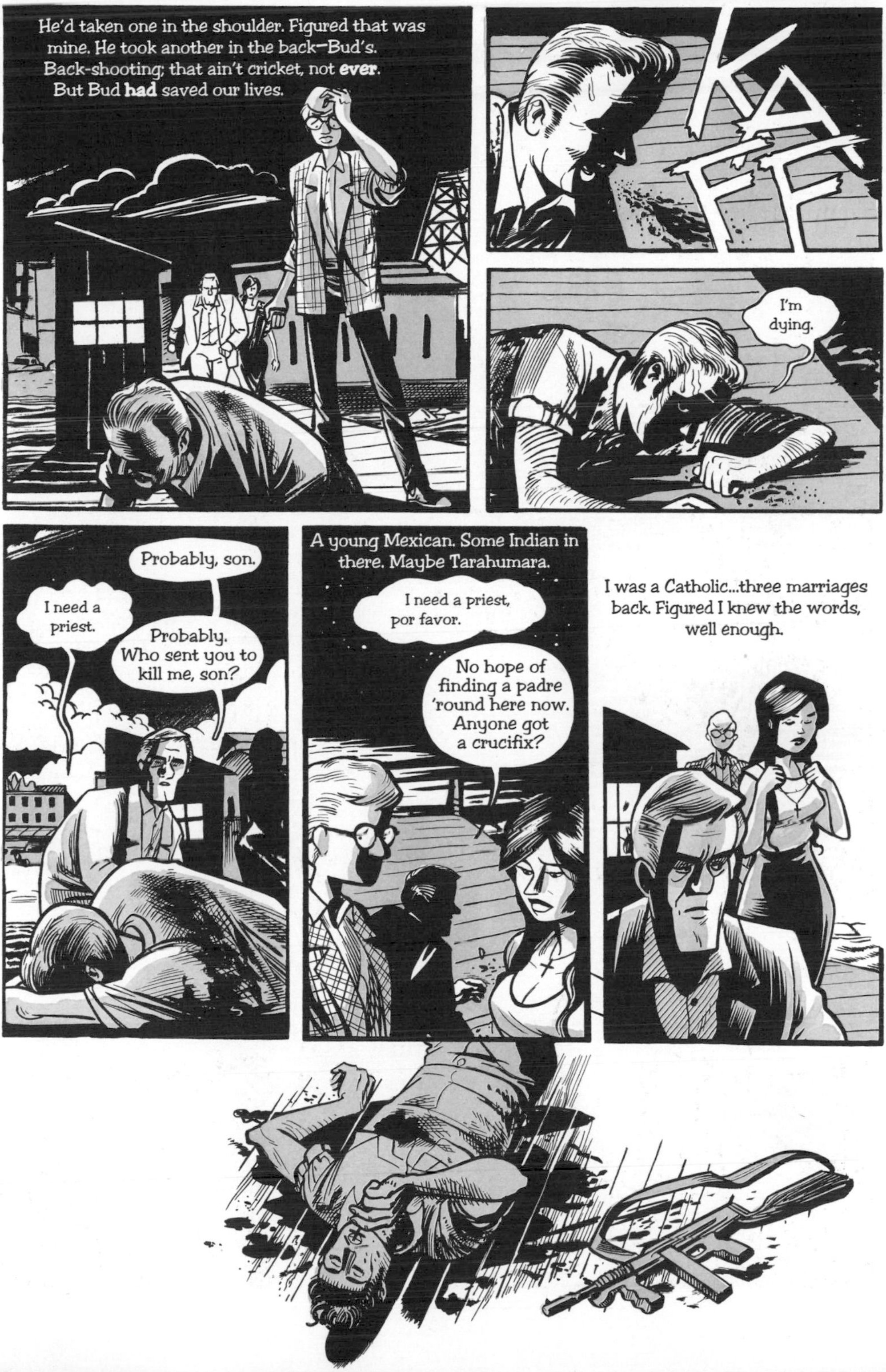
He'd taken one in the shoulder. Figured that was mine. He took another in the back—Bud's. Back-shooting; that ain't cricket, not **ever**. But Bud **had** saved our lives.
KAFF
I'm dying.
I need a priest.
Probably, son.
Probably. Who sent you to kill me, son?
A young Mexican. Some Indian in there. Maybe Tarahumara.
I need a priest, por favor.
No hope of finding a padre 'round here now. Anyone got a crucifix?
I was a Catholic...three marriages back. Figured I knew the words, well enough.

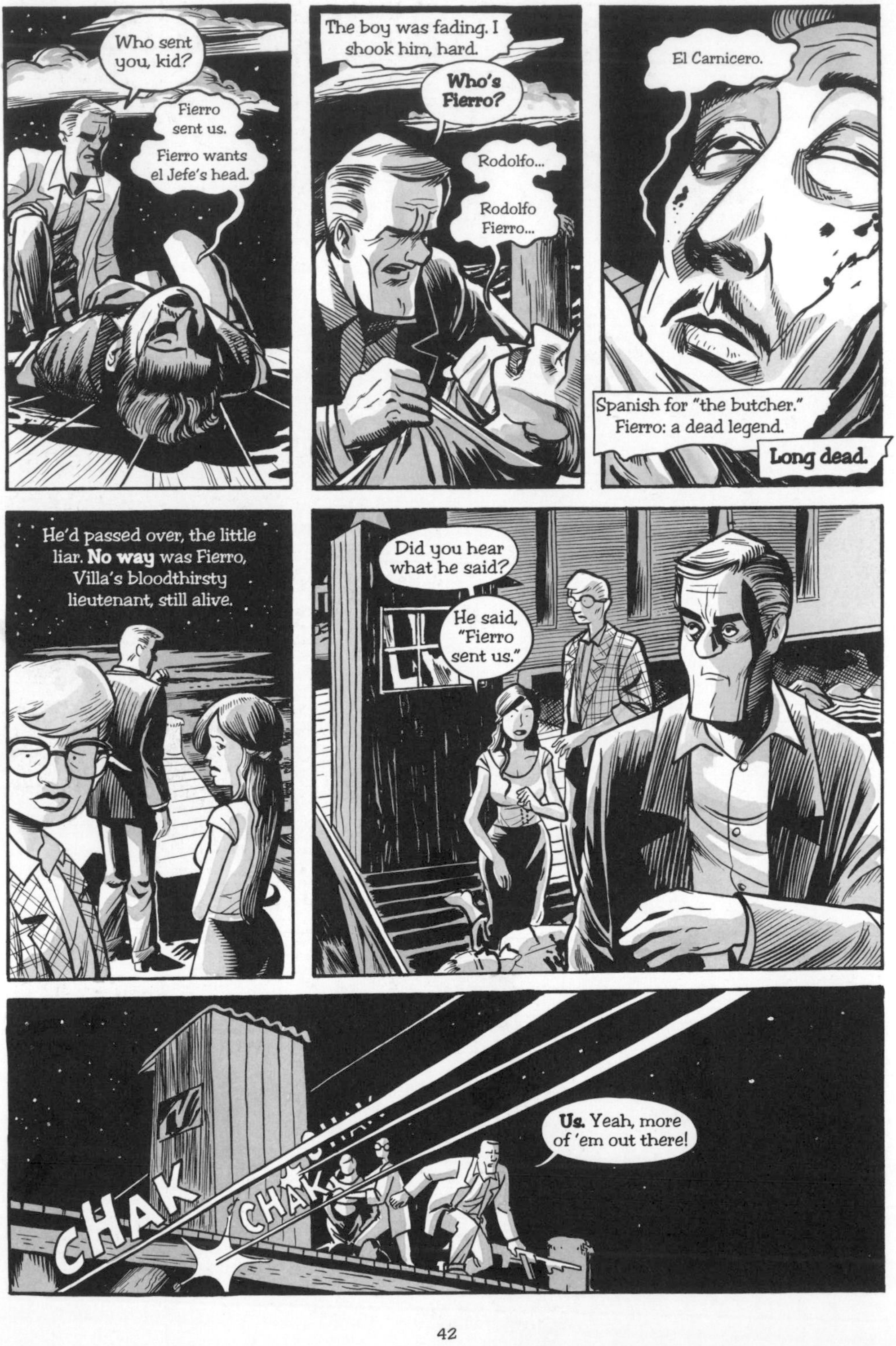
Who sent you, kid?
Fierro sent us.
Fierro wants el Jefe's head.
The boy was fading. I shook him, hard.
Who's Fierro?
Rodolfo...
Rodolfo Fierro...
El Carnicero.
Spanish for "the butcher." Fierro: a dead legend.
Long dead.
He'd passed over, the little liar. **No way** was Fierro, Villa's bloodthirsty lieutenant, still alive.
Did you hear what he said?
He said, "Fierro sent us."
Us. Yeah, more of 'em out there!
CHAK
CHAK

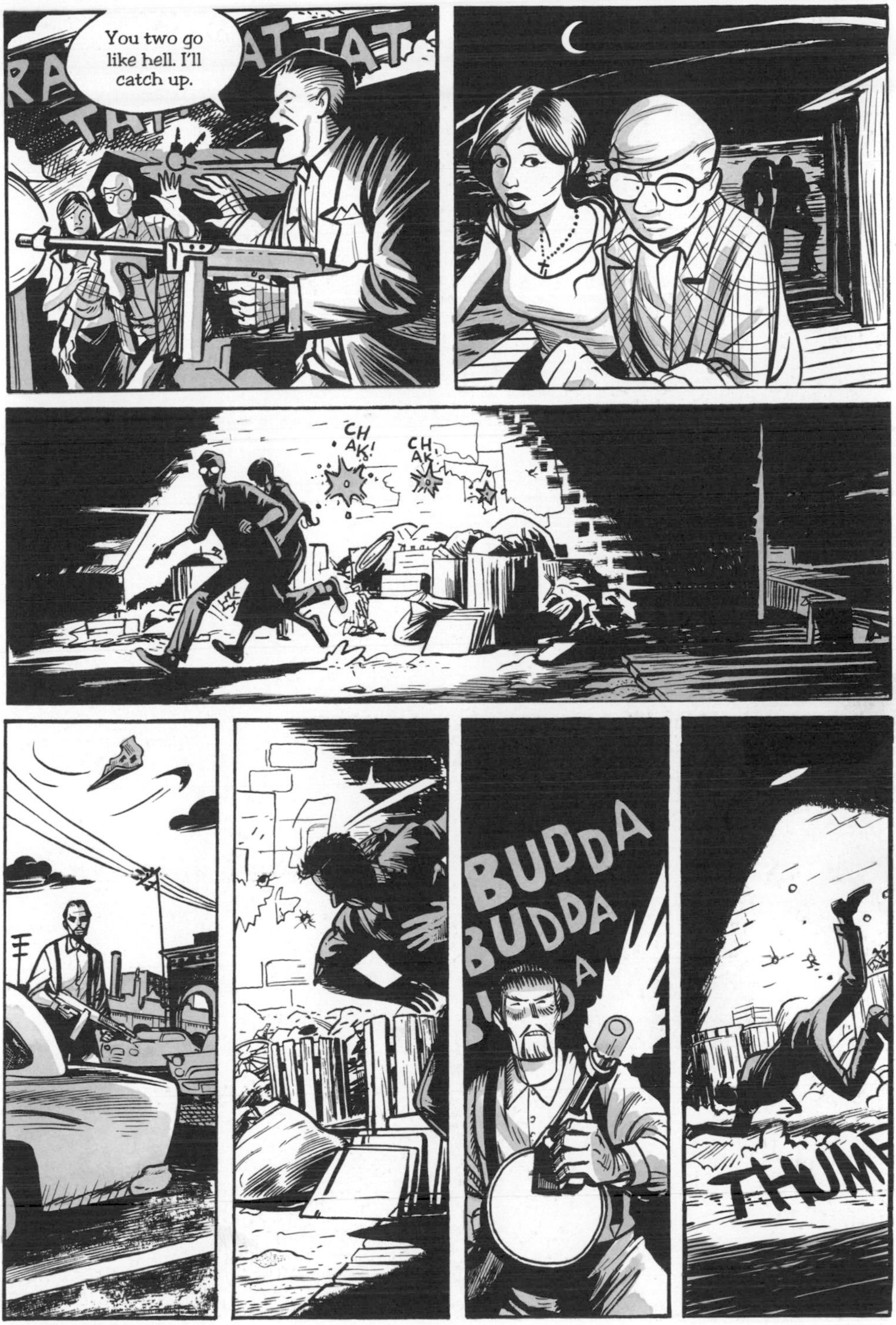

You two go like hell. I'll catch up.
CH AK!
CH AK!
BUDDA
BUDDA
THUMP

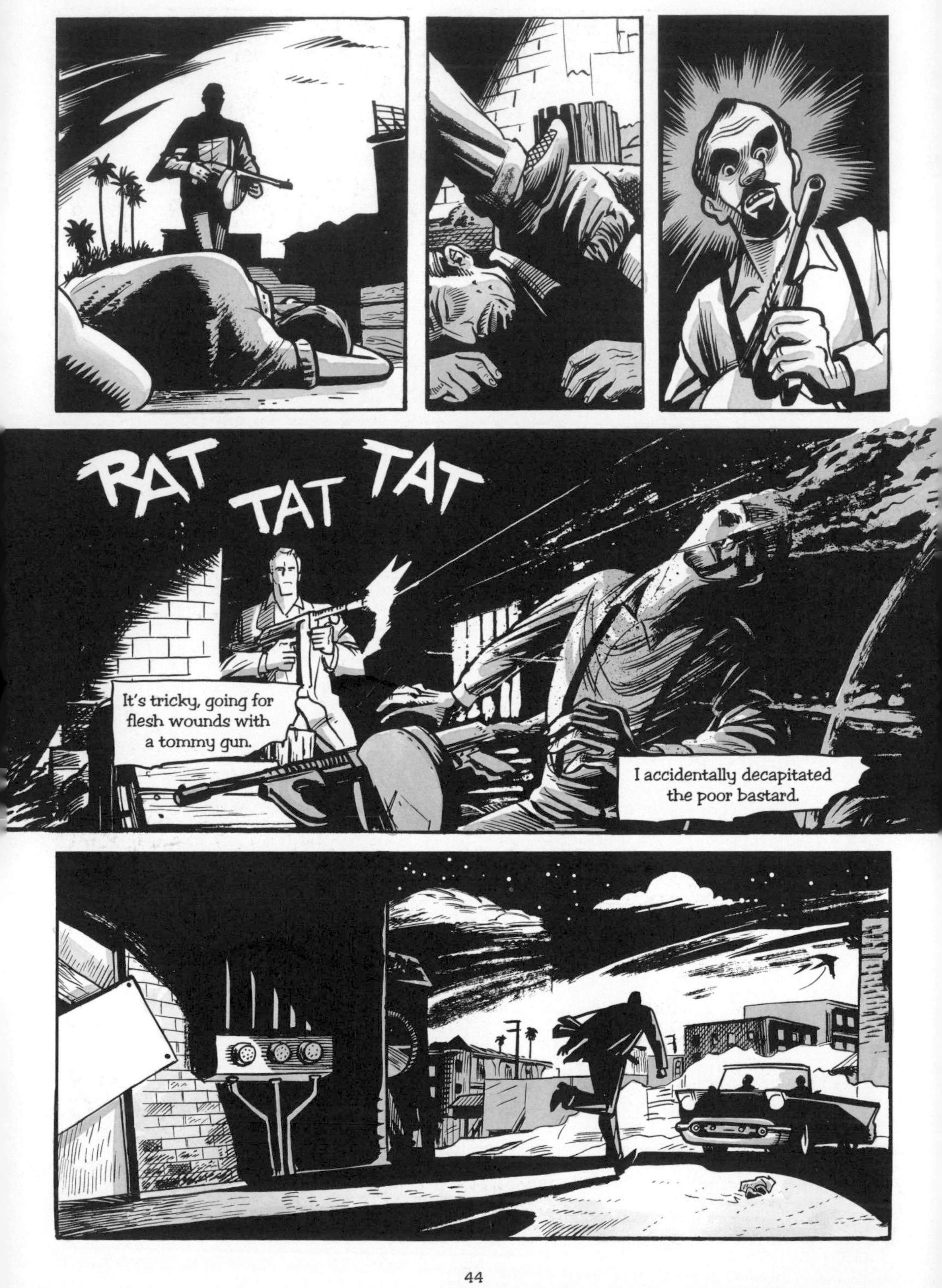
RAT TAT TAT
It's tricky, going for flesh wounds with a tommy gun.
I accidentally decapitated the poor bastard.

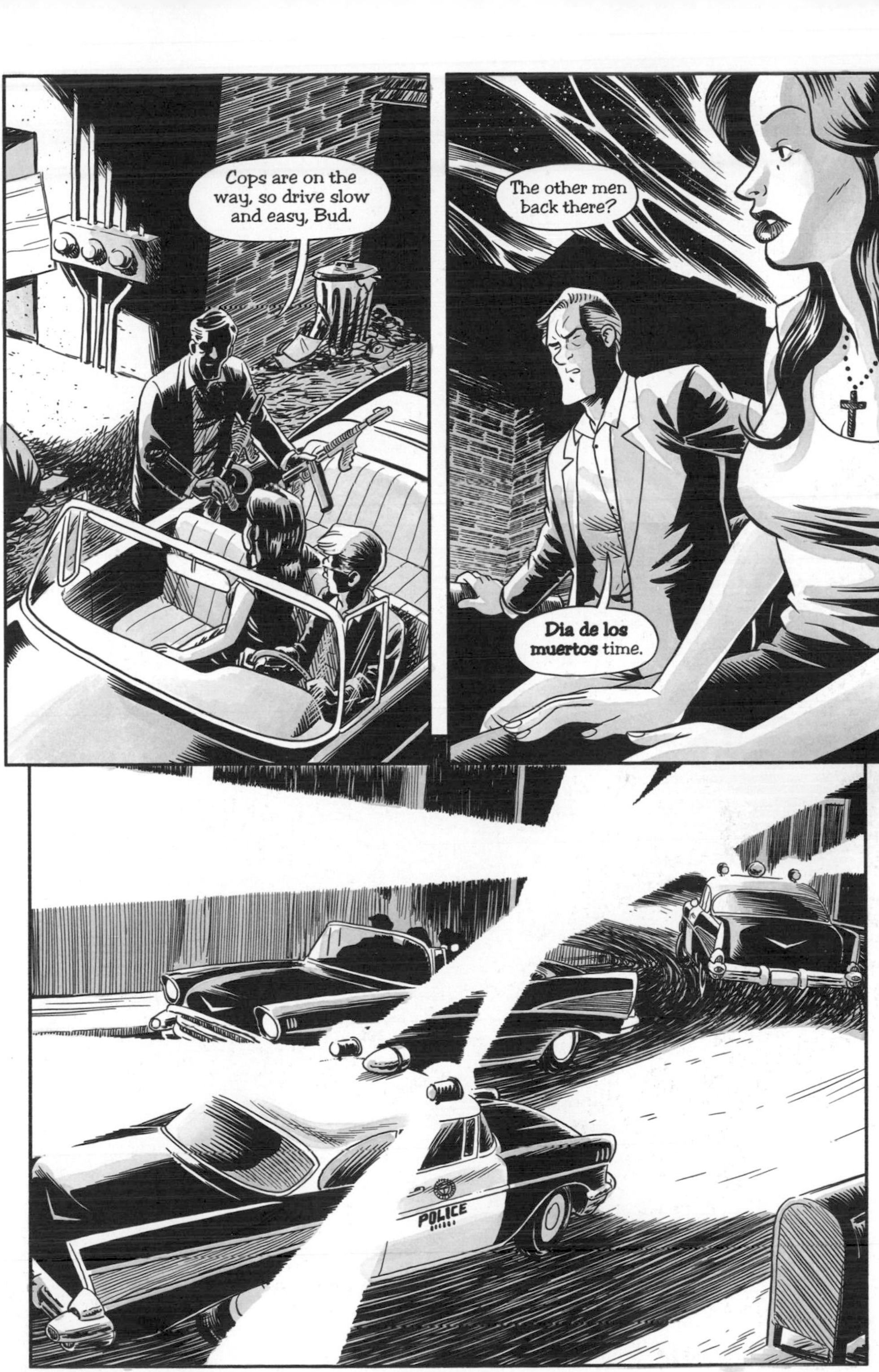
Cops are on the way, so drive slow and easy, Bud.
The other men back there?
Dia de los muertos time.
POLICE

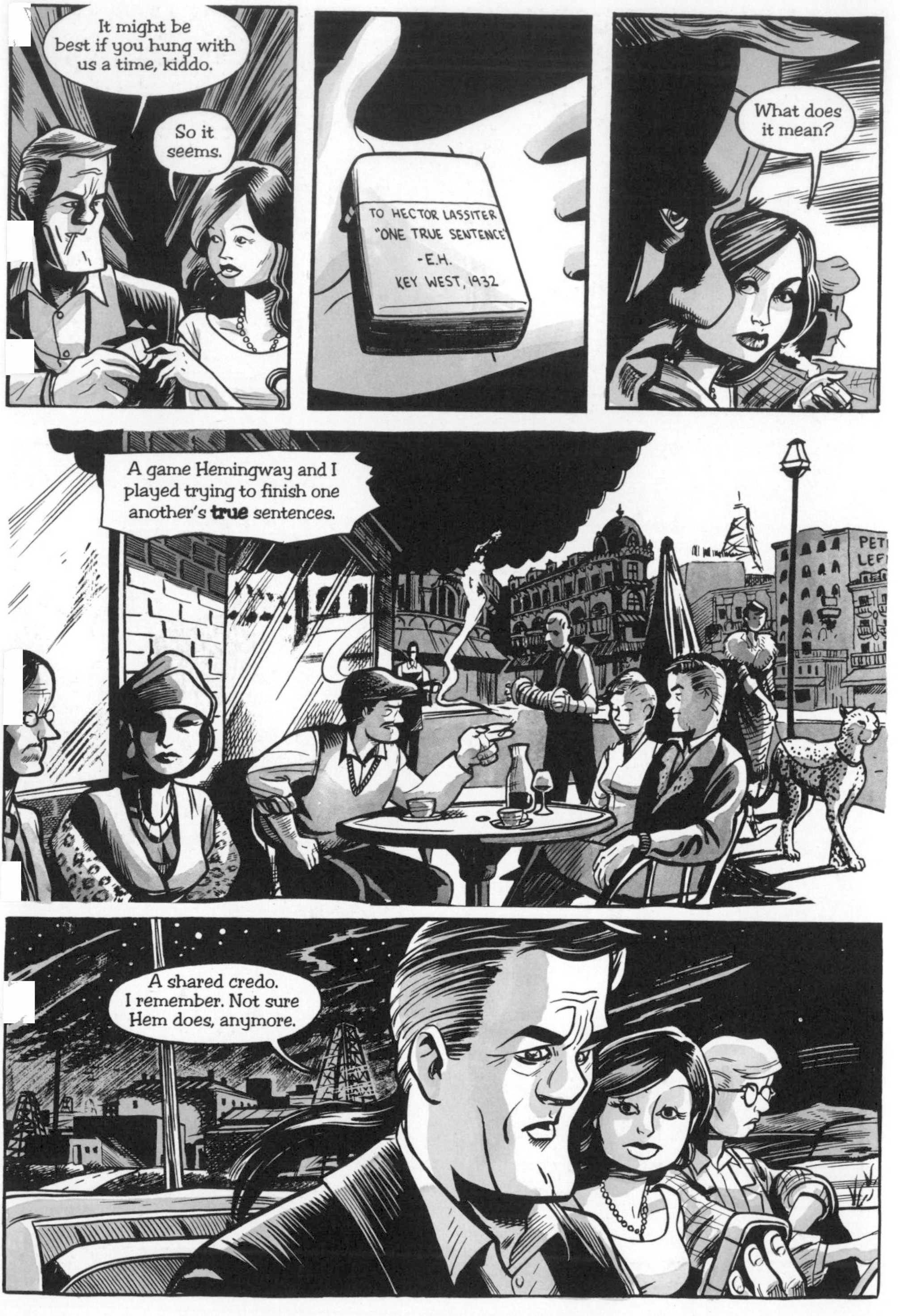
It might be best if you hung with us a time, kiddo.
So it seems.
TO HECTOR LASSITER
"ONE TRUE SENTENCE"
-E.H.
KEY WEST, 1932
What does it mean?
A game Hemingway and I played trying to finish one another's **true** sentences.
A shared credo. I remember. Not sure Hem does, anymore.

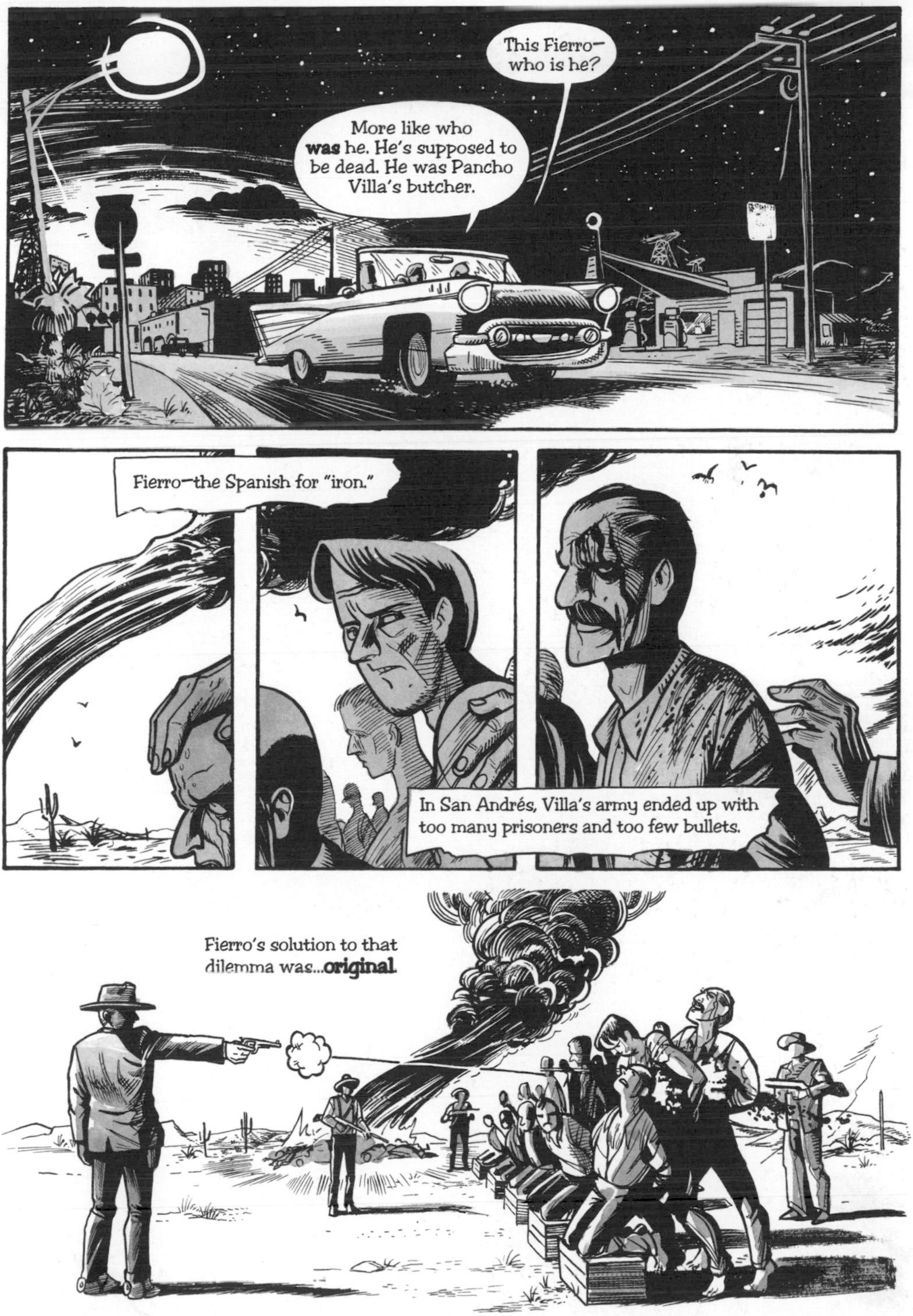
This Fierro—who is he?
More like who **was** he. He's supposed to be dead. He was Pancho Villa's butcher.
Fierro—the Spanish for "iron."
In San Andrés, Villa's army ended up with too many prisoners and too few bullets.
Fierro's solution to that dilemma was...**original**.

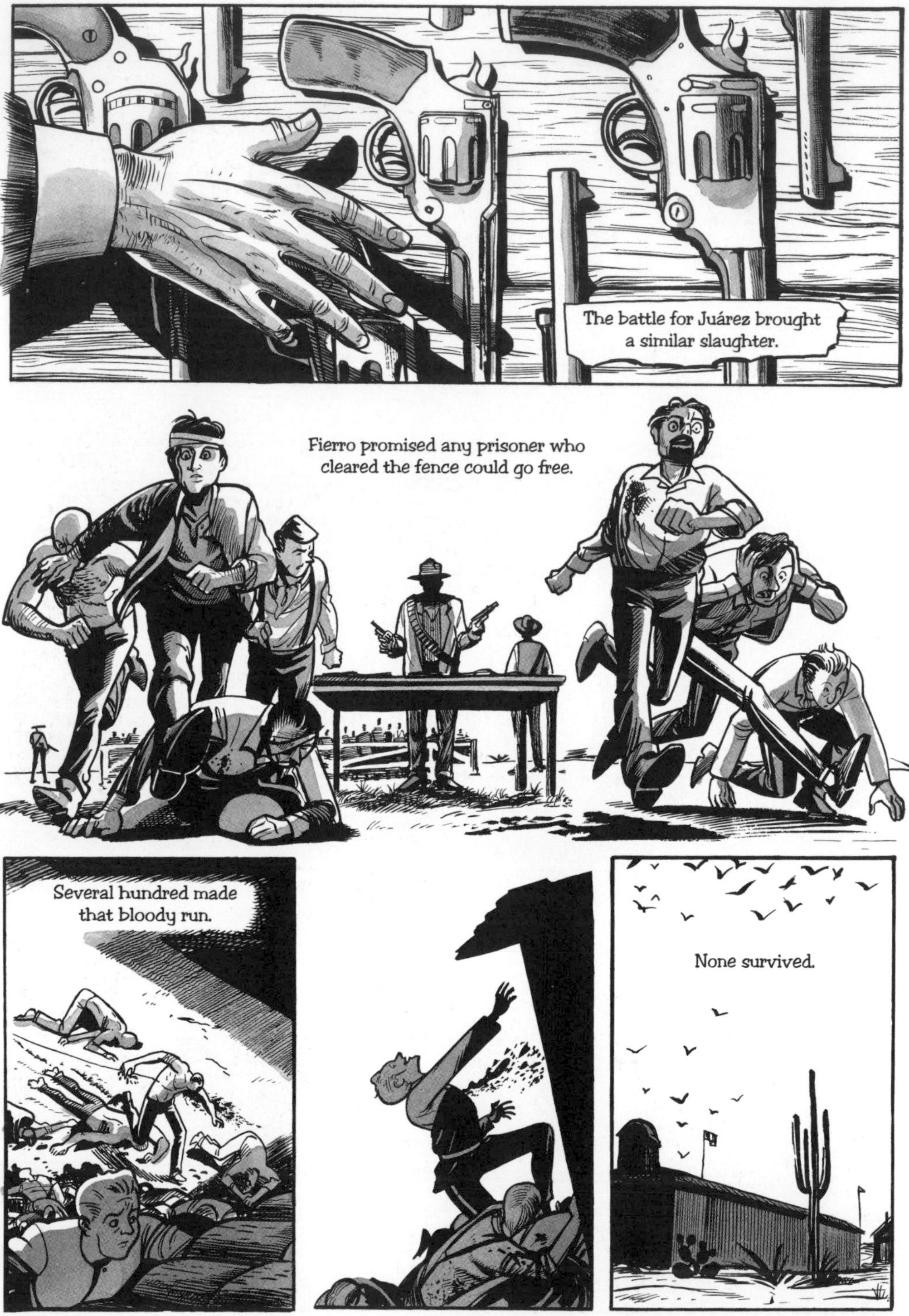
The battle for Juárez brought a similar slaughter.
Fierro promised any prisoner who cleared the fence could go free.
Several hundred made that bloody run.
None survived.

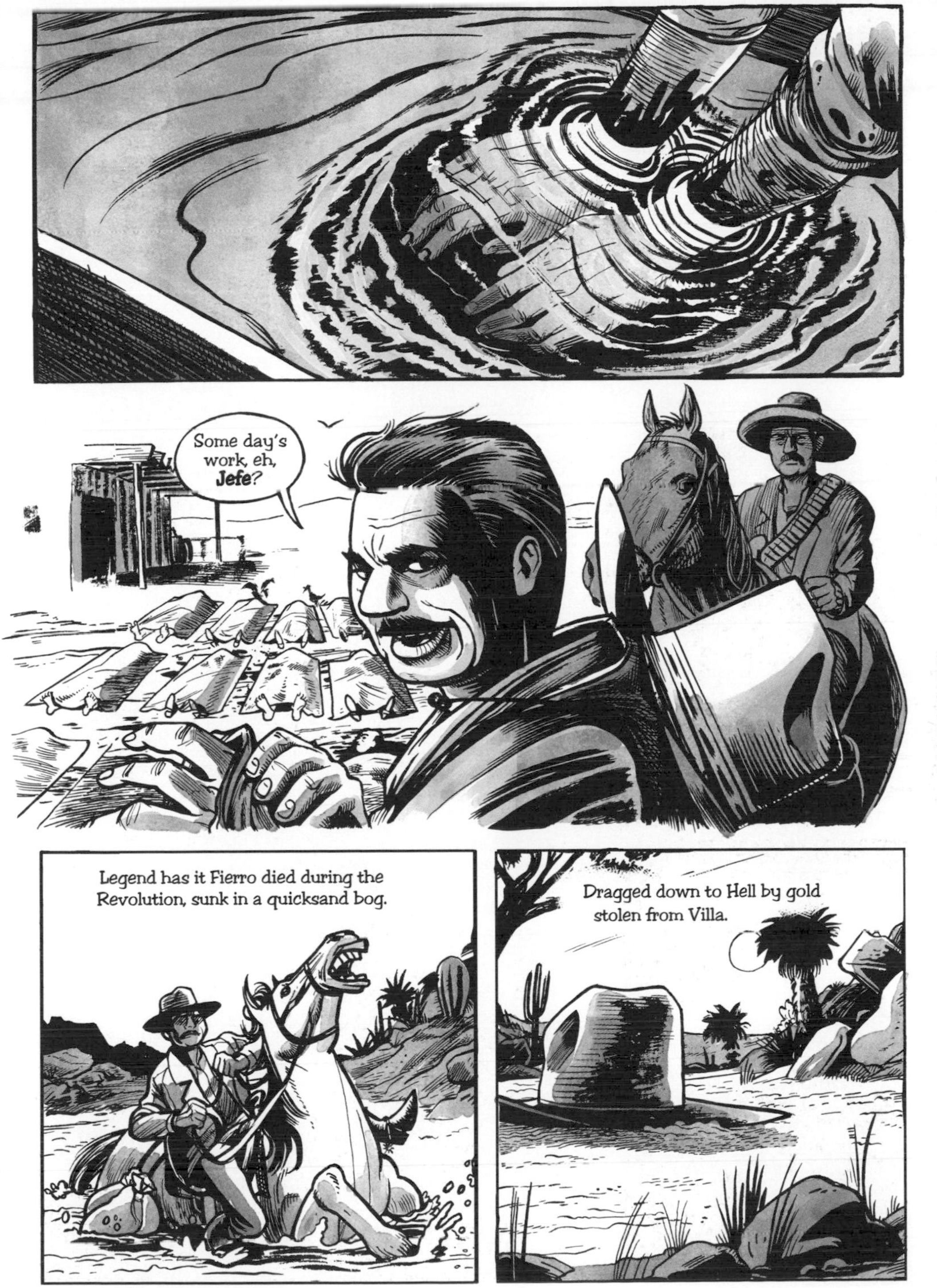

Some day's work, eh, **Jefe**?
Legend has it Fierro died during the Revolution, sunk in a quicksand bog.
Dragged down to Hell by gold stolen from Villa.

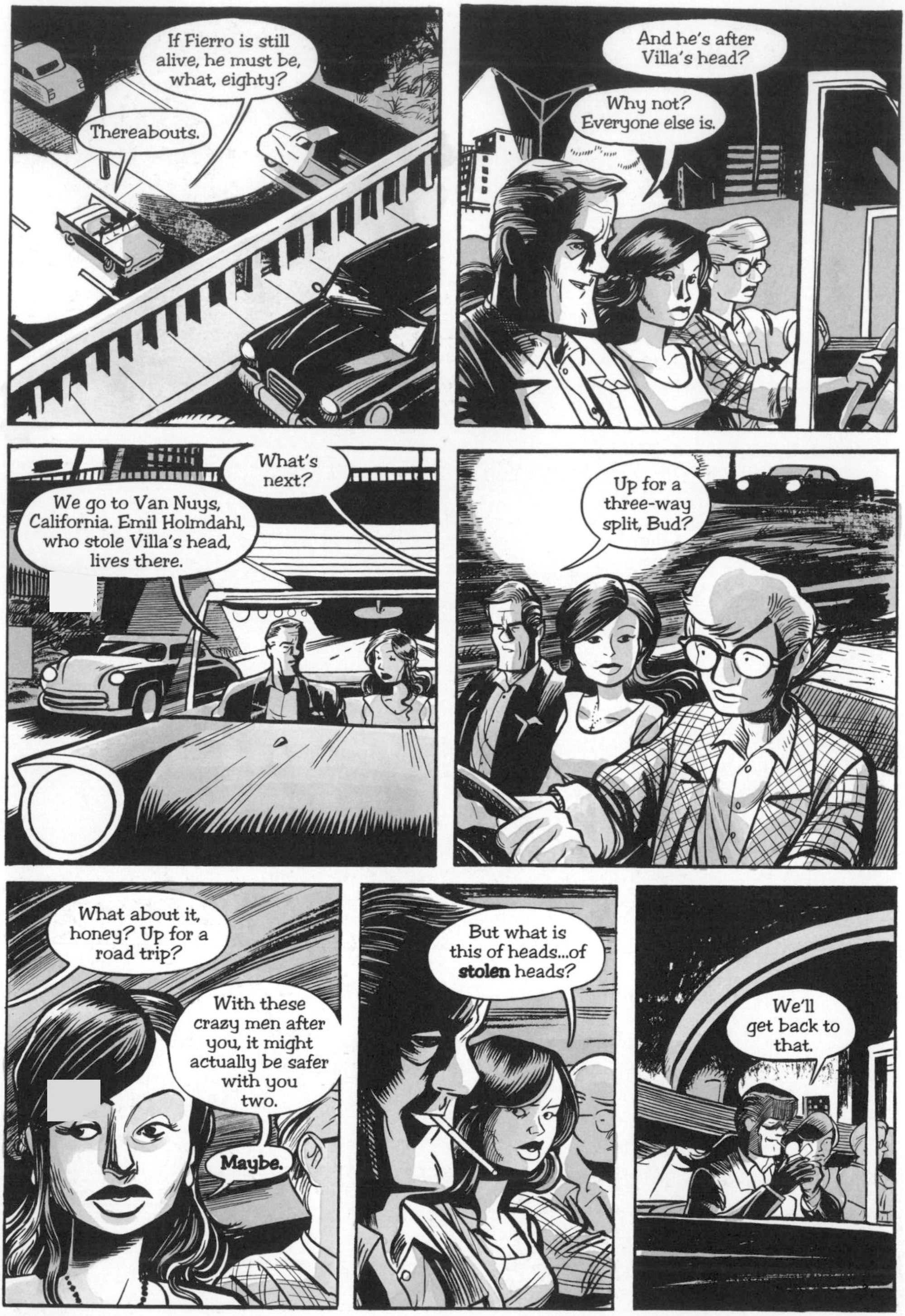
If Fierro is still alive, he must be, what, eighty?
Thereabouts.
And he's after Villa's head?
Why not? Everyone else is.
What's next?
We go to Van Nuys, California. Emil Holmdahl, who stole Villa's head, lives there.
Up for a three-way split, Bud?
What about it, honey? Up for a road trip?
With these crazy men after you, it might actually be safer with you two.
Maybe.
But what is this of heads...of **stolen** heads?
We'll get back to that.

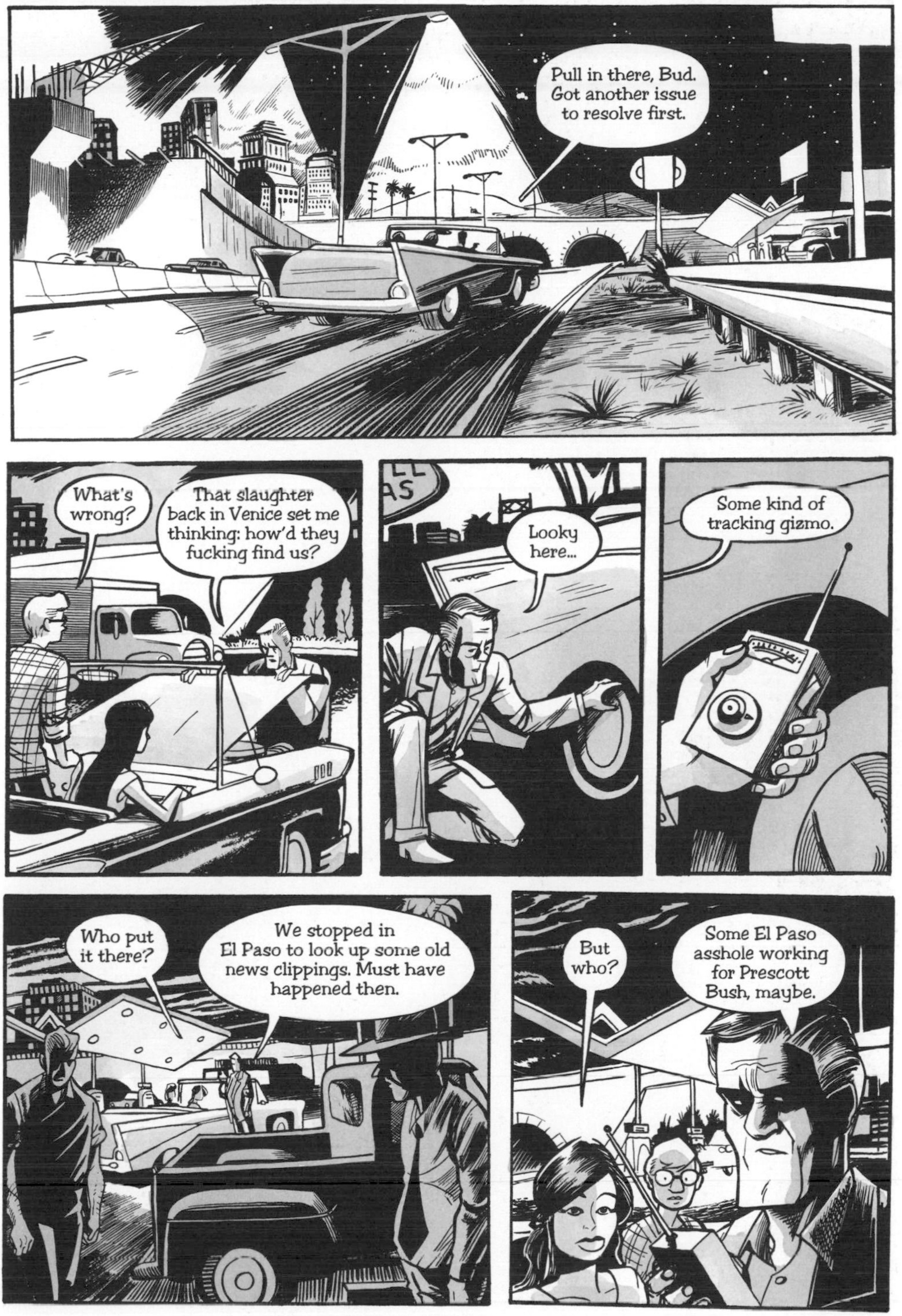
Pull in there, Bud. Got another issue to resolve first.
What's wrong?
That slaughter back in Venice set me thinking: how'd they fucking find us?
Looky here...
Some kind of tracking gizmo.
Who put it there?
We stopped in El Paso to look up some old news clippings. Must have happened then.
But who?
Some El Paso asshole working for Prescott Bush, maybe.

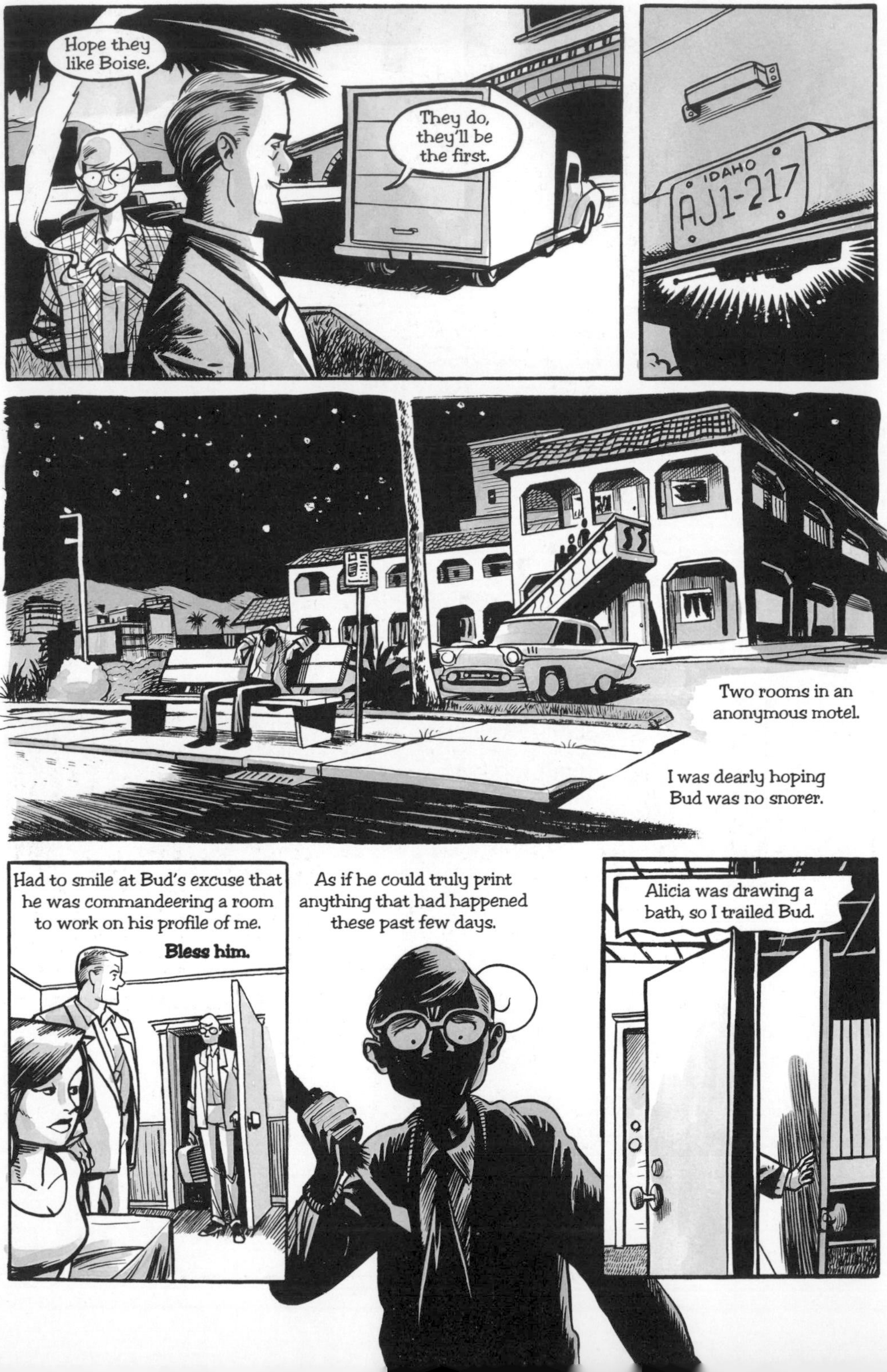

Hope they like Boise.
They do, they'll be the first.
IDAHO
AJ1-217
Two rooms in an anonymous motel.
I was dearly hoping Bud was no snorer.
Had to smile at Bud's excuse that he was commandeering a room to work on his profile of me.
Bless him.
As if he could truly print anything that had happened these past few days.
Alicia was drawing a bath, so I trailed Bud.

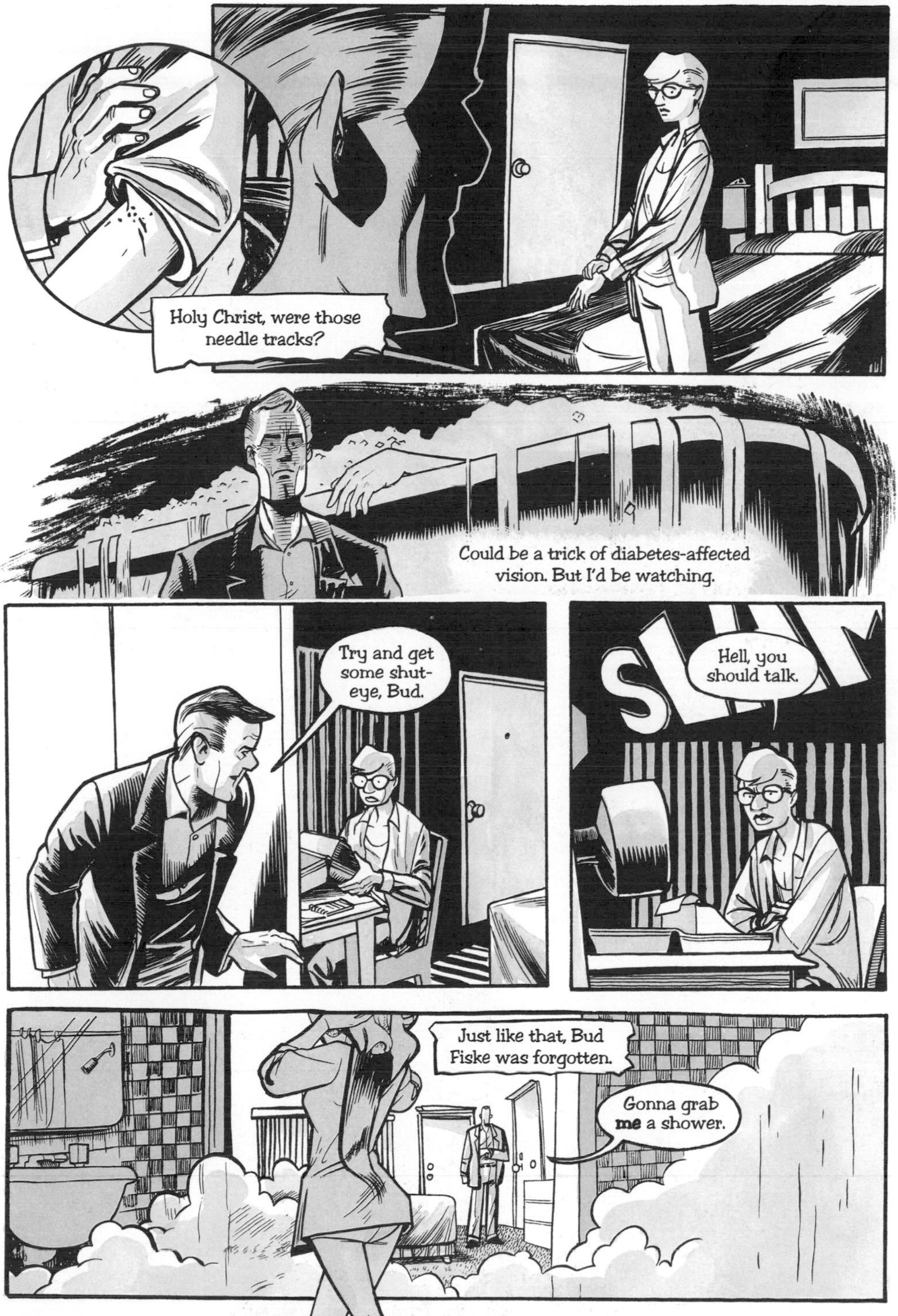
Holy Christ, were those needle tracks?
Could be a trick of diabetes-affected vision. But I'd be watching.
Try and get some shut-eye, Bud.
Hell, you should talk.
Just like that, Bud Fiske was forgotten.
Gonna grab **me** a shower.

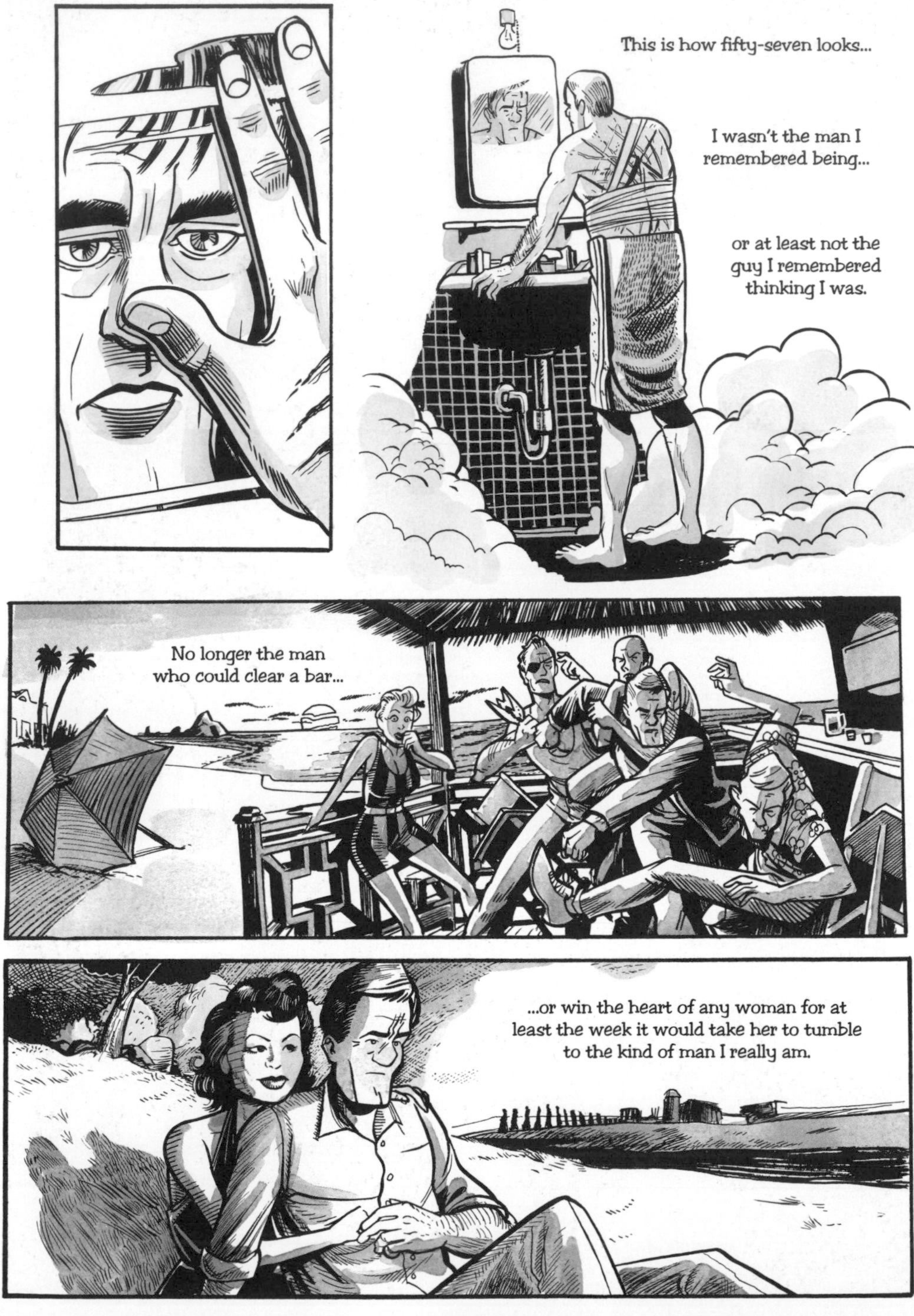
This is how fifty-seven looks...
I wasn't the man I remembered being...
or at least not the guy I remembered thinking I was.
No longer the man who could clear a bar...
...or win the heart of any woman for at least the week it would take her to tumble to the kind of man I really am.

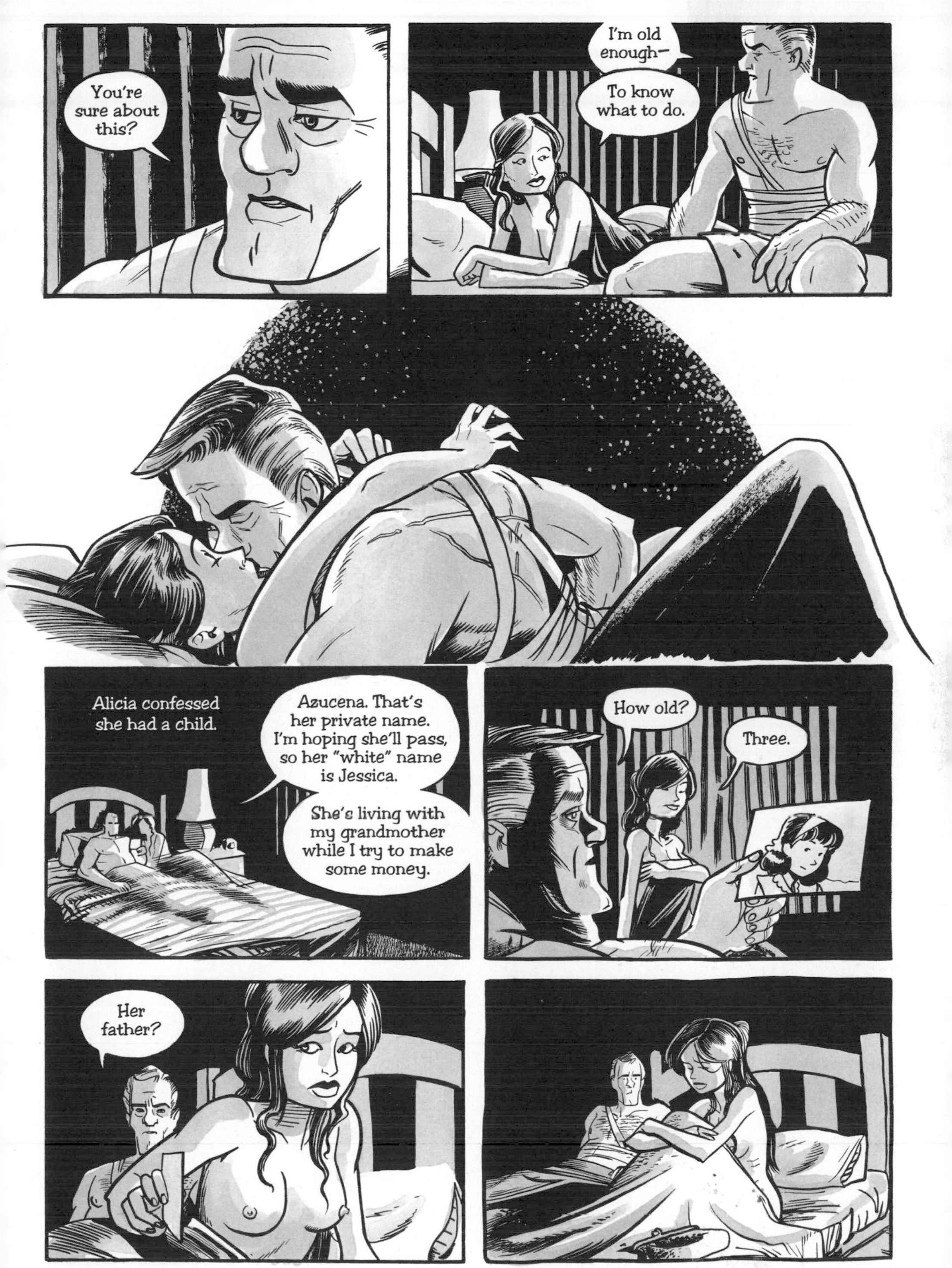
You're sure about this?
I'm old enough—
To know what to do.
Alicia confessed she had a child.
Azucena. That's her private name. I'm hoping she'll pass, so her "white" name is Jessica.
She's living with my grandmother while I try to make some money.
How old?
Three.
Her father?

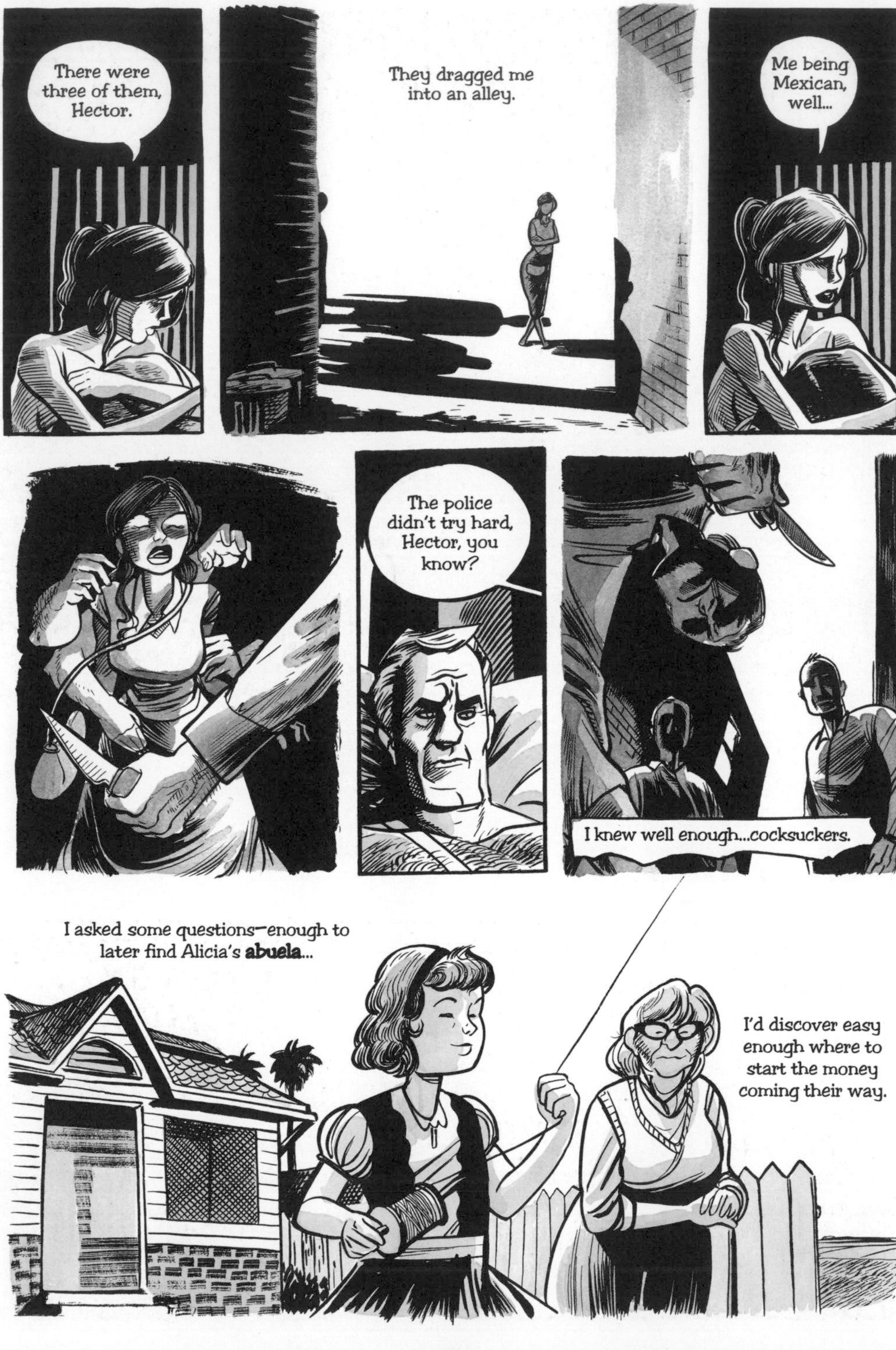

There were three of them, Hector.
They dragged me into an alley.
Me being Mexican, well...
The police didn't try hard, Hector, you know?
I knew well enough...cocksuckers.
I asked some questions—enough to later find Alicia's **abuela**...
I'd discover easy enough where to start the money coming their way.

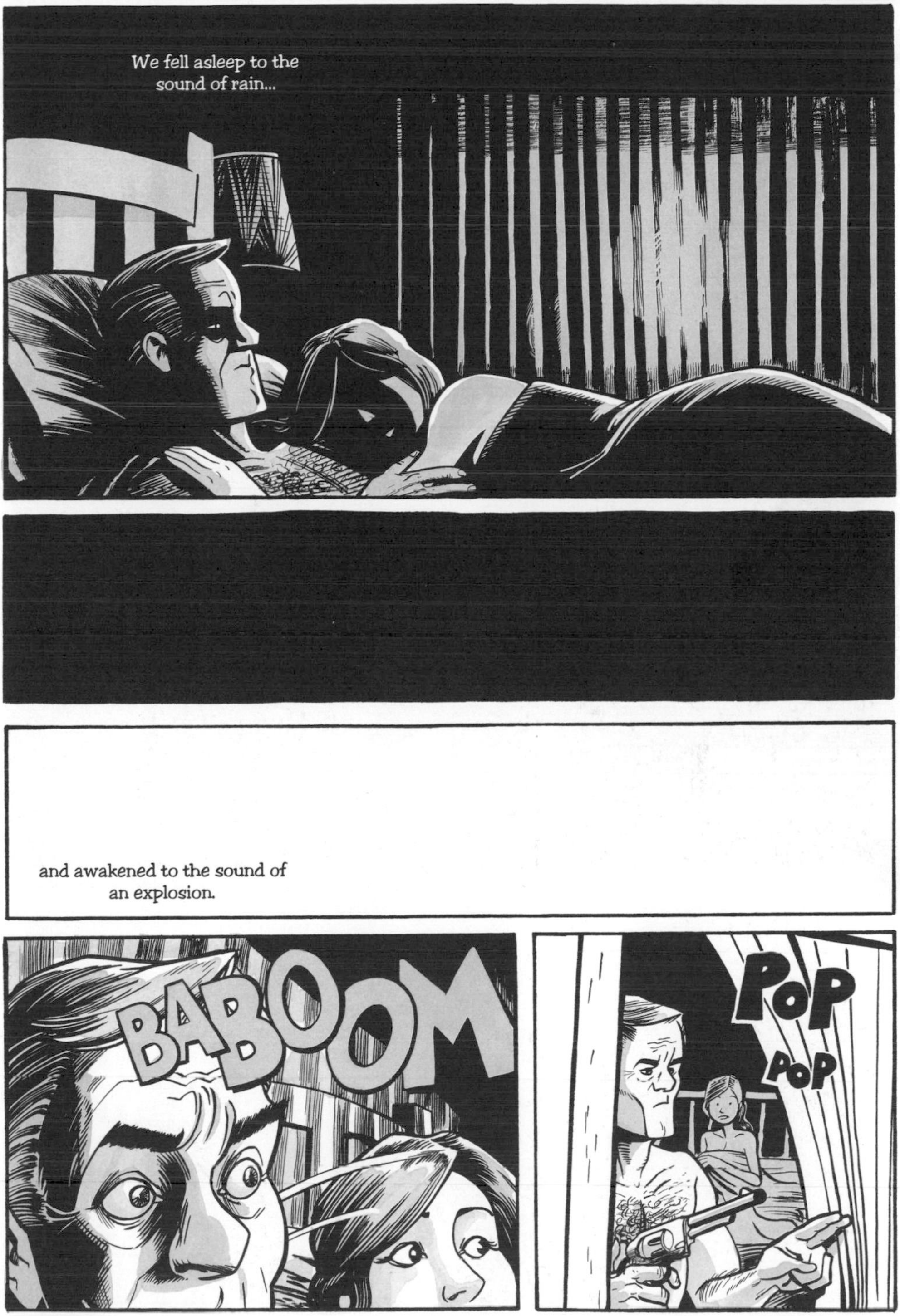

We fell asleep to the sound of rain...
and awakened to the sound of an explosion.
BABOOM
POP
POP

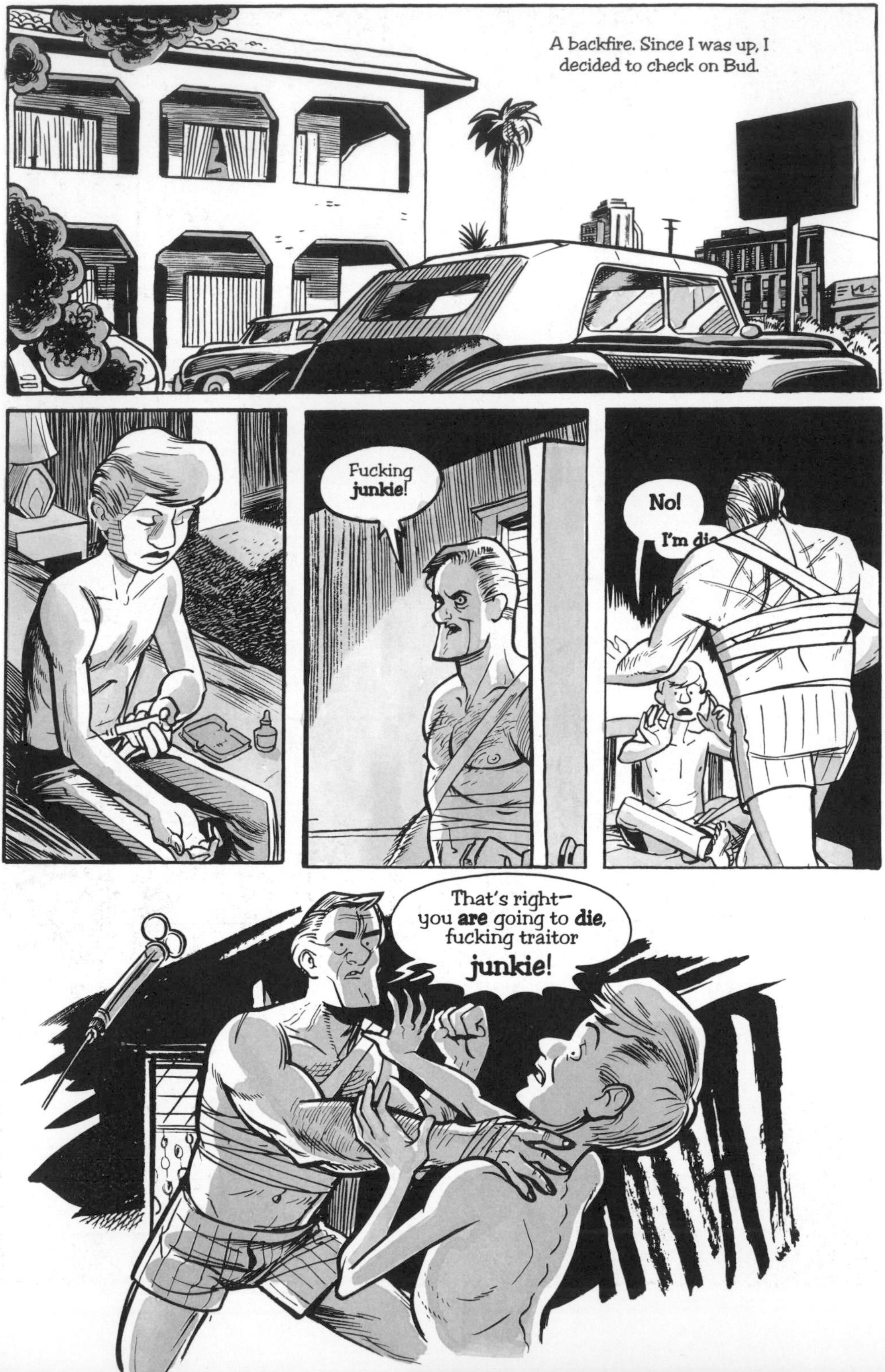

A backfire. Since I was up, I decided to check on Bud.
Fucking **junkie**!
No!
That's right— you **are** going to **die**, fucking traitor **junkie**!

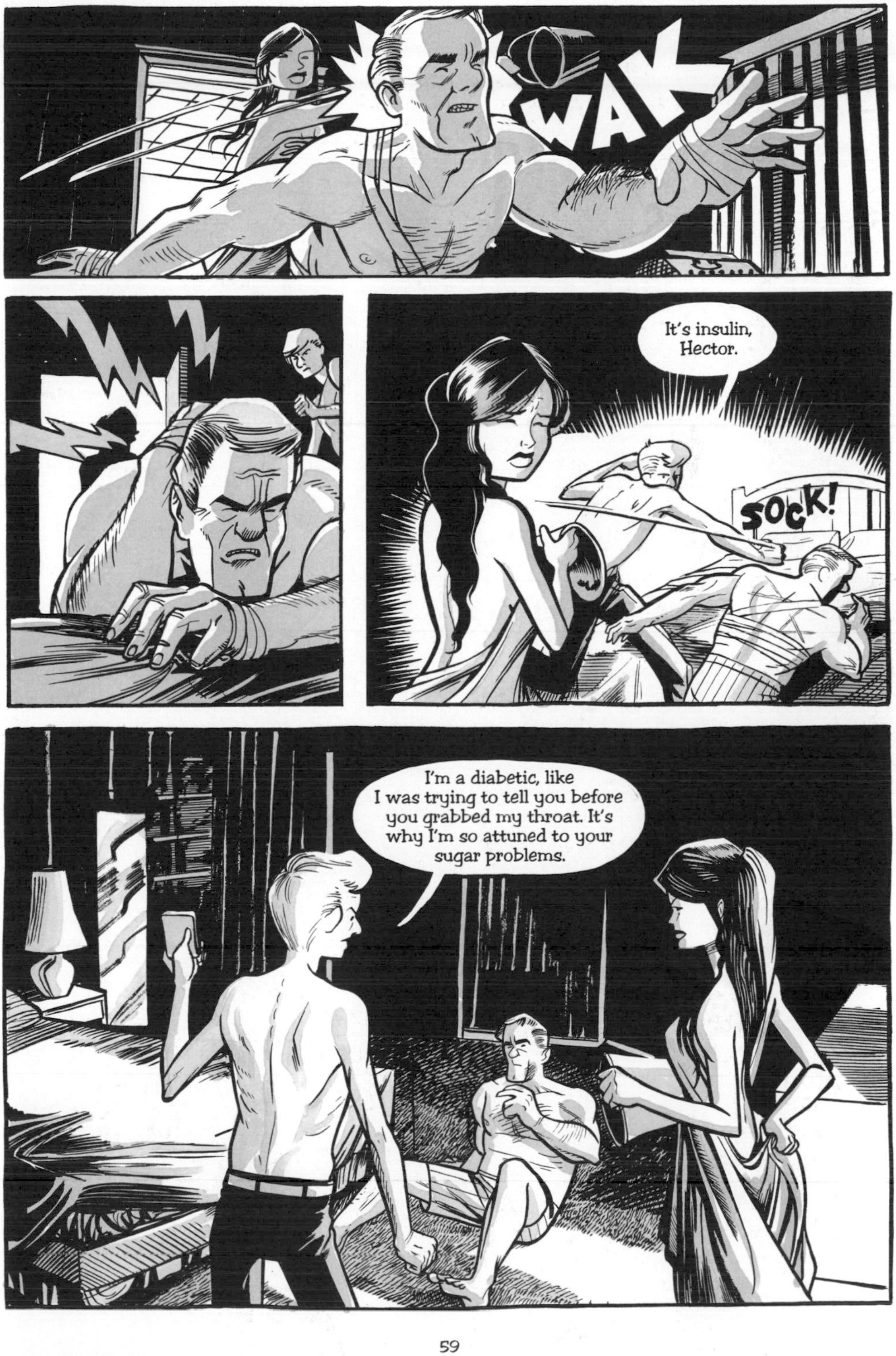

WAK
It's insulin, Hector.
SOCK!
I'm a diabetic, like I was trying to tell you before you grabbed my throat. It's why I'm so attuned to your sugar problems.

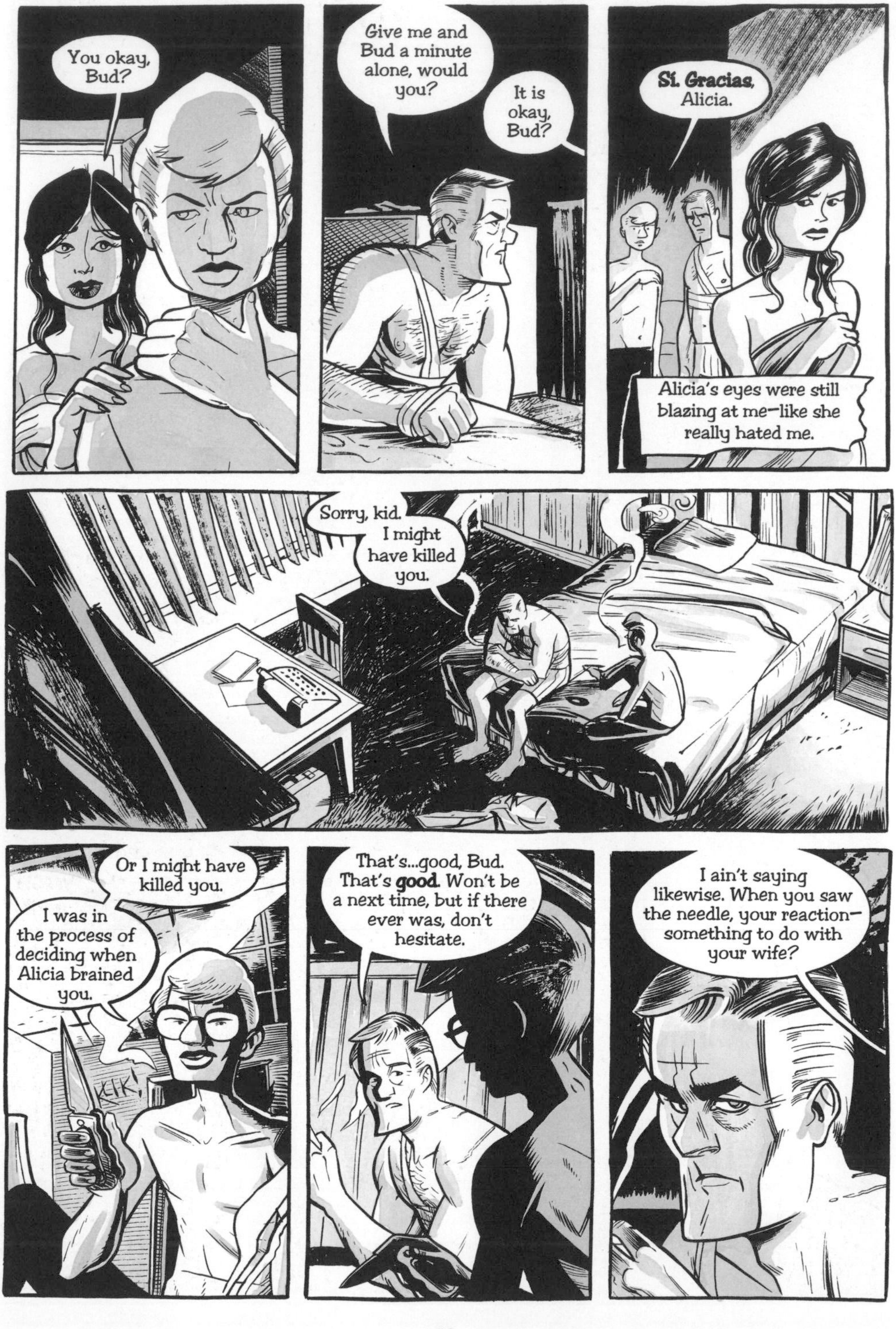
You okay, Bud?
Give me and Bud a minute alone, would you?
It is okay, Bud?
Sí. Gracias, Alicia.
Alicia's eyes were still blazing at me—like she really hated me.
Sorry, kid. I might have killed you.
Or I might have killed you.
I was in the process of deciding when Alicia brained you.
KLIK!
That's...good, Bud. That's good. Won't be a next time, but if there ever was, don't hesitate.
I ain't saying likewise. When you saw the needle, your reaction—something to do with your wife?

My wife was an addict.

I didn't know until doctors told me...and then told me what it did to my daughter. Maria's addiction killed Dolores, really.

And that's all I'll say about any of that.

I'll talk to Alicia. See if I can smooth it over.

I'll owe you large, kid.

Hell, maybe Bud would succeed. He was a poet, after all...

Do you deliberately make a mess of your life just to keep yourself interested?

Kid, you may be the first to really get my sorry act.

What a terrible way to live. You can't live in the moment all the time, Hector. Need to give it a rest now and again.

No way, Bud. Gotta feed the beast...only way the muse will spread her legs for you.

It's the price we writers pay.

All of us.

Bud left, looking **real** dubious.

61

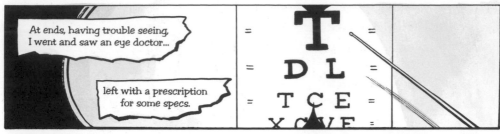

At ends, having trouble seeing, I went and saw an eye doctor...

left with a prescription for some specs.

Saw a regular doctor, too... He ran me through tests...

said he'd call in a few days with the verdict on my possible diabetes.

Turned out he was a reader of mine...

Try and take it easier. Lay off the alcohol...and no more fights.

Don't confuse me with my characters, Doc.

That's good advice. You should listen to yourself, Mr. Lassiter.

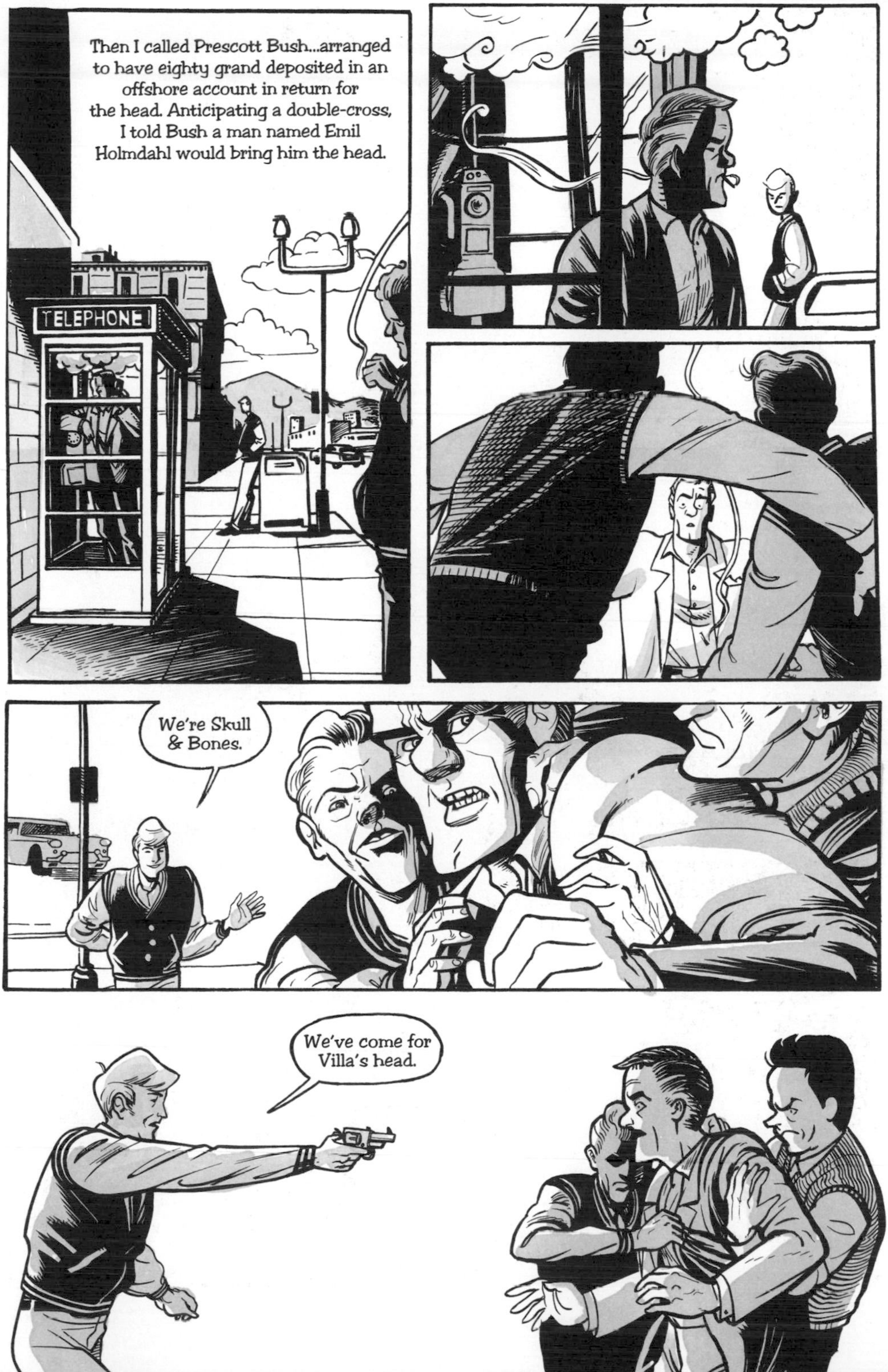
Then I called Prescott Bush...arranged to have eighty grand deposited in an offshore account in return for the head. Anticipating a double-cross, I told Bush a man named Emil Holmdahl would bring him the head.
TELEPHONE
We're Skull & Bones.
We've come for Villa's head.

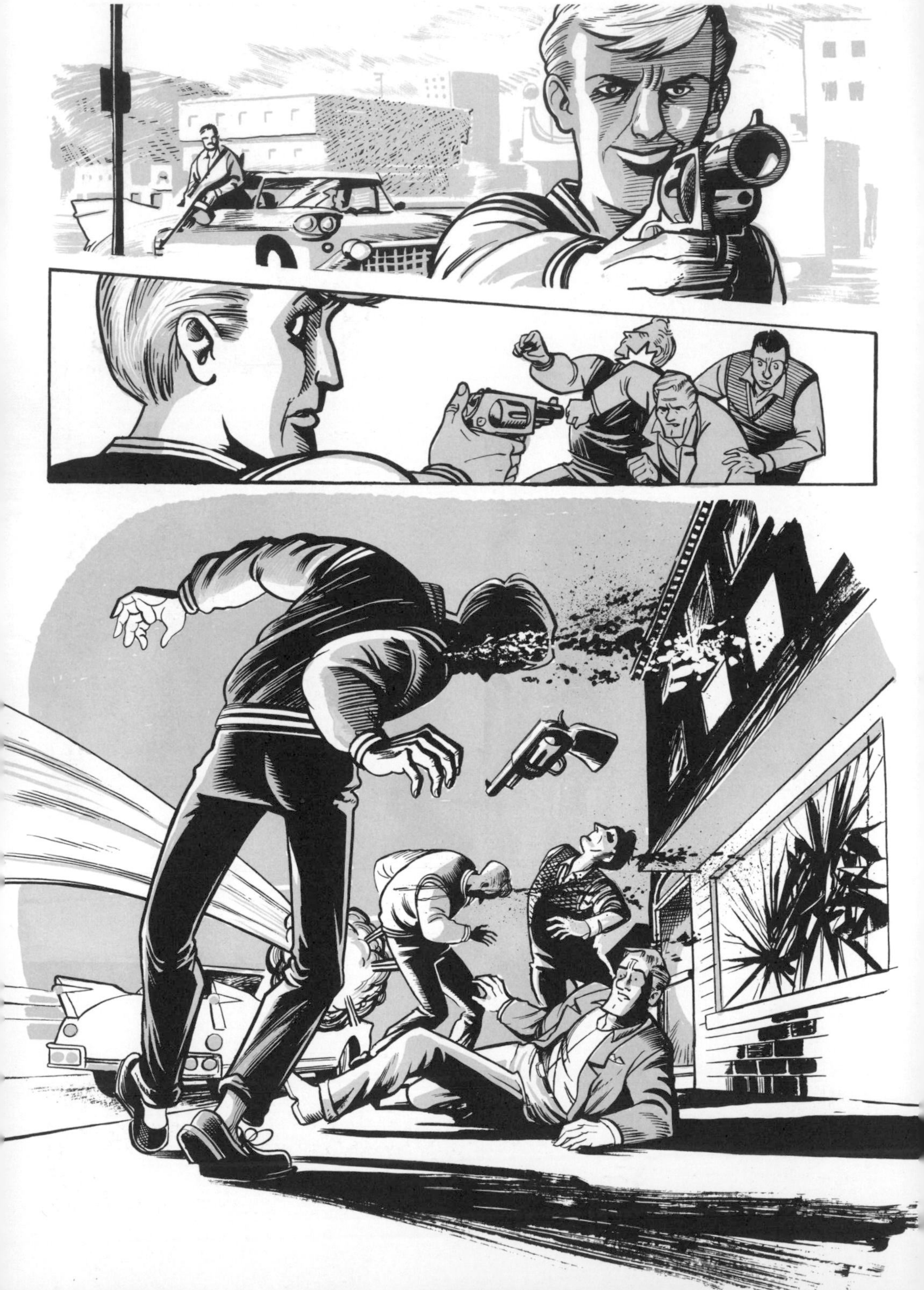

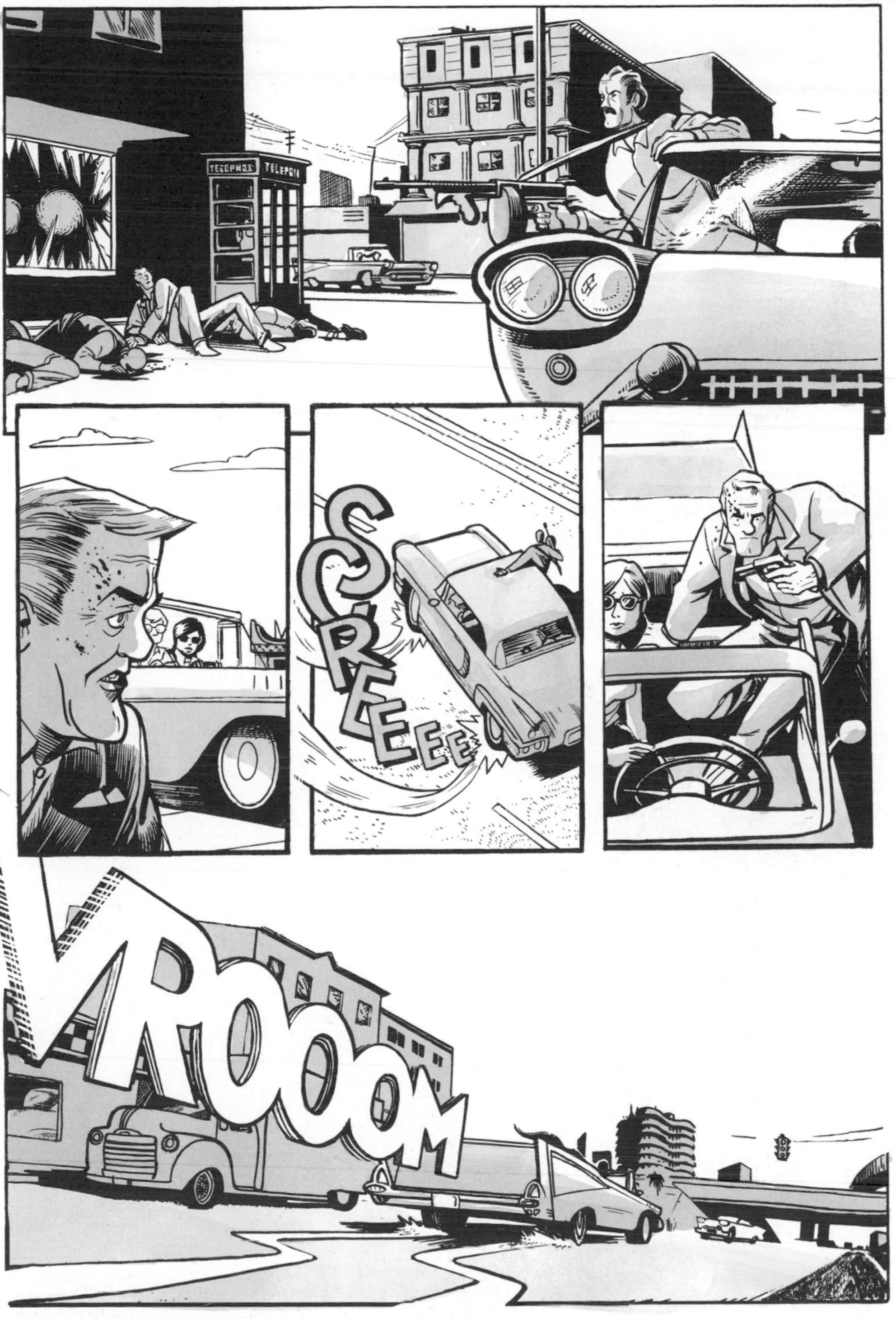
SCREEEE
VROOOM

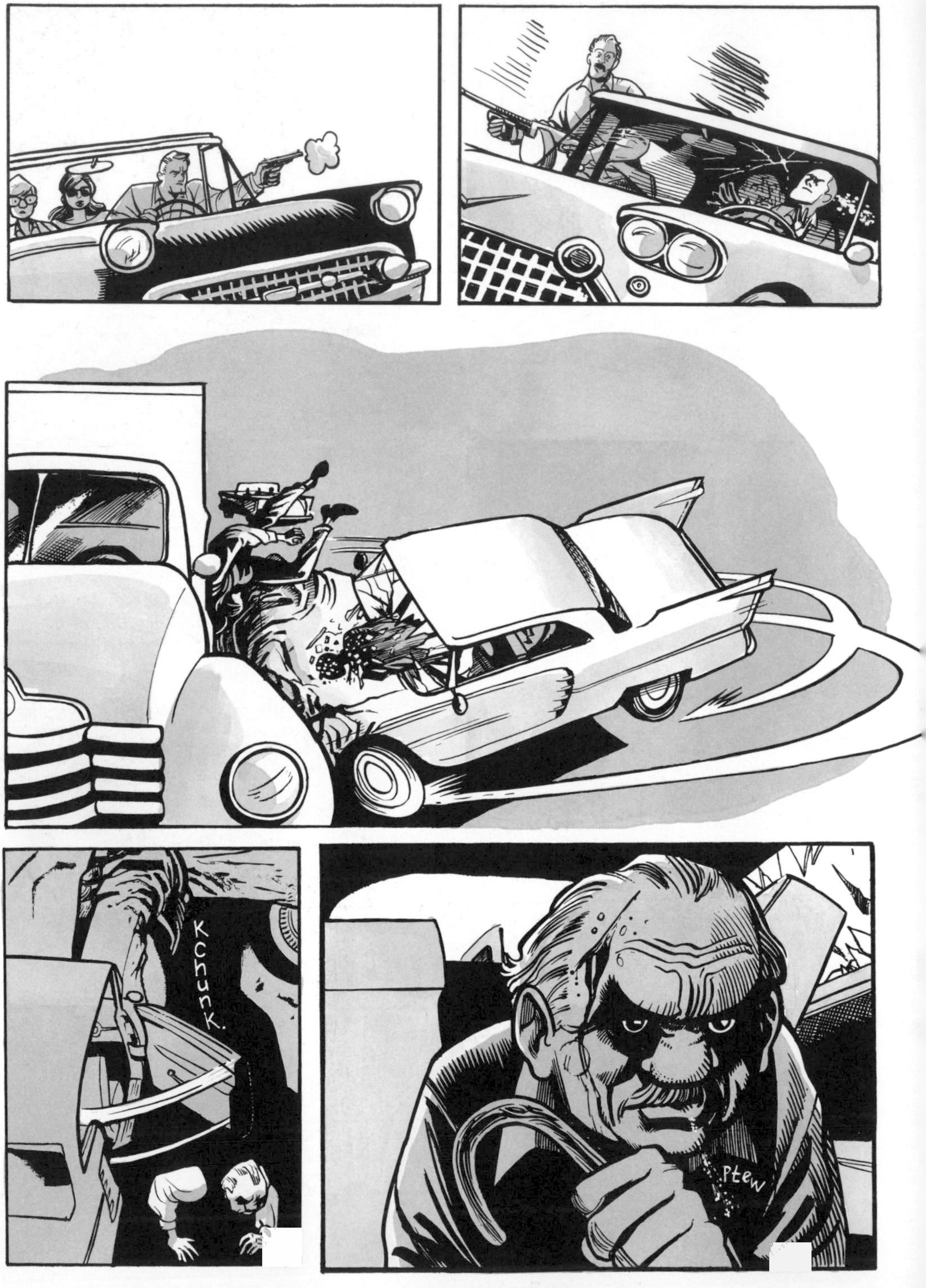
Kchunk.
Ptew

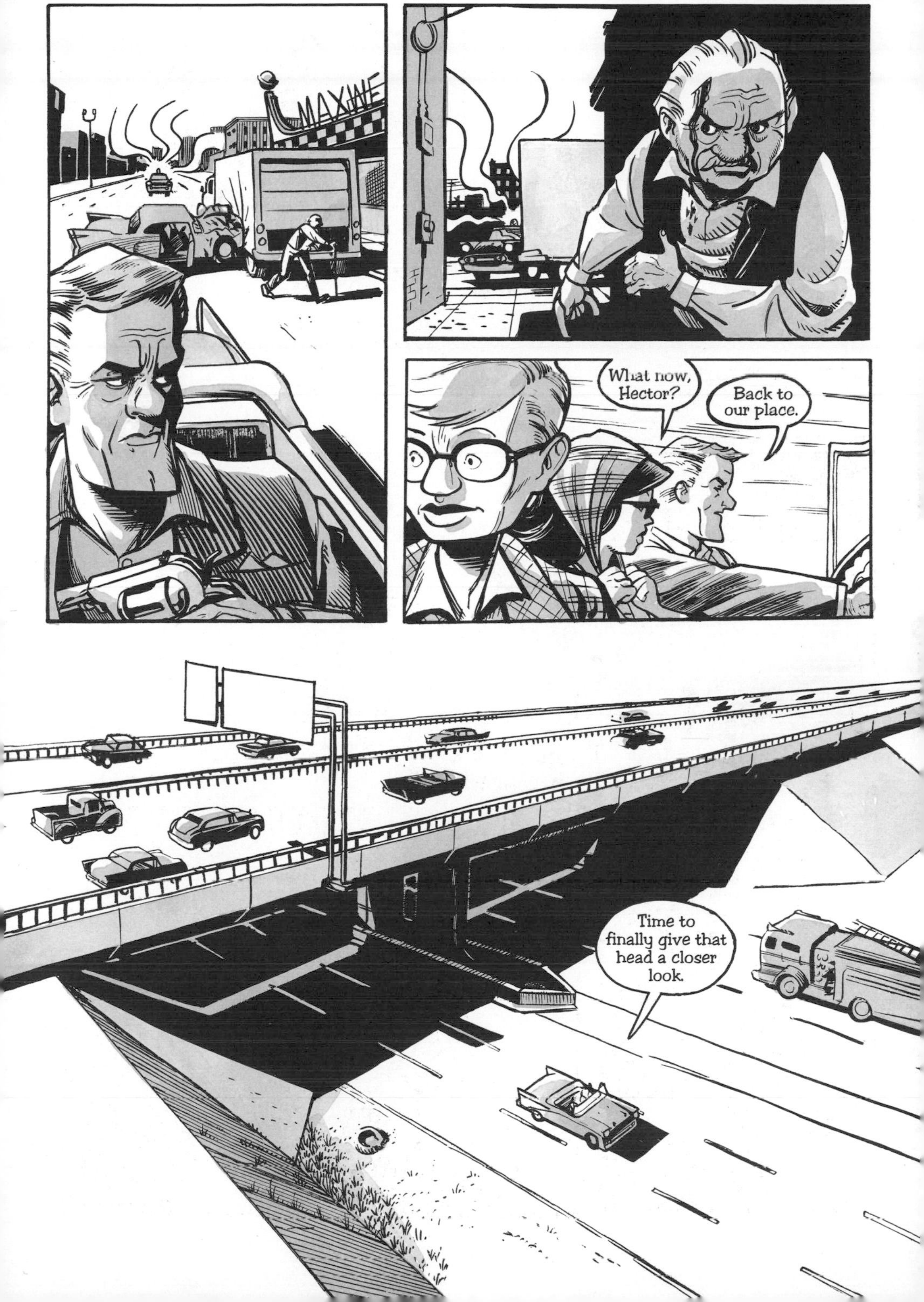
MAXINE
What now, Hector?
Back to our place.
Time to finally give that head a closer look.

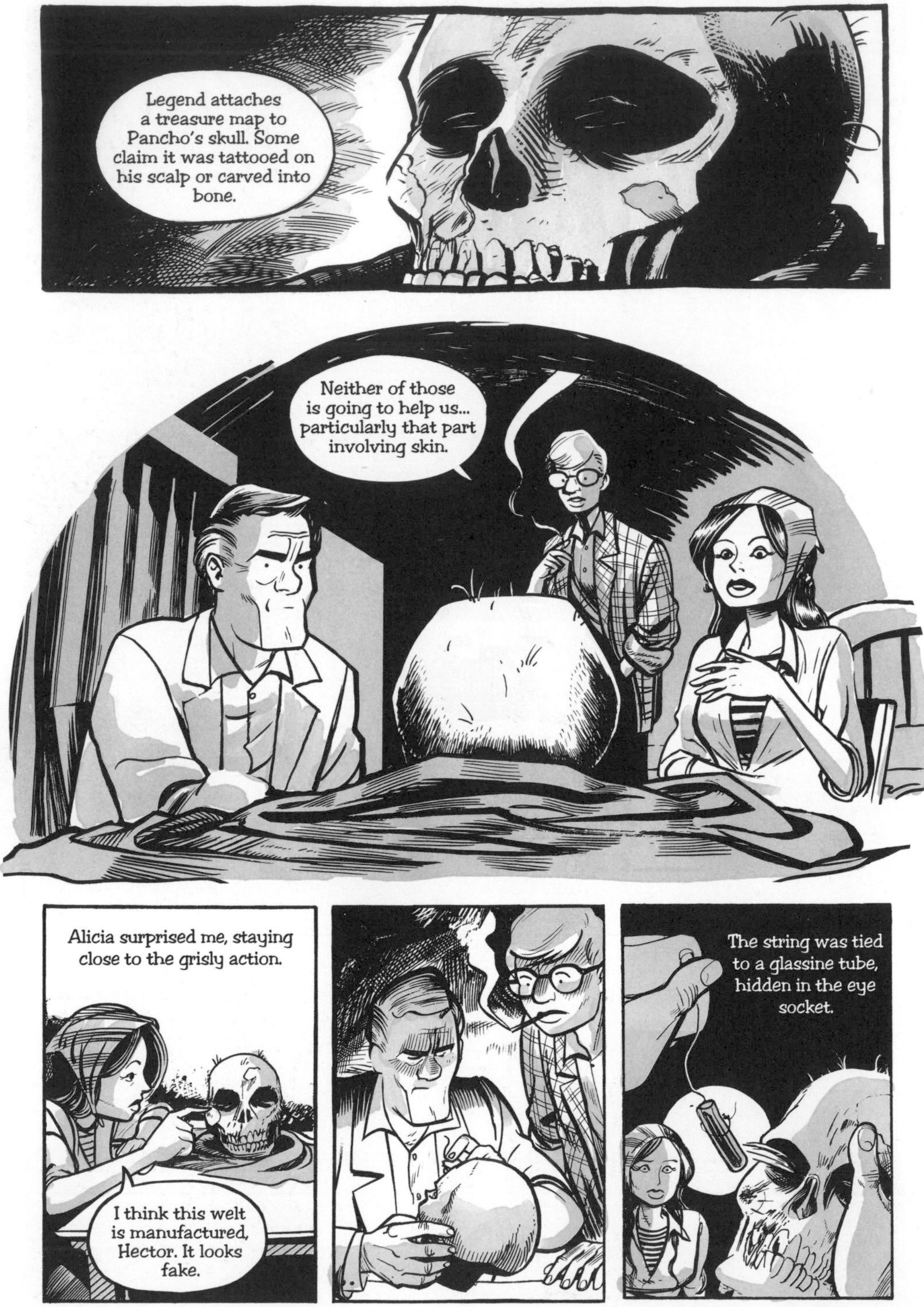

Legend attaches a treasure map to Pancho's skull. Some claim it was tattooed on his scalp or carved into bone.
Neither of those is going to help us... particularly that part involving skin.
Alicia surprised me, staying close to the grisly action.
I think this welt is manufactured, Hector. It looks fake.
The string was tied to a glassine tube, hidden in the eye socket.

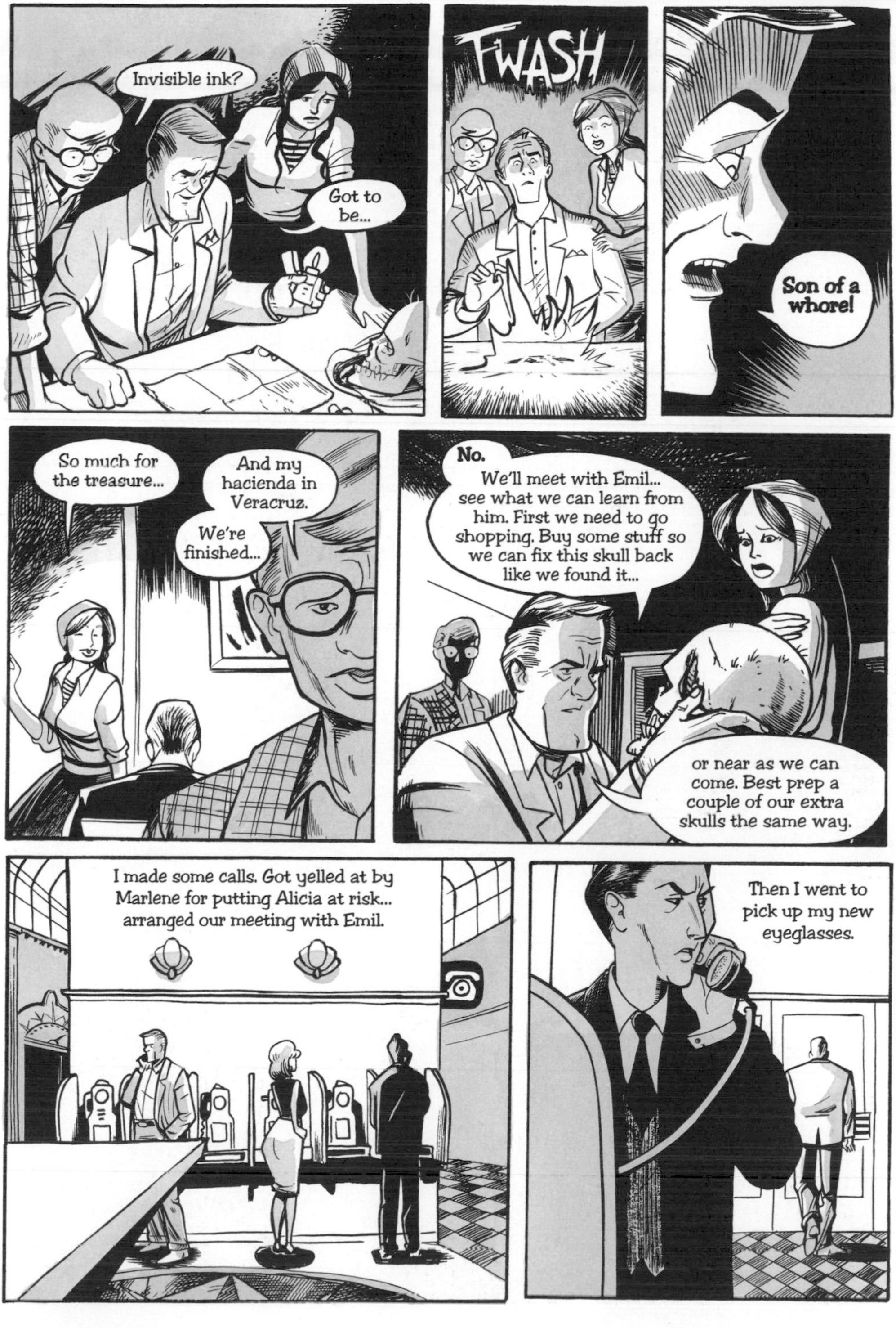

Invisible ink?
Got to be...
FWASH
Son of a whore!
So much for the treasure...
And my hacienda in Veracruz.
We're finished...
No.
We'll meet with Emil... see what we can learn from him. First we need to go shopping. Buy some stuff so we can fix this skull back like we found it...
or near as we can come. Best prep a couple of our extra skulls the same way.
I made some calls. Got yelled at by Marlene for putting Alicia at risk... arranged our meeting with Emil.
Then I went to pick up my new eyeglasses.

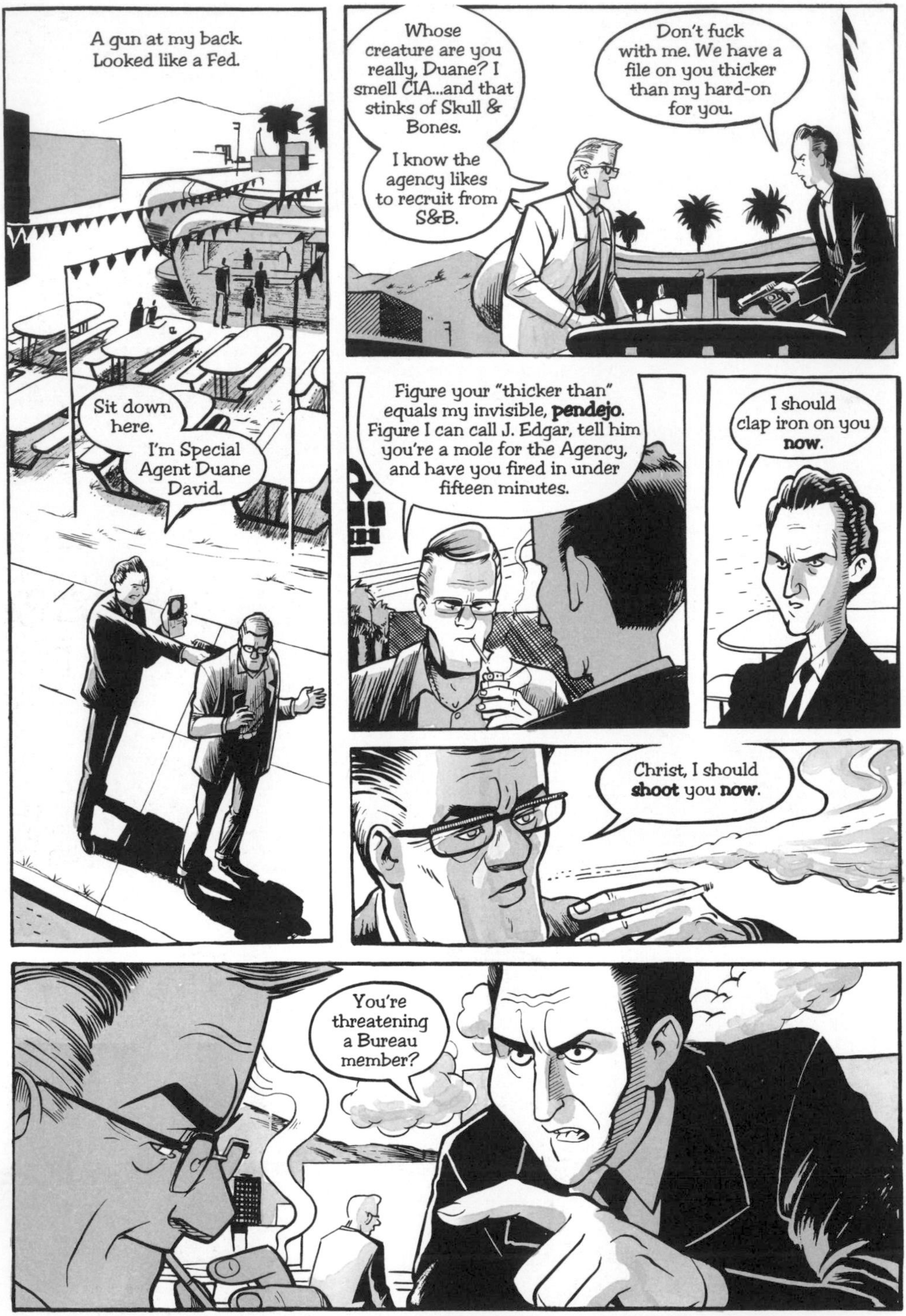
A gun at my back. Looked like a Fed.
Sit down here.
I'm Special Agent Duane David.
Whose creature are you really, Duane? I smell CIA...and that stinks of Skull & Bones.
I know the agency likes to recruit from S&B.
Don't fuck with me. We have a file on you thicker than my hard-on for you.
Figure your "thicker than" equals my invisible, **pendejo**. Figure I can call J. Edgar, tell him you're a mole for the Agency, and have you fired in under fifteen minutes.
I should clap iron on you **now**.
Christ, I should **shoot** you **now**.
You're threatening a Bureau member?

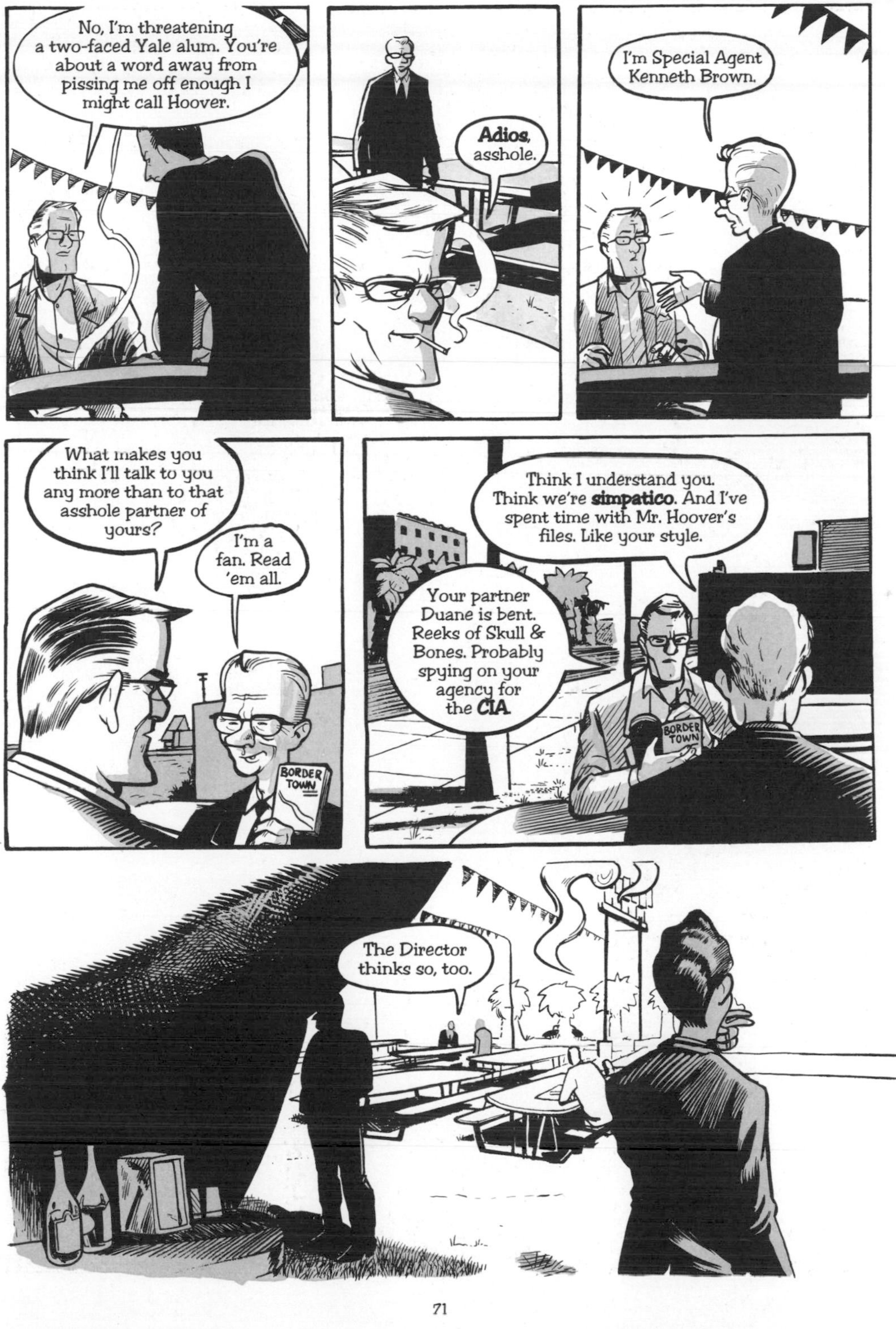
No, I'm threatening a two-faced Yale alum. You're about a word away from pissing me off enough I might call Hoover.
Adios, asshole.
I'm Special Agent Kenneth Brown.
What makes you think I'll talk to you any more than to that asshole partner of yours?
I'm a fan. Read 'em all.
BORDER TOWN
Think I understand you. Think we're simpatico. And I've spent time with Mr. Hoover's files. Like your style.
Your partner Duane is bent. Reeks of Skull & Bones. Probably spying on your agency for the CIA.
BORDER TOWN
The Director thinks so, too.

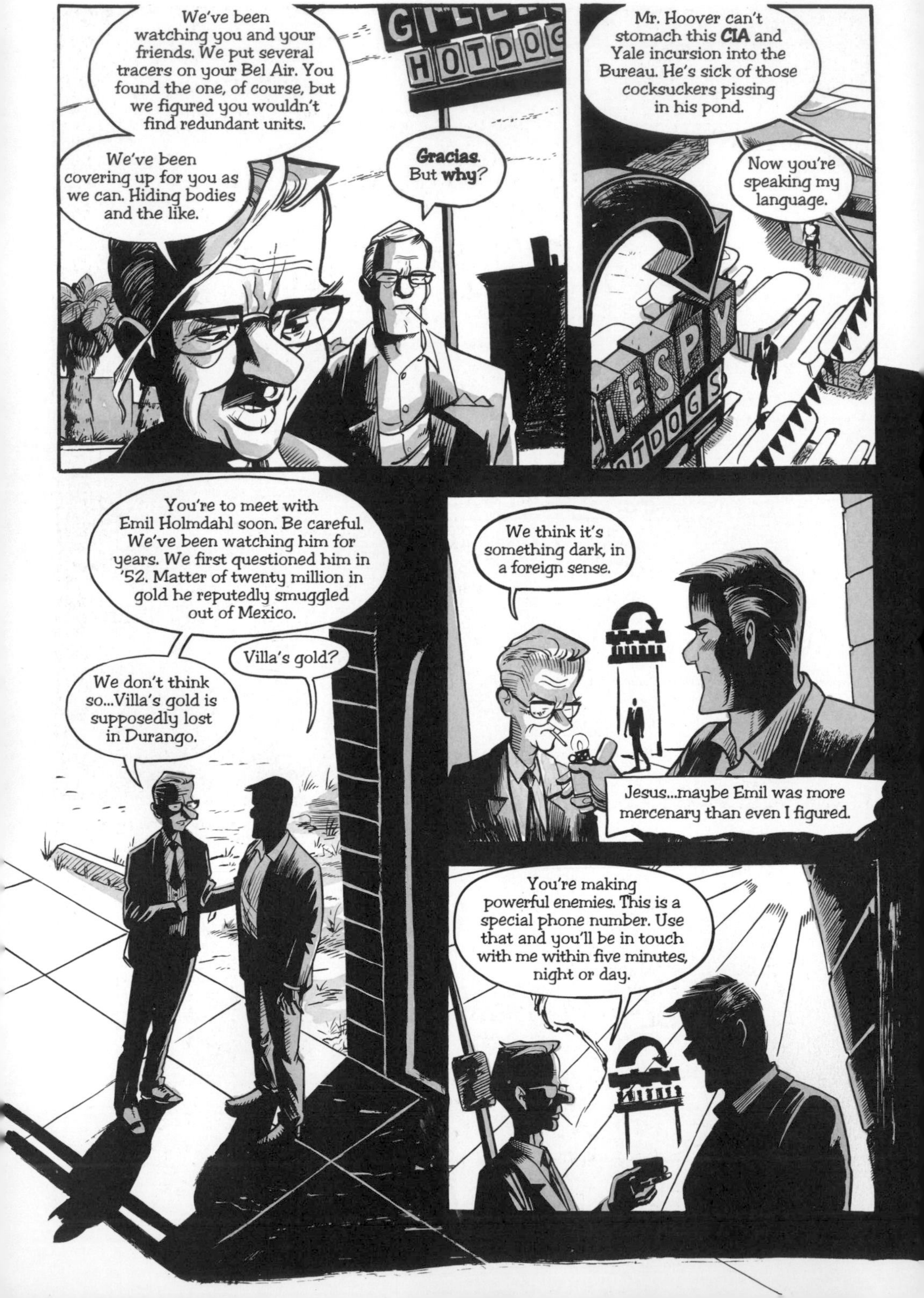

We've been watching you and your friends. We put several tracers on your Bel Air. You found the one, of course, but we figured you wouldn't find redundant units.
We've been covering up for you as we can. Hiding bodies and the like.
Gracias. But why?
HOTDOG
Mr. Hoover can't stomach this CIA and Yale incursion into the Bureau. He's sick of those cocksuckers pissing in his pond.
Now you're speaking my language.
LESPY
You're to meet with Emil Holmdahl soon. Be careful. We've been watching him for years. We first questioned him in '52. Matter of twenty million in gold he reputedly smuggled out of Mexico.
Villa's gold?
We don't think so...Villa's gold is supposedly lost in Durango.
We think it's something dark, in a foreign sense.
Jesus...maybe Emil was more mercenary than even I figured.
You're making powerful enemies. This is a special phone number. Use that and you'll be in touch with me within five minutes, night or day.

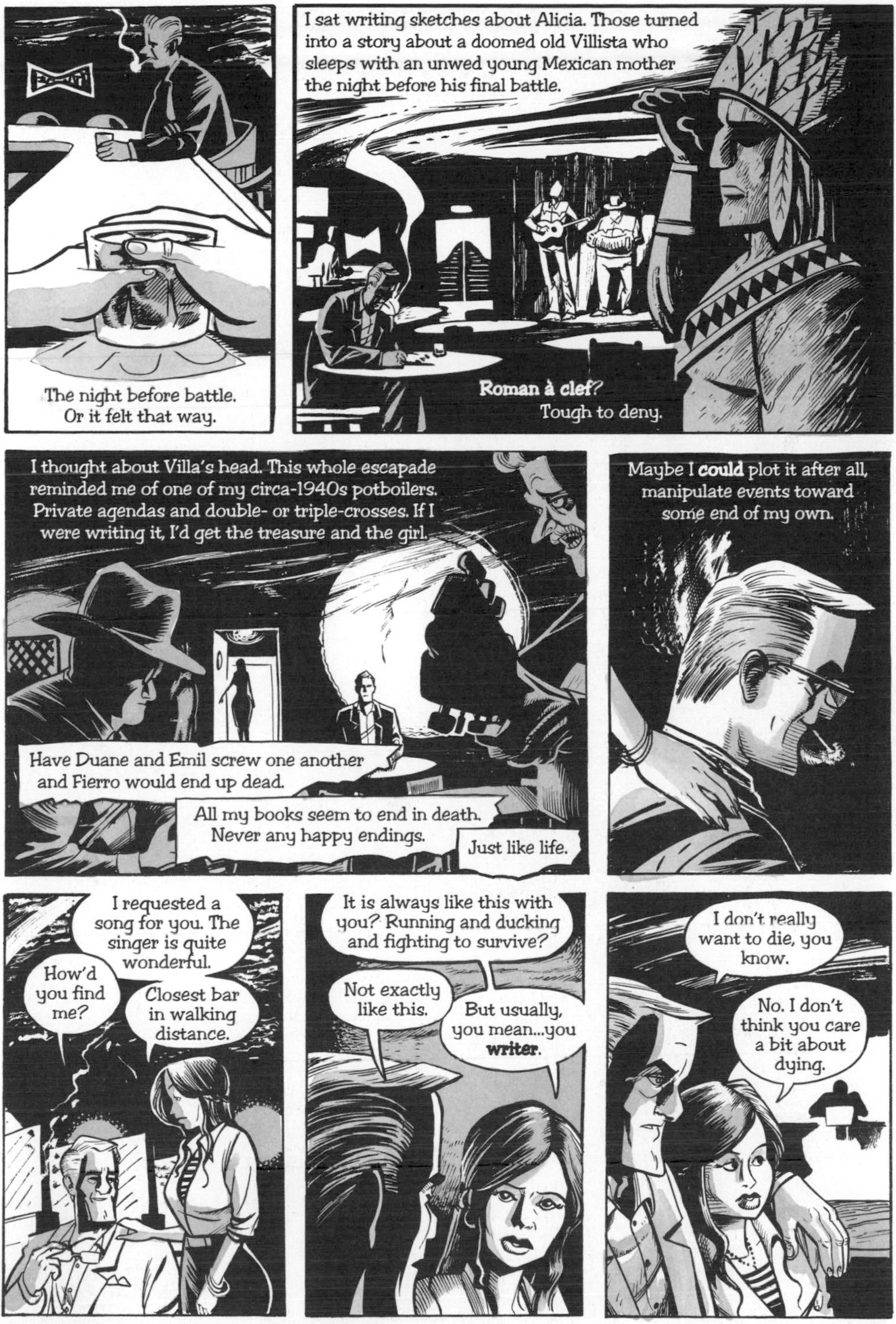
The night before battle.
Or it felt that way.
I sat writing sketches about Alicia. Those turned into a story about a doomed old Villista who sleeps with an unwed young Mexican mother the night before his final battle.
Roman à clef?
Tough to deny.
I thought about Villa's head. This whole escapade reminded me of one of my circa-1940s potboilers. Private agendas and double- or triple-crosses. If I were writing it, I'd get the treasure and the girl.
Have Duane and Emil screw one another and Fierro would end up dead.
All my books seem to end in death. Never any happy endings.
Just like life.
Maybe I **could** plot it after all, manipulate events toward some end of my own.
I requested a song for you. The singer is quite wonderful.
How'd you find me?
Closest bar in walking distance.
It is always like this with you? Running and ducking and fighting to survive?
Not exactly like this.
But usually, you mean...you **writer**.
I don't really want to die, you know.
No. I don't think you care a bit about dying.

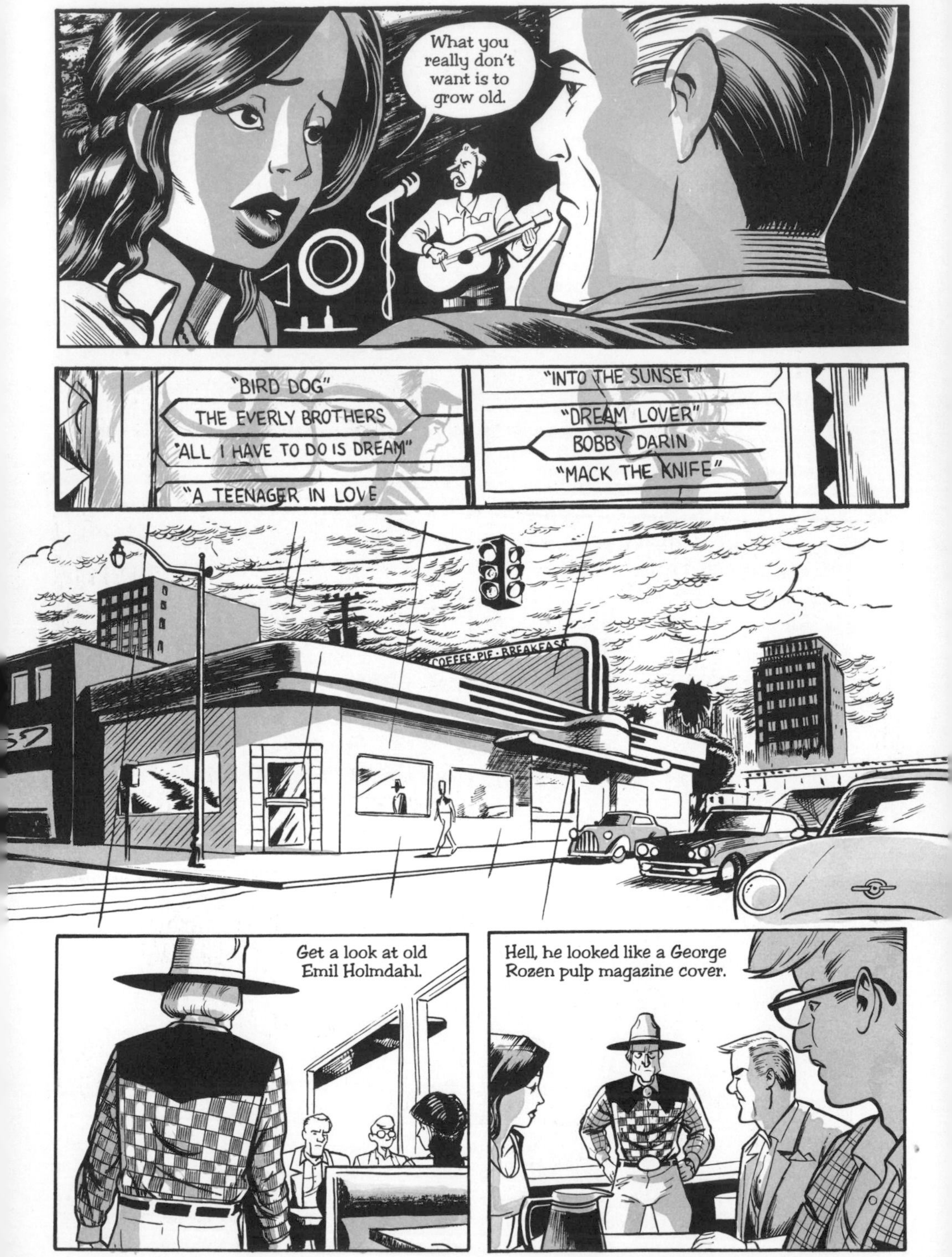
What you really don't want is to grow old.
"BIRD DOG"
THE EVERLY BROTHERS
"ALL I HAVE TO DO IS DREAM"
"A TEENAGER IN LOVE
"INTO THE SUNSET"
"DREAM LOVER"
BOBBY DARIN
"MACK THE KNIFE"
COFFEE · PIE · BREAKFAST
Get a look at old Emil Holmdahl.
Hell, he looked like a George Rozen pulp magazine cover.

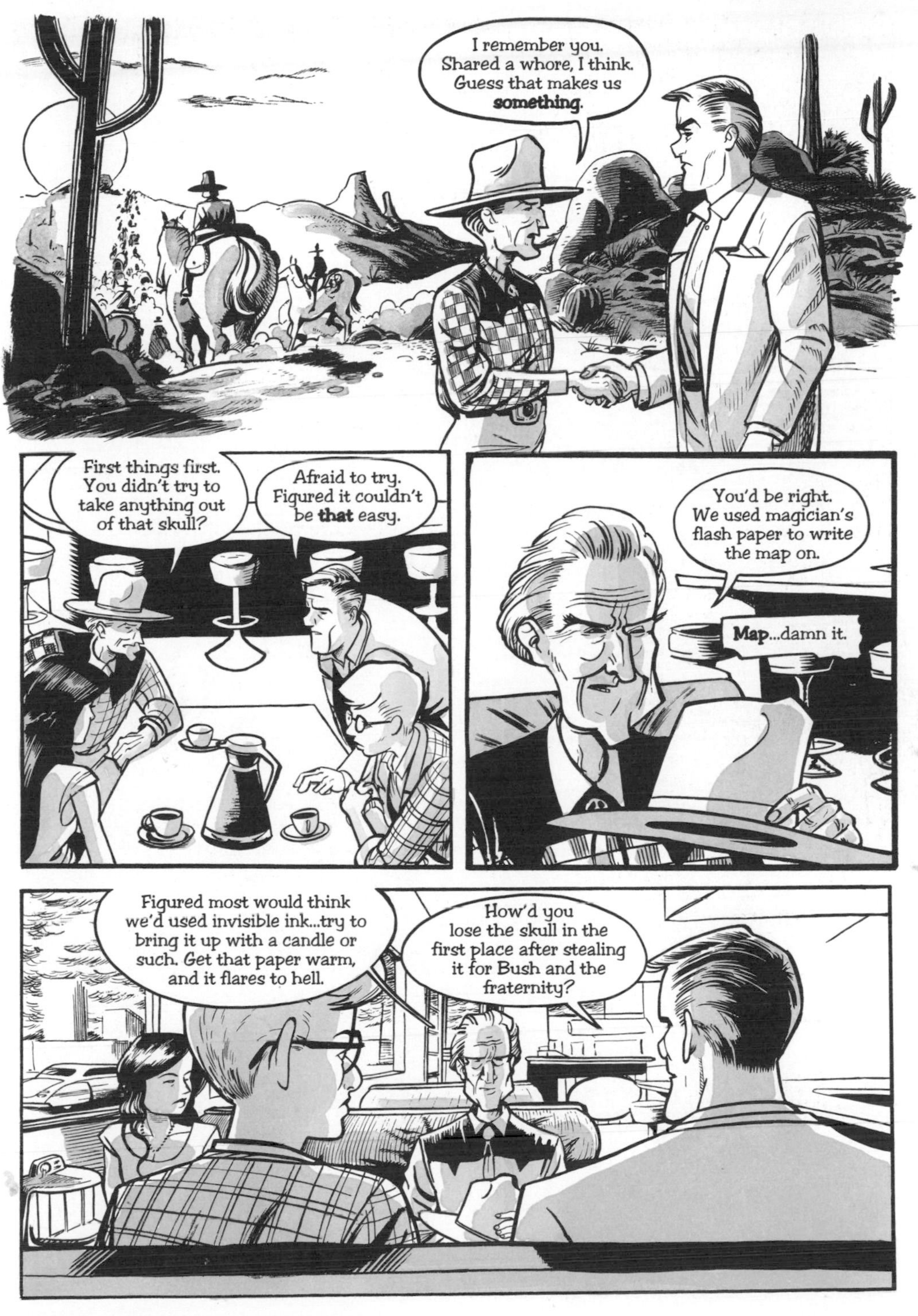
I remember you. Shared a whore, I think. Guess that makes us **something**.
First things first. You didn't try to take anything out of that skull?
Afraid to try. Figured it couldn't be **that** easy.
You'd be right. We used magician's flash paper to write the map on.
Map...damn it.
Figured most would think we'd used invisible ink...try to bring it up with a candle or such. Get that paper warm, and it flares to hell.
How'd you lose the skull in the first place after stealing it for Bush and the fraternity?

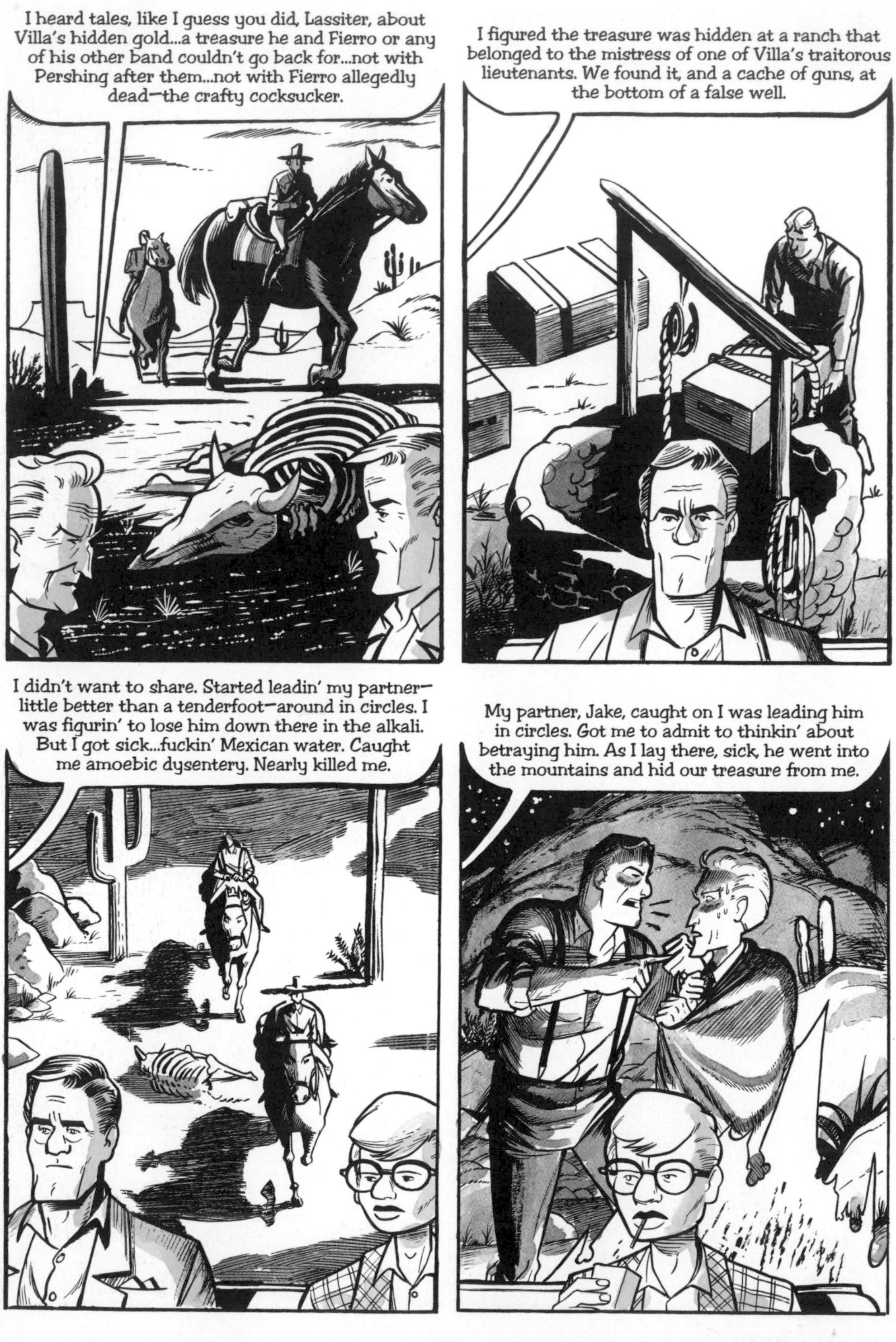

I heard tales, like I guess you did, Lassiter, about Villa's hidden gold...a treasure he and Fierro or any of his other band couldn't go back for...not with Pershing after them...not with Fierro allegedly dead—the crafty cocksucker.
I figured the treasure was hidden at a ranch that belonged to the mistress of one of Villa's traitorous lieutenants. We found it, and a cache of guns, at the bottom of a false well.
I didn't want to share. Started leadin' my partner—little better than a tenderfoot—around in circles. I was figurin' to lose him down there in the alkali. But I got sick...fuckin' Mexican water. Caught me amoebic dysentery. Nearly killed me.
My partner, Jake, caught on I was leading him in circles. Got me to admit to thinkin' about betraying him. As I lay there, sick, he went into the mountains and hid our treasure from me.

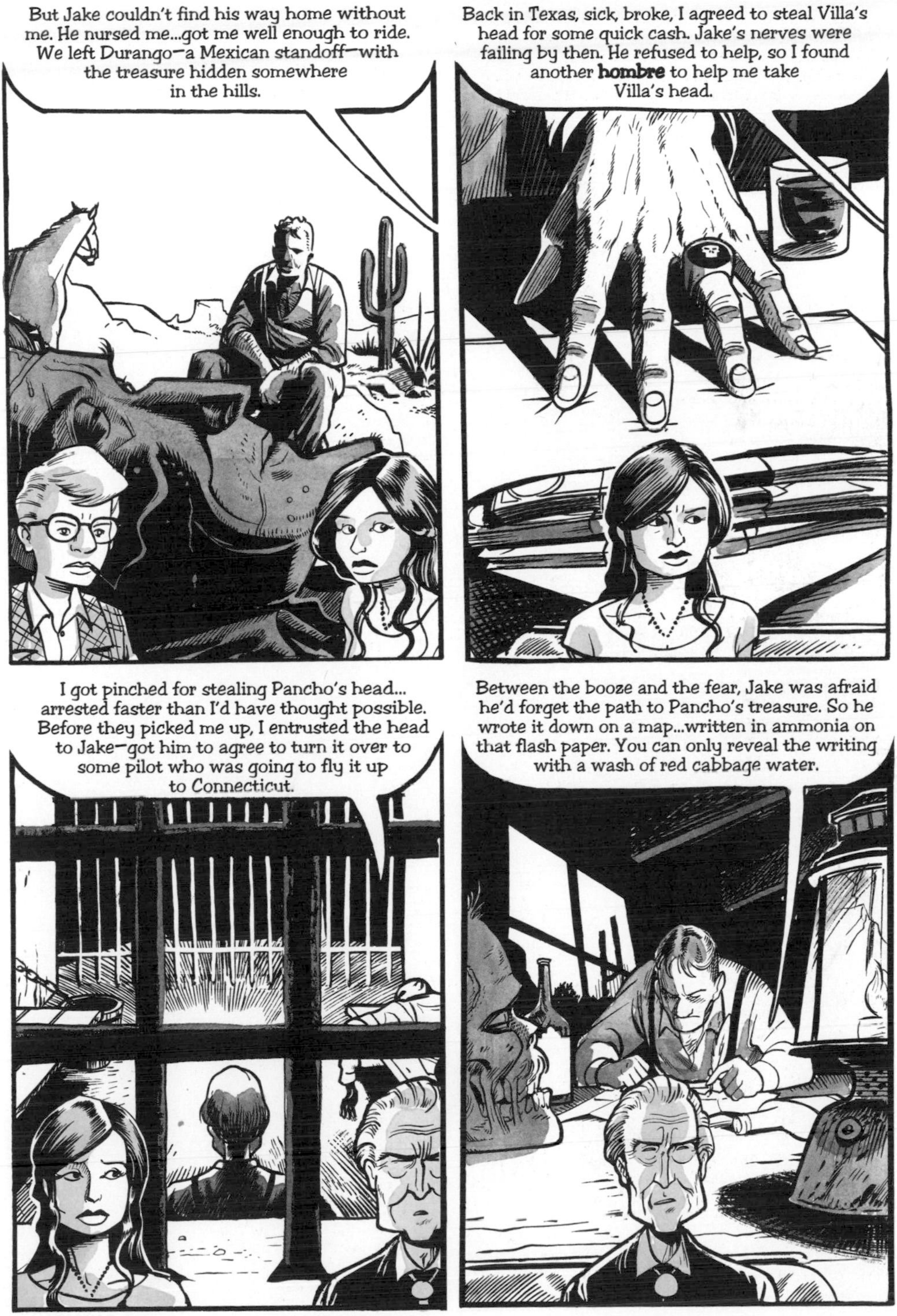

But Jake couldn't find his way home without me. He nursed me...got me well enough to ride. We left Durango—a Mexican standoff—with the treasure hidden somewhere in the hills.
Back in Texas, sick, broke, I agreed to steal Villa's head for some quick cash. Jake's nerves were failing by then. He refused to help, so I found another **hombre** to help me take Villa's head.
I got pinched for stealing Pancho's head... arrested faster than I'd have thought possible. Before they picked me up, I entrusted the head to Jake—got him to agree to turn it over to some pilot who was going to fly it up to Connecticut.
Between the booze and the fear, Jake was afraid he'd forget the path to Pancho's treasure. So he wrote it down on a map...written in ammonia on that flash paper. You can only reveal the writing with a wash of red cabbage water.

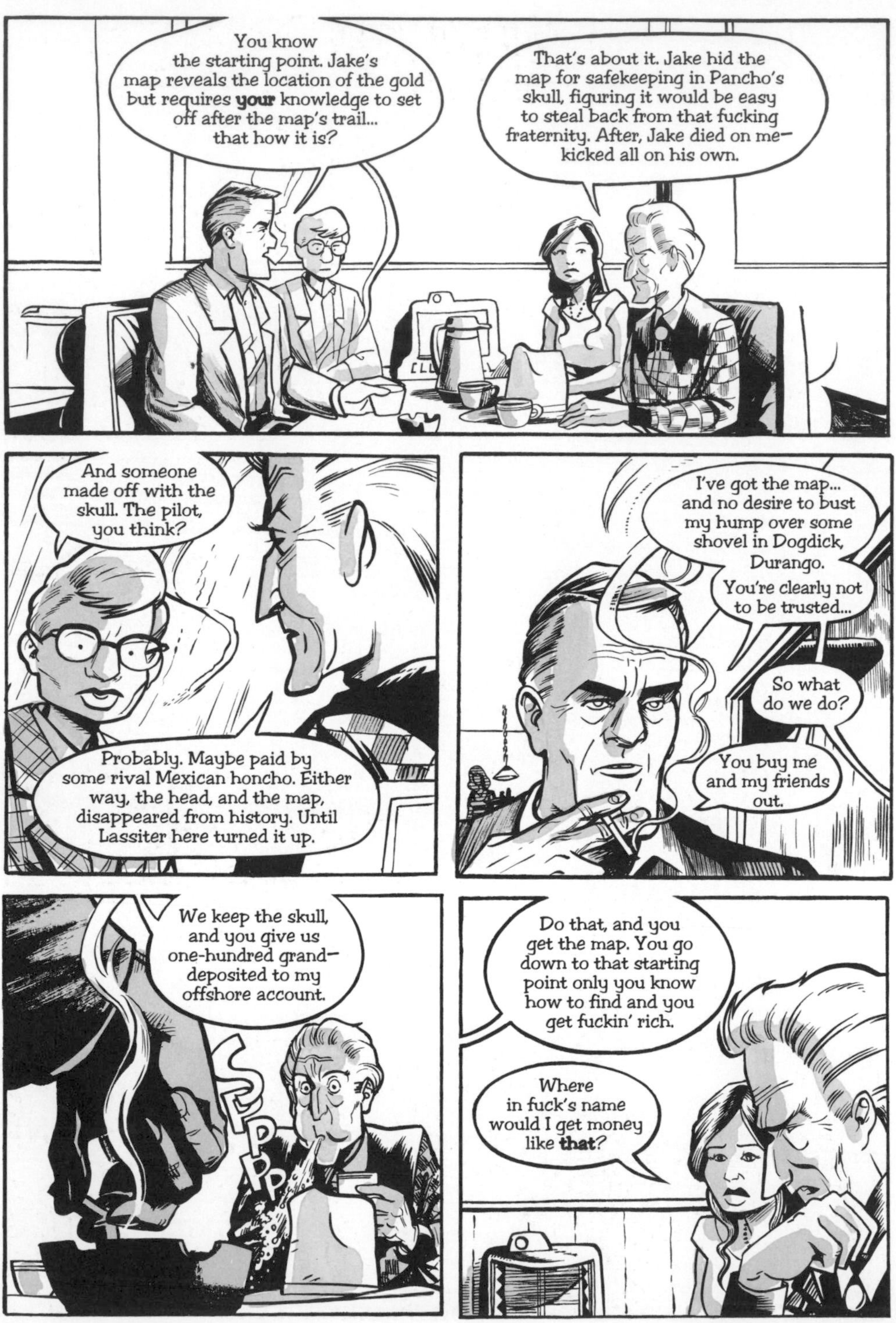
You know the starting point. Jake's map reveals the location of the gold but requires **your** knowledge to set off after the map's trail... that how it is?
That's about it. Jake hid the map for safekeeping in Pancho's skull, figuring it would be easy to steal back from that fucking fraternity. After, Jake died on me—kicked all on his own.
And someone made off with the skull. The pilot, you think?
Probably. Maybe paid by some rival Mexican honcho. Either way, the head, and the map, disappeared from history. Until Lassiter here turned it up.
I've got the map... and no desire to bust my hump over some shovel in Dogdick, Durango.
You're clearly not to be trusted...
So what do we do?
You buy me and my friends out.
We keep the skull, and you give us one-hundred grand—deposited to my offshore account.
SPPPP
Do that, and you get the map. You go down to that starting point only you know how to find and you get fuckin' rich.
Where in fuck's name would I get money like **that**?

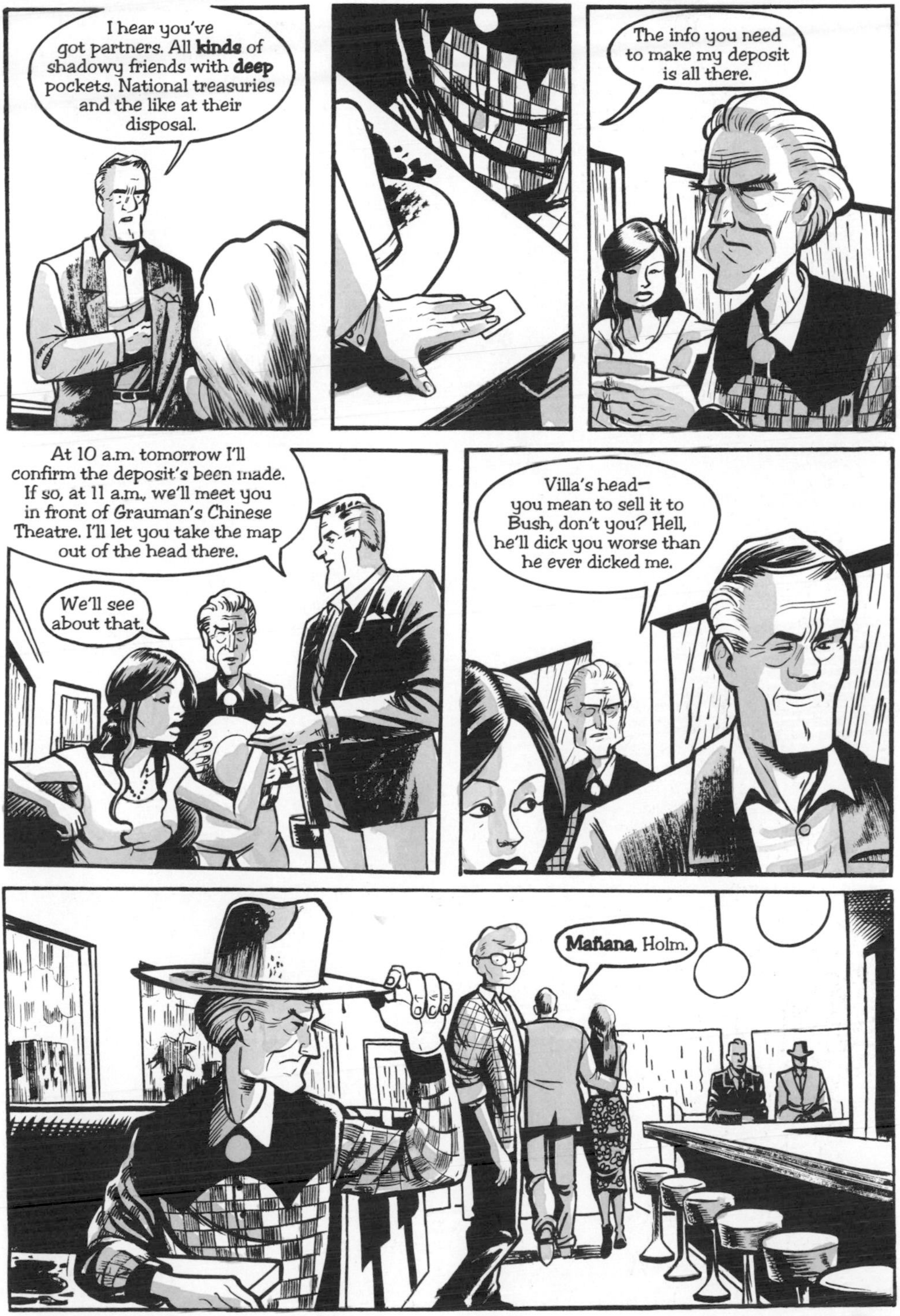
I hear you've got partners. All **kinds** of shadowy friends with **deep** pockets. National treasuries and the like at their disposal.
The info you need to make my deposit is all there.
At 10 a.m. tomorrow I'll confirm the deposit's been made. If so, at 11 a.m., we'll meet you in front of Grauman's Chinese Theatre. I'll let you take the map out of the head there.
We'll see about that.
Villa's head— you mean to sell it to Bush, don't you? Hell, he'll dick you worse than he ever dicked me.
Mañana, Holm.

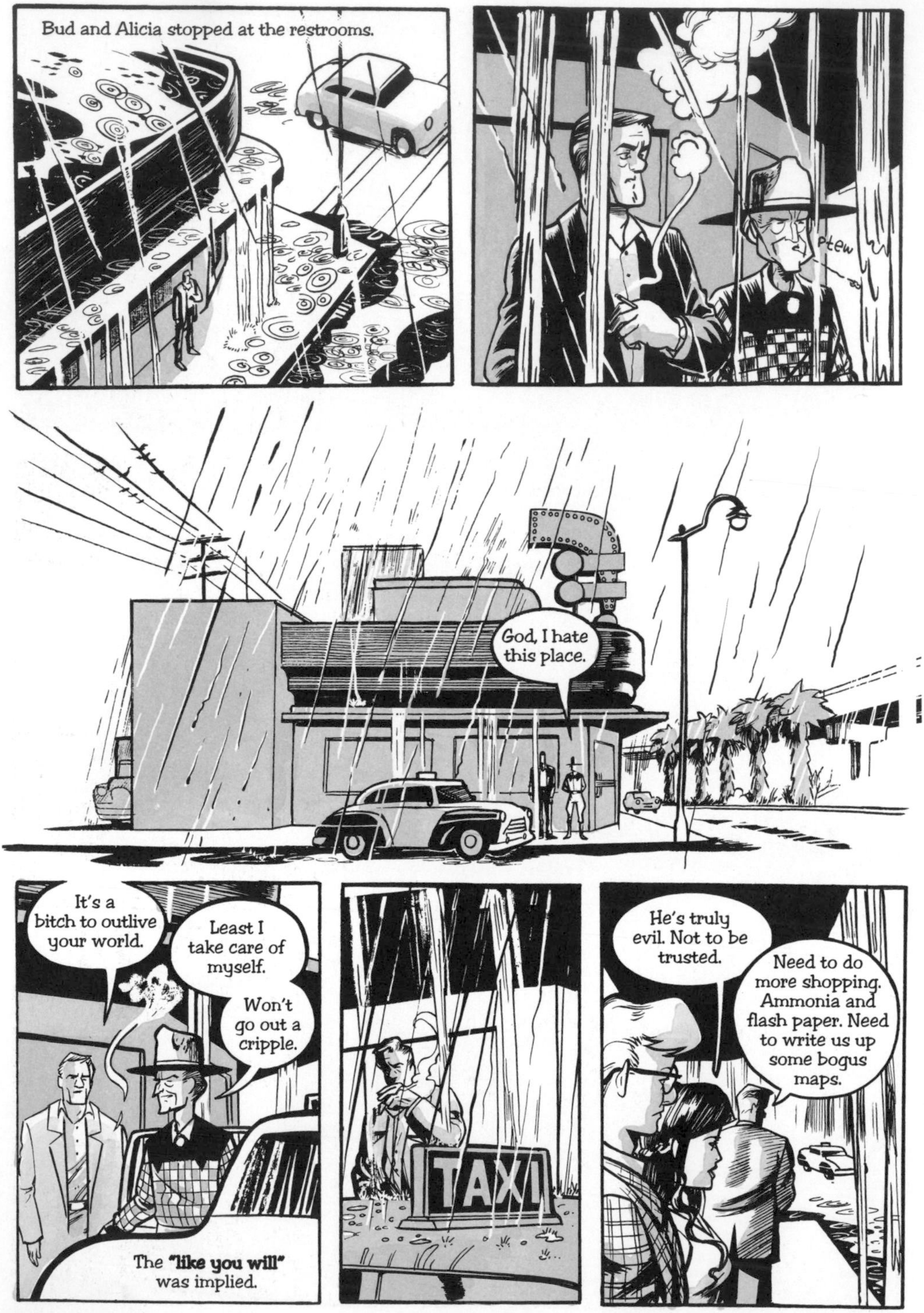
Bud and Alicia stopped at the restrooms.
ptew
God, I hate this place.
It's a bitch to outlive your world.
Least I take care of myself.
Won't go out a cripple.
The "like you will" was implied.
TAXI
He's truly evil. Not to be trusted.
Need to do more shopping. Ammonia and flash paper. Need to write us up some bogus maps.

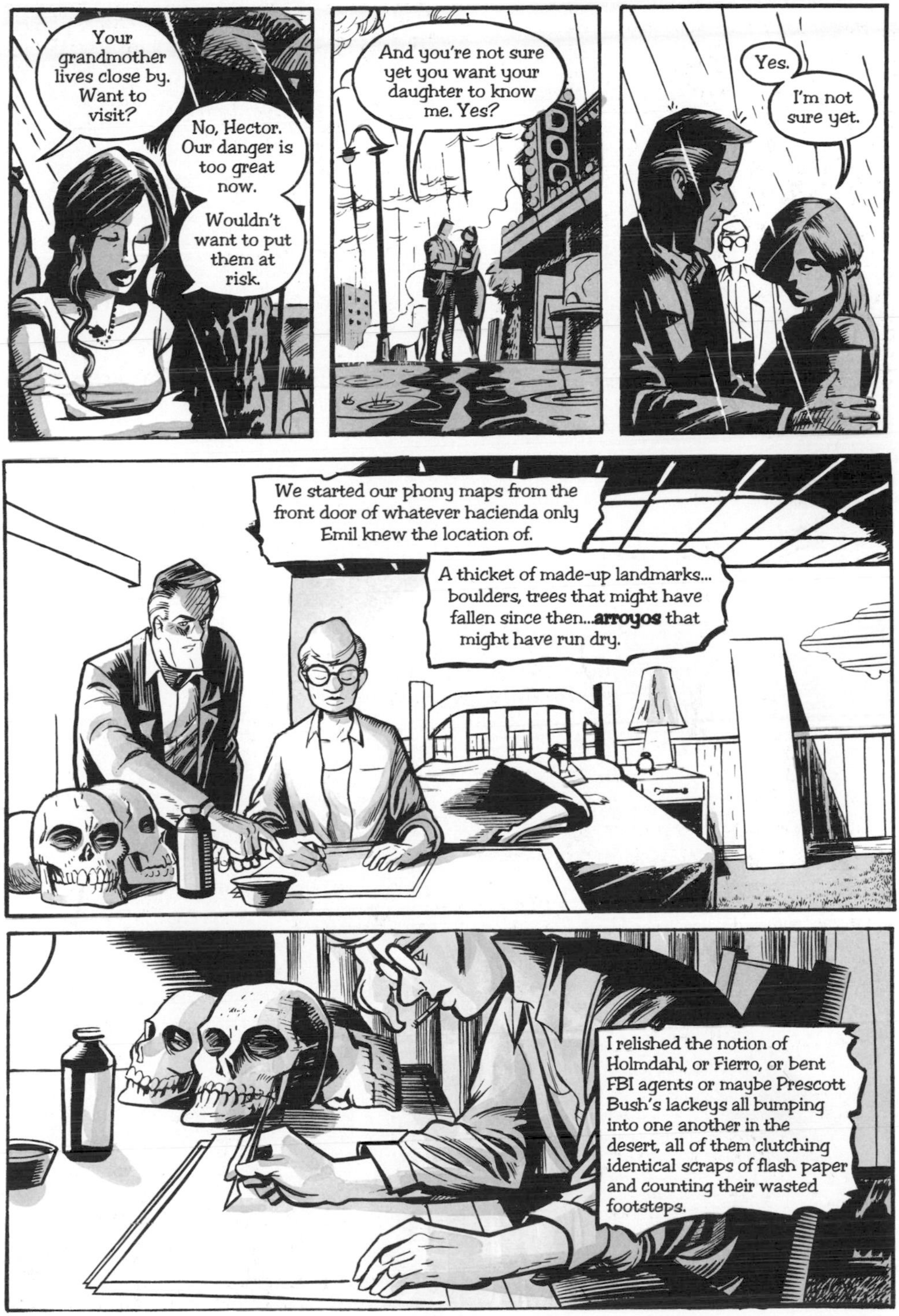
Your grandmother lives close by. Want to visit?
No, Hector. Our danger is too great now.
Wouldn't want to put them at risk.
And you're not sure yet you want your daughter to know me. Yes?
Yes.
I'm not sure yet.
We started our phony maps from the front door of whatever hacienda only Emil knew the location of.
A thicket of made-up landmarks... boulders, trees that might have fallen since then...**arroyos** that might have run dry.
I relished the notion of Holmdahl, or Fierro, or bent FBI agents or maybe Prescott Bush's lackeys all bumping into one another in the desert, all of them clutching identical scraps of flash paper and counting their wasted footsteps.

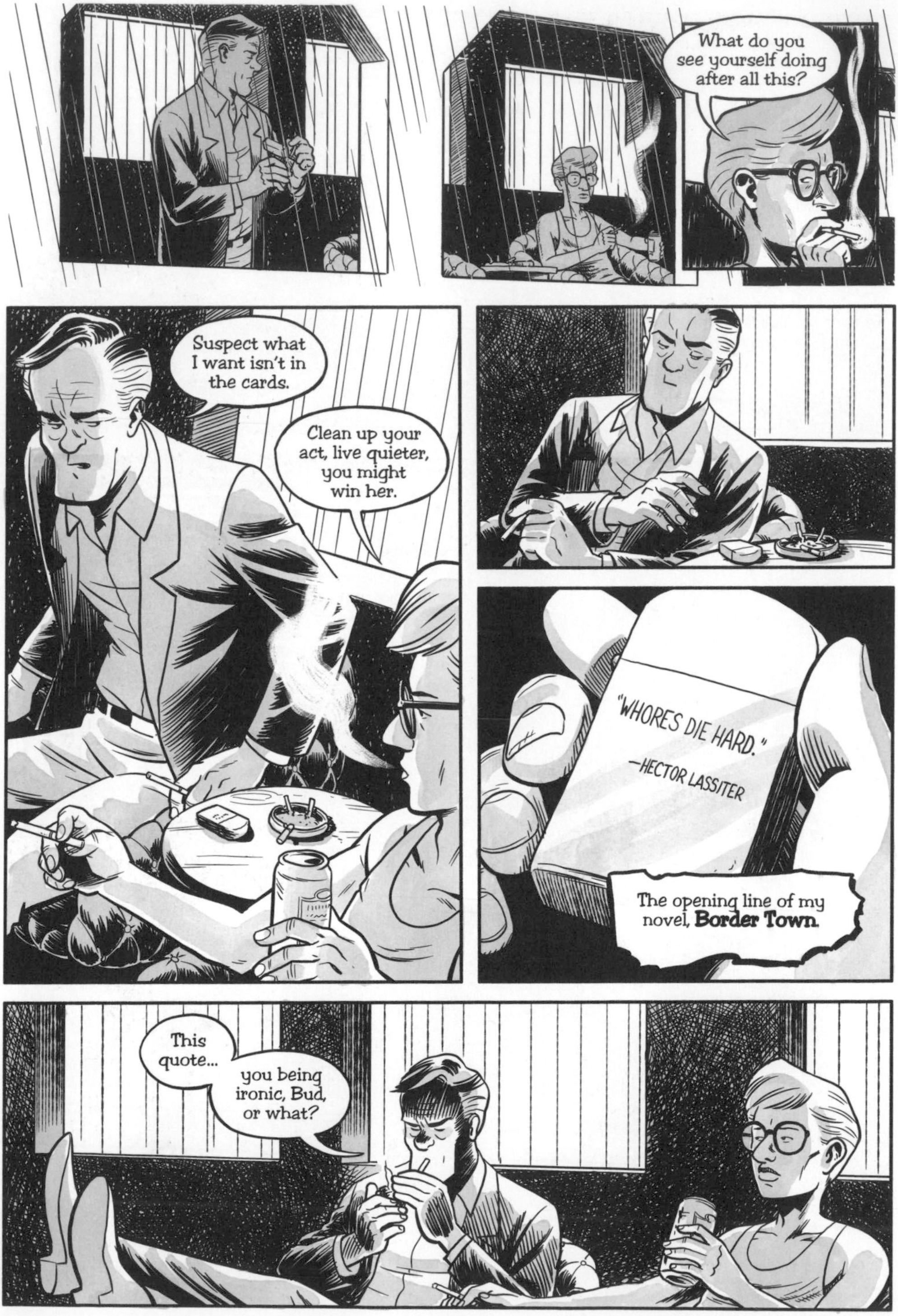
What do you see yourself doing after all this?
Suspect what I want isn't in the cards.
Clean up your act, live quieter, you might win her.
"WHORES DIE HARD."
—HECTOR LASSITER
The opening line of my novel, **Border Town**.
This quote...
you being ironic, Bud, or what?

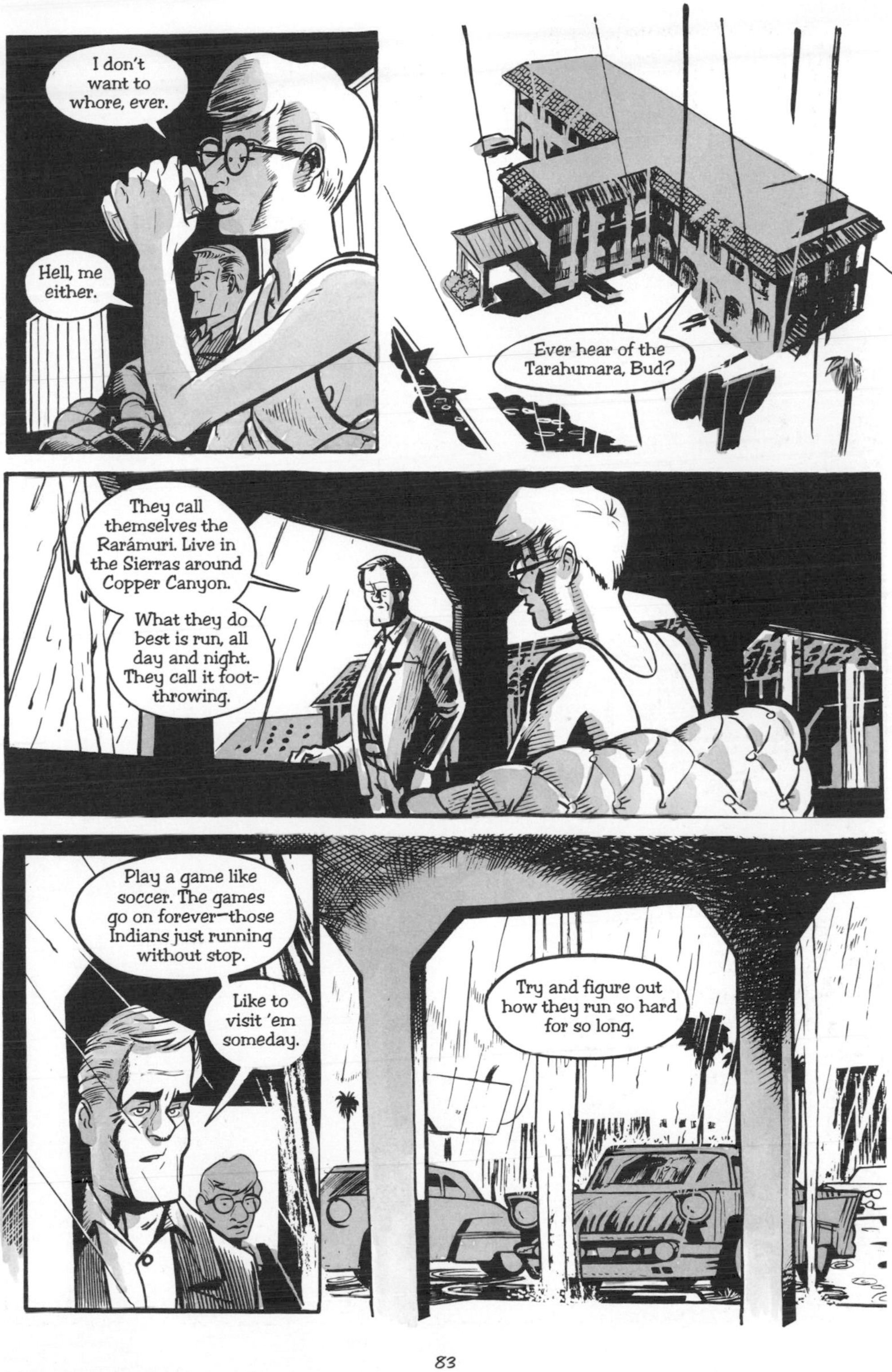
I don't want to whore, ever.
Hell, me either.
Ever hear of the Tarahumara, Bud?
They call themselves the Rarámuri. Live in the Sierras around Copper Canyon.
What they do best is run, all day and night. They call it foot-throwing.
Play a game like soccer. The games go on forever—those Indians just running without stop.
Like to visit 'em someday.
Try and figure out how they run so hard for so long.

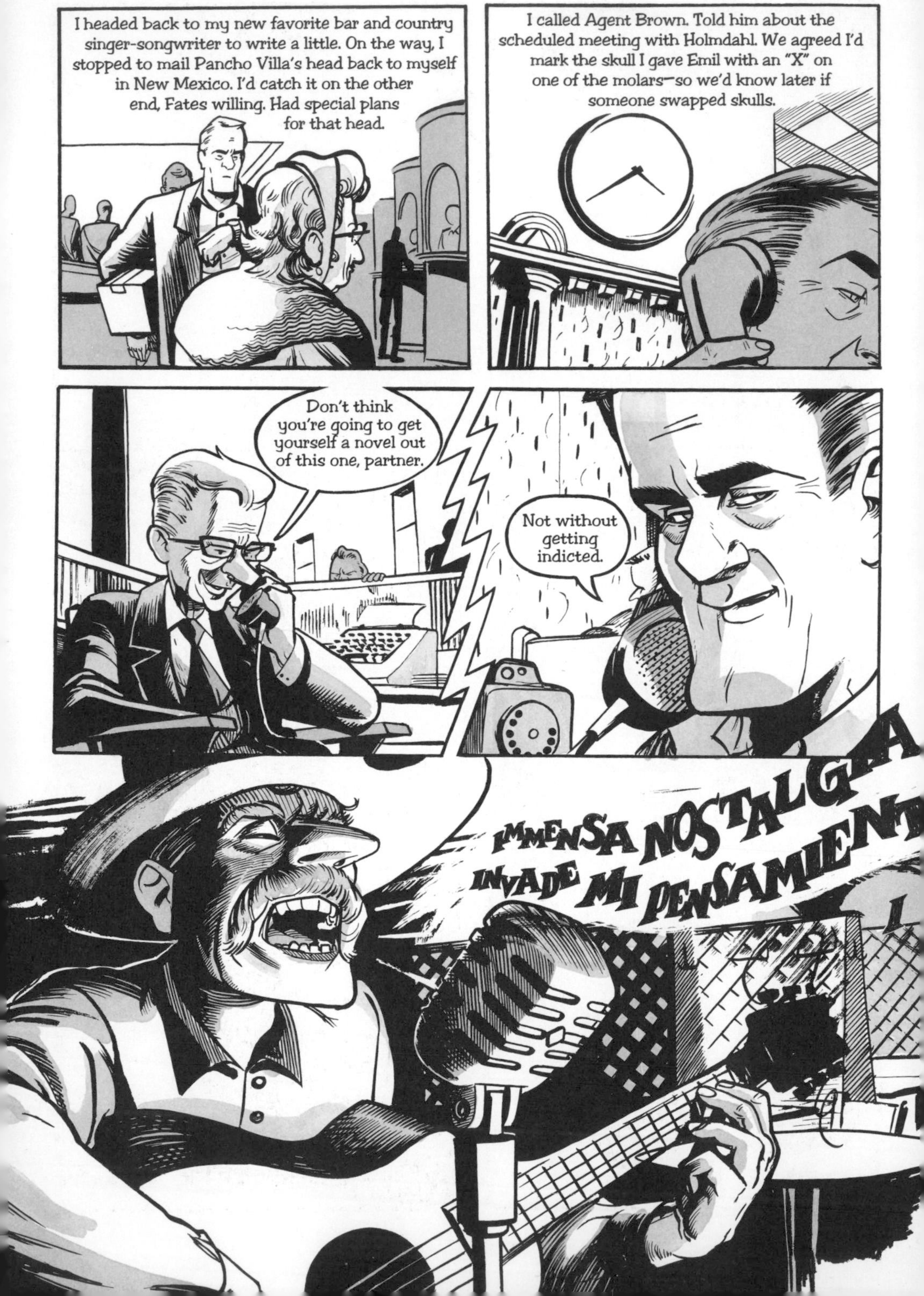
I headed back to my new favorite bar and country singer-songwriter to write a little. On the way, I stopped to mail Pancho Villa's head back to myself in New Mexico. I'd catch it on the other end, Fates willing. Had special plans for that head.
I called Agent Brown. Told him about the scheduled meeting with Holmdahl. We agreed I'd mark the skull I gave Emil with an "X" on one of the molars—so we'd know later if someone swapped skulls.
Don't think you're going to get yourself a novel out of this one, partner.
Not without getting indicted.
IMMENSA NOSTALGIA INVADE MI PENSAMIENT

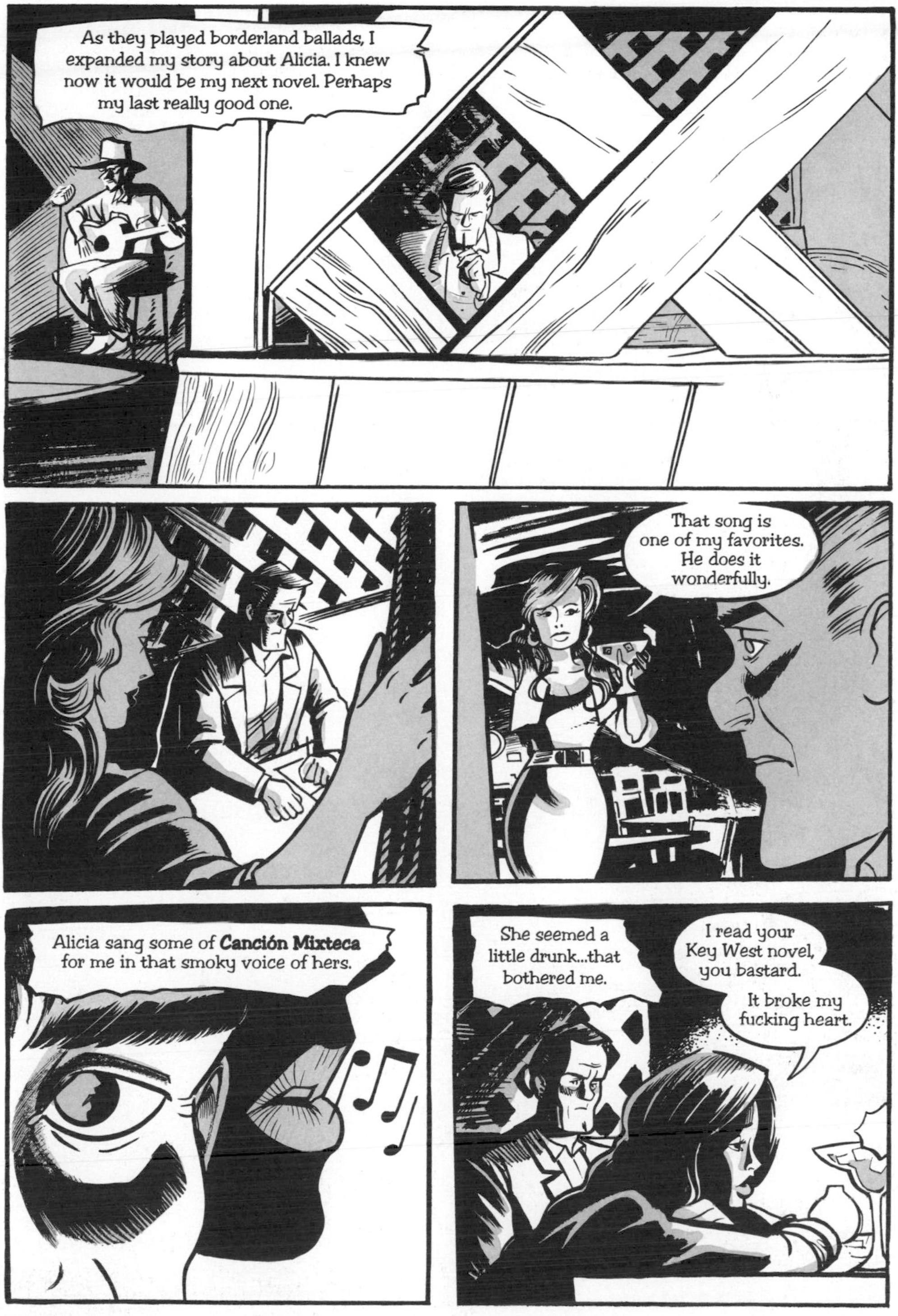
As they played borderland ballads, I expanded my story about Alicia. I knew now it would be my next novel. Perhaps my last really good one.
That song is one of my favorites. He does it wonderfully.
Alicia sang some of **Canción Mixteca** for me in that smoky voice of hers.
She seemed a little drunk...that bothered me.
I read your Key West novel, you bastard.
It broke my fucking heart.

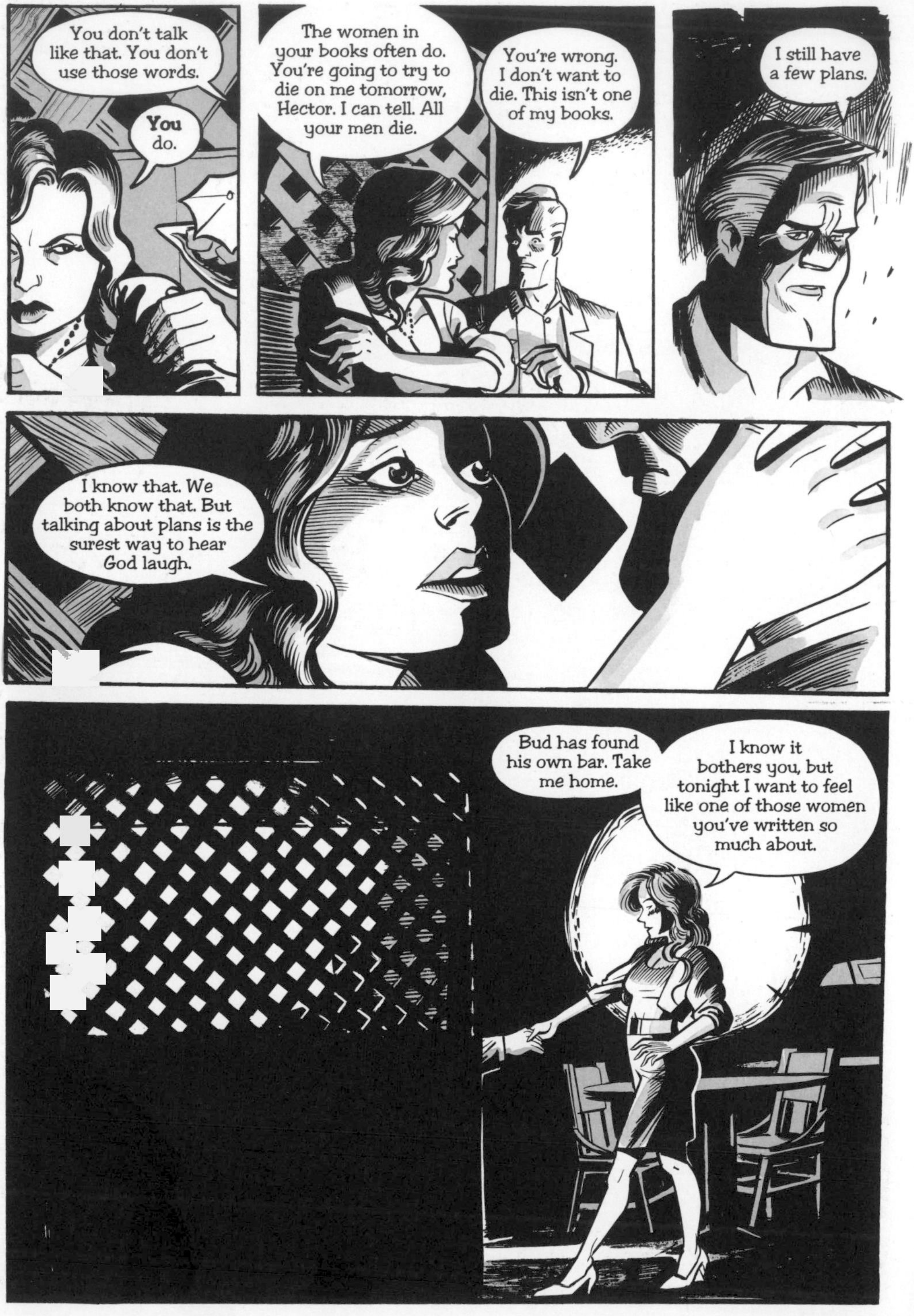
You don't talk like that. You don't use those words.
You do.
The women in your books often do. You're going to try to die on me tomorrow, Hector. I can tell. All your men die.
You're wrong. I don't want to die. This isn't one of my books.
I still have a few plans.
I know that. We both know that. But talking about plans is the surest way to hear God laugh.
Bud has found his own bar. Take me home.
I know it bothers you, but tonight I want to feel like one of those women you've written so much about.

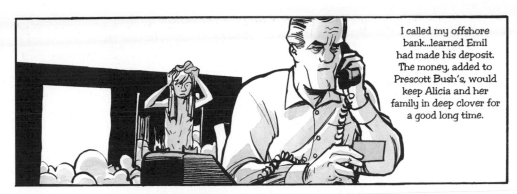

I called my offshore bank...learned Emil had made his deposit. The money, added to Prescott Bush's, would keep Alicia and her family in deep clover for a good long time.
Alicia awakened with a sore throat. We stopped for some honey she could use to spike her thermos of chamomile tea.
HOLLYWOOD
ABBOT BROS. GROCERS
HONEY

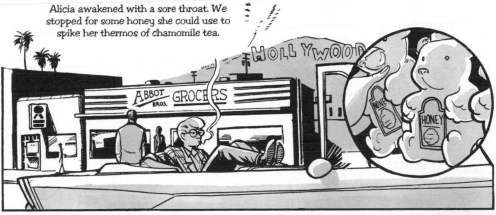

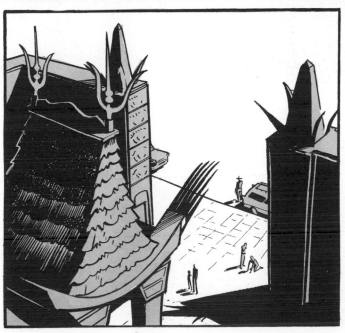

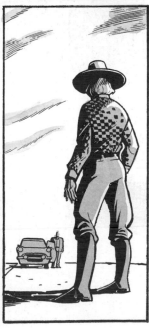

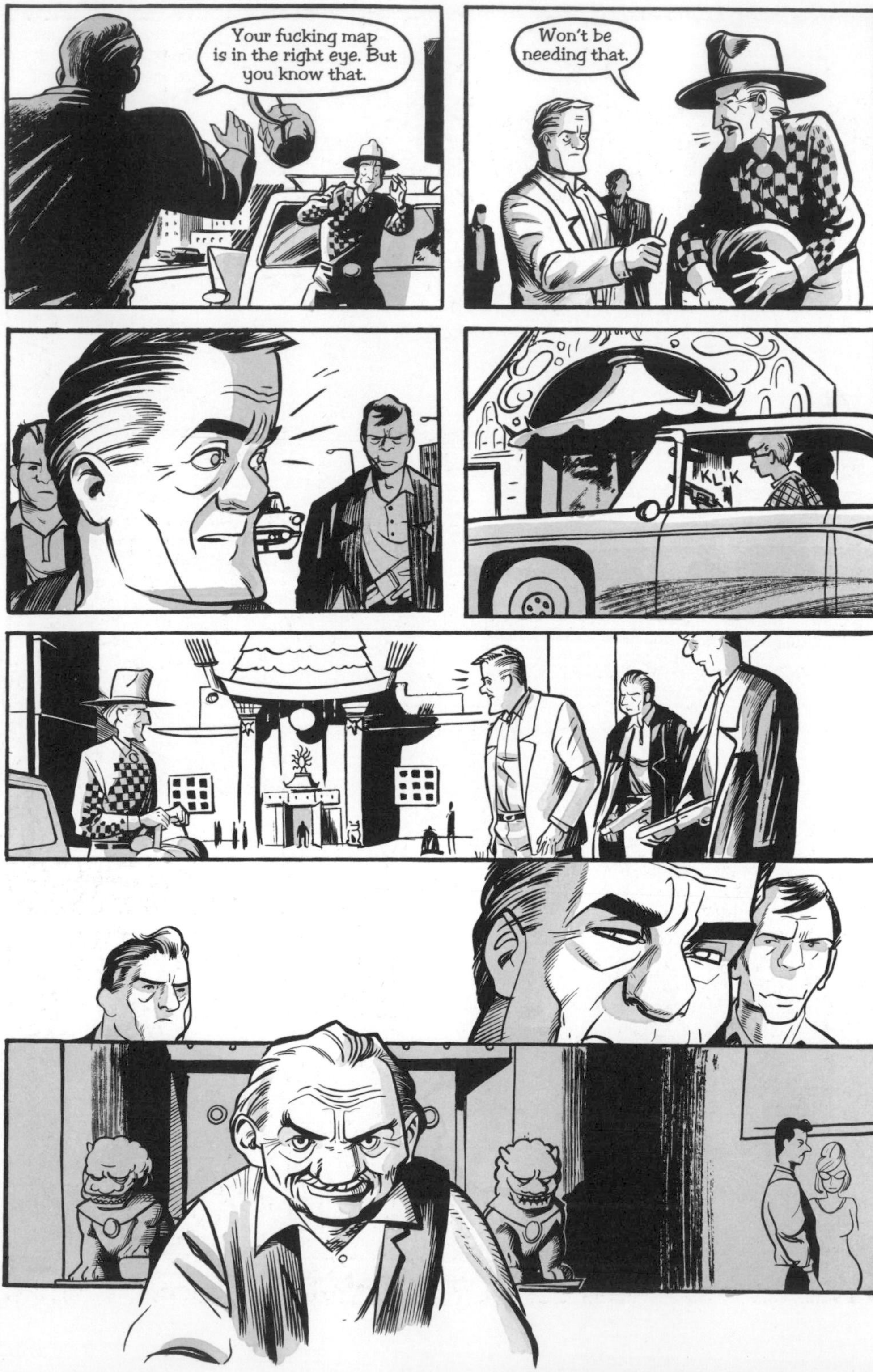
Your fucking map is in the right eye. But you know that.
Won't be needing that.
KLIK

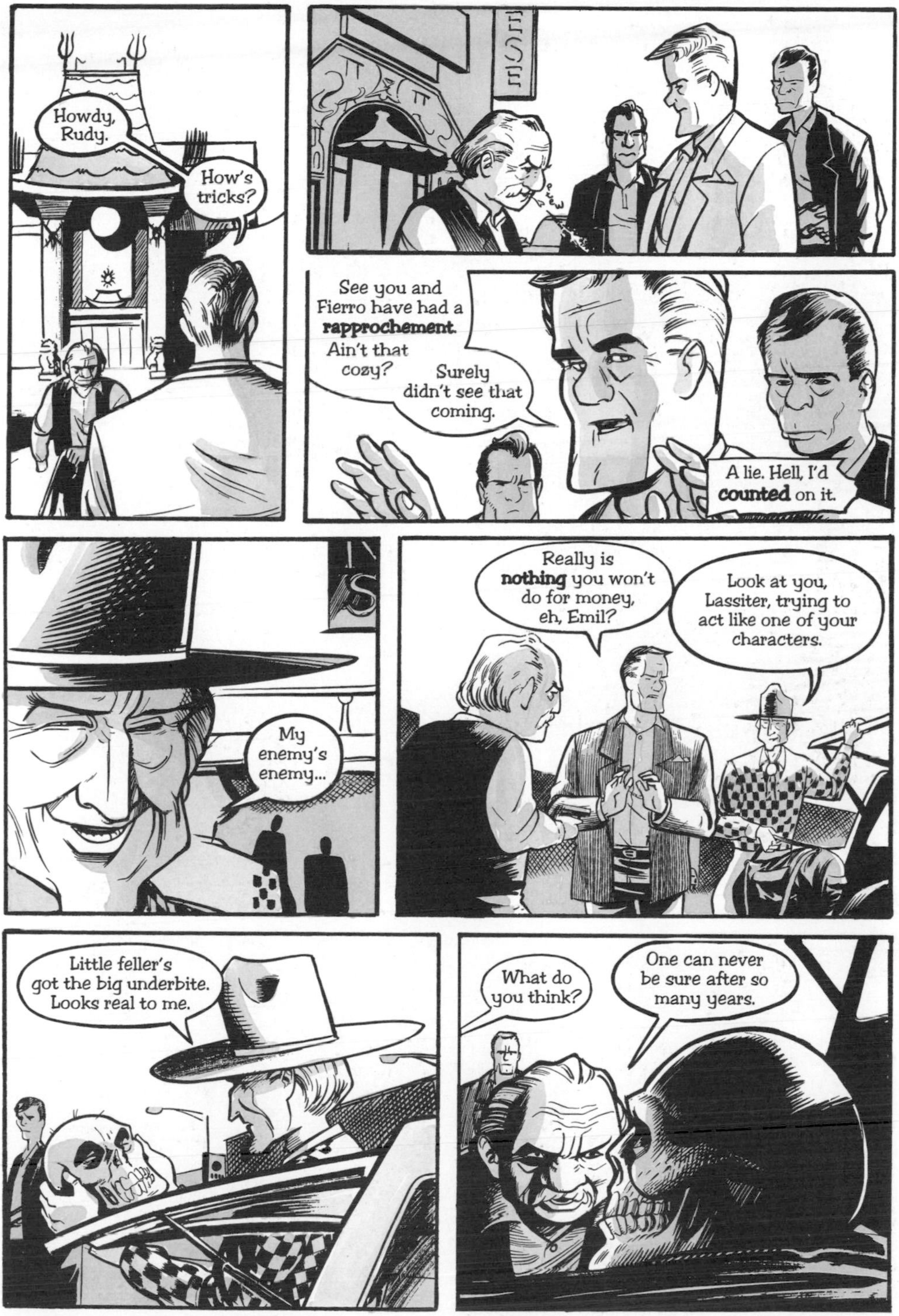
Howdy, Rudy.
How's tricks?
See you and Fierro have had a **rapprochement**. Ain't that cozy?
Surely didn't see that coming.
A lie. Hell, I'd **counted** on it.
My enemy's enemy...
Really is **nothing** you won't do for money, eh, Emil?
Look at you, Lassiter, trying to act like one of your characters.
Little feller's got the big underbite. Looks real to me.
What do you think?
One can never be sure after so many years.

This I keep.

The head?

I **think** it is real.

Give Lassiter his gun back. That ain't cricket. Never a man's gun or his horse.

Fuck you, gringo—this gun is worth much money.

Empty the bullets and give it back, asshole.

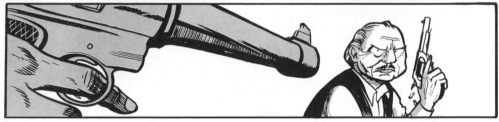

We'll meet again, I promise you.

God, I **hope** so.

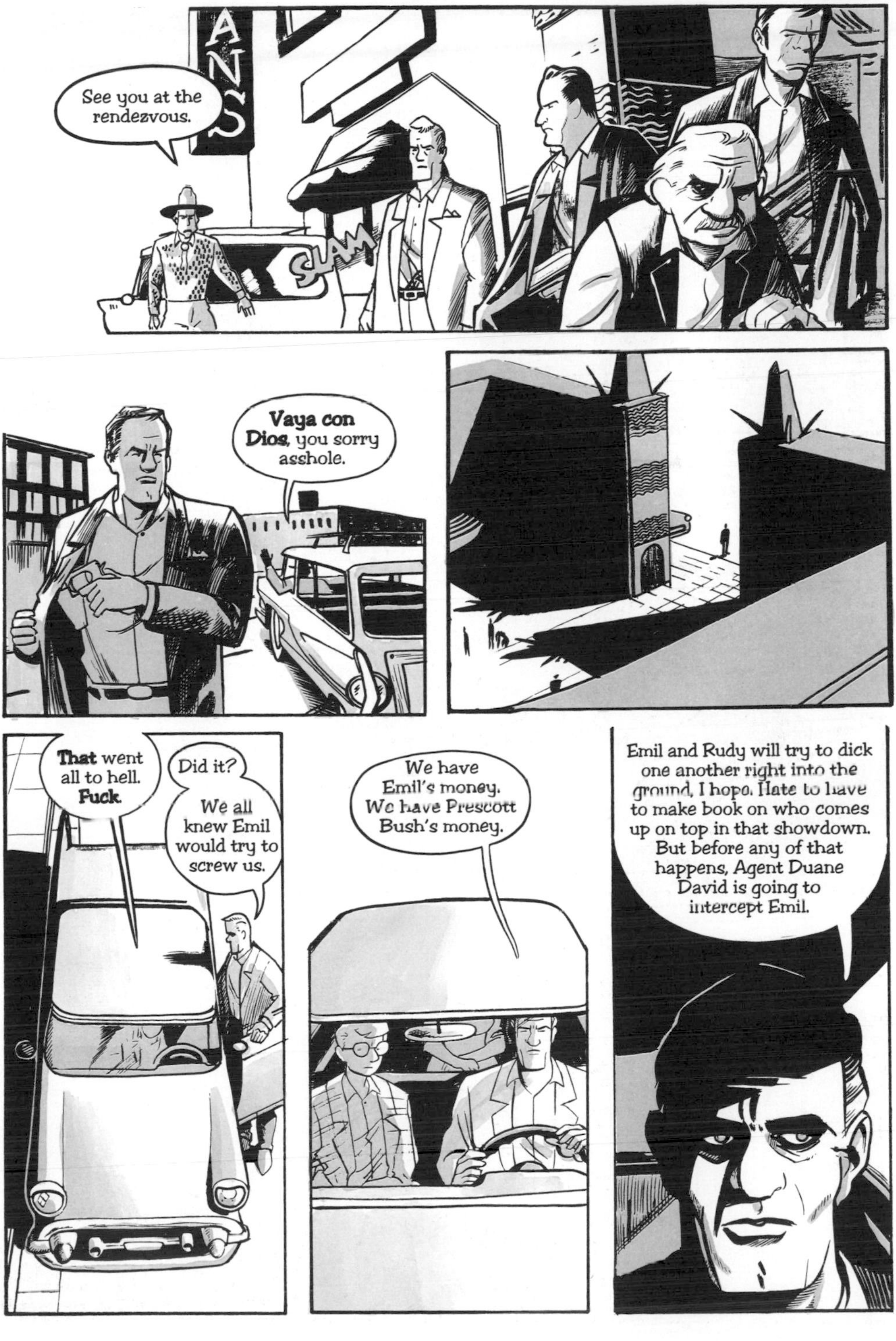
See you at the rendezvous.
ANS
SLAM
Vaya con Dios, you sorry asshole.
That went all to hell. Fuck.
Did it?
We all knew Emil would try to screw us.
We have Emil's money. We have Prescott Bush's money.
Emil and Rudy will try to dick one another right into the ground, I hope. Hate to have to make book on who comes up on top in that showdown. But before any of that happens, Agent Duane David is going to intercept Emil.

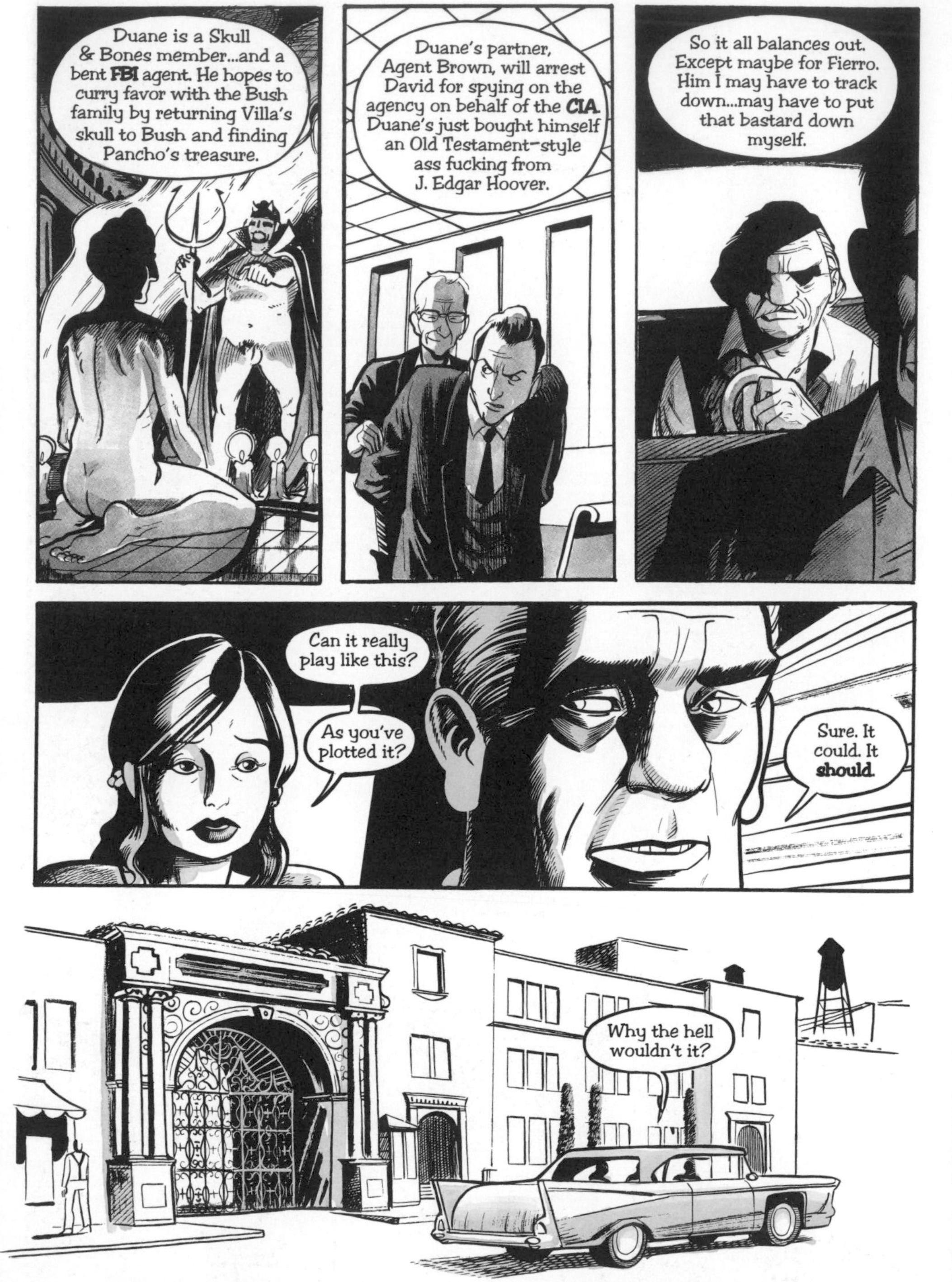
Duane is a Skull & Bones member...and a bent FBI agent. He hopes to curry favor with the Bush family by returning Villa's skull to Bush and finding Pancho's treasure.
Duane's partner, Agent Brown, will arrest David for spying on the agency on behalf of the CIA. Duane's just bought himself an Old Testament-style ass fucking from J. Edgar Hoover.
So it all balances out. Except maybe for Fierro. Him I may have to track down...may have to put that bastard down myself.
Can it really play like this?
As you've plotted it?
Sure. It could. It **should**.
Why the hell wouldn't it?

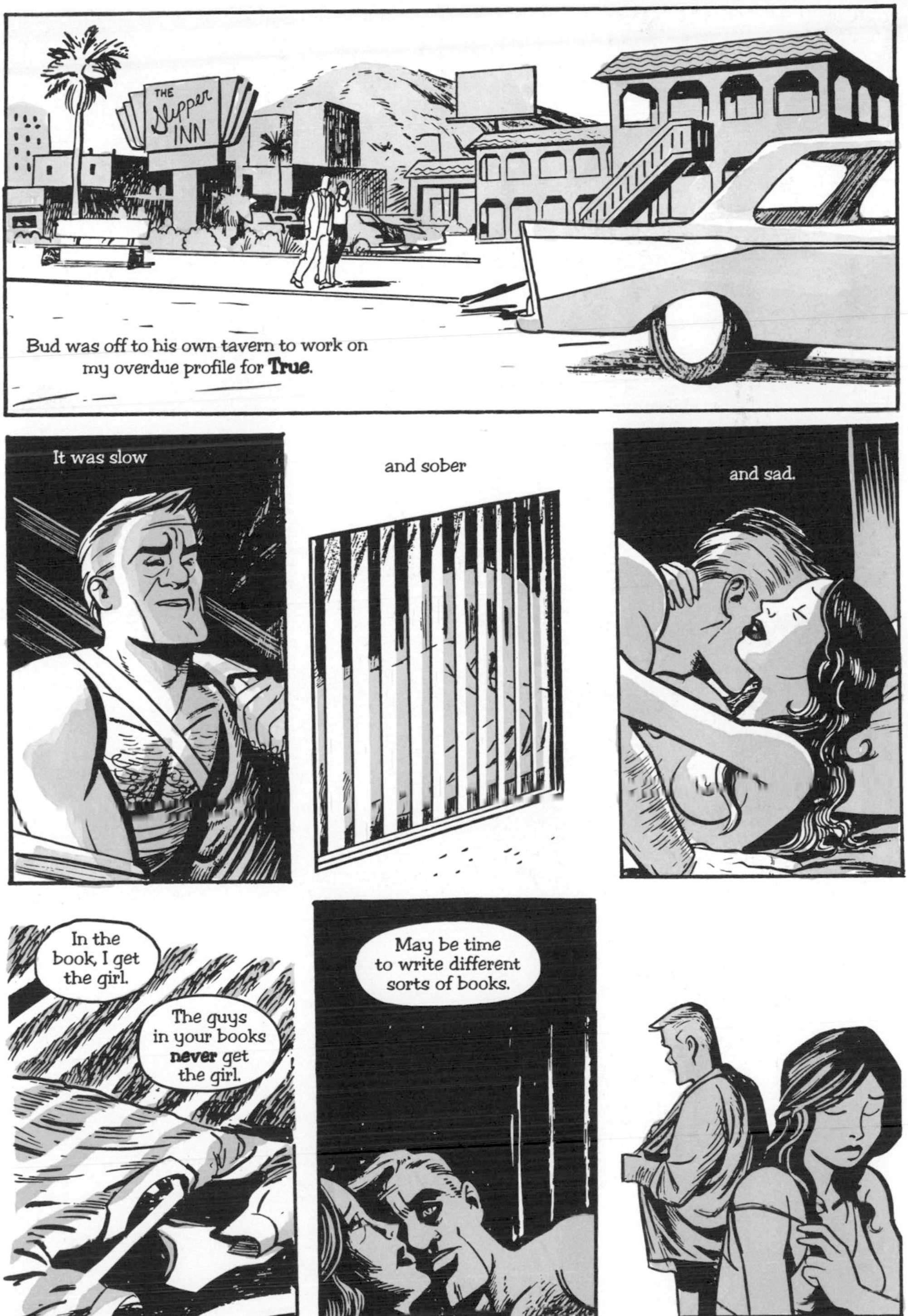
THE Slipper INN
Bud was off to his own tavern to work on my overdue profile for **True**.
It was slow
and sober
and sad.
In the book, I get the girl.
The guys in your books **never** get the girl.
May be time to write different sorts of books.

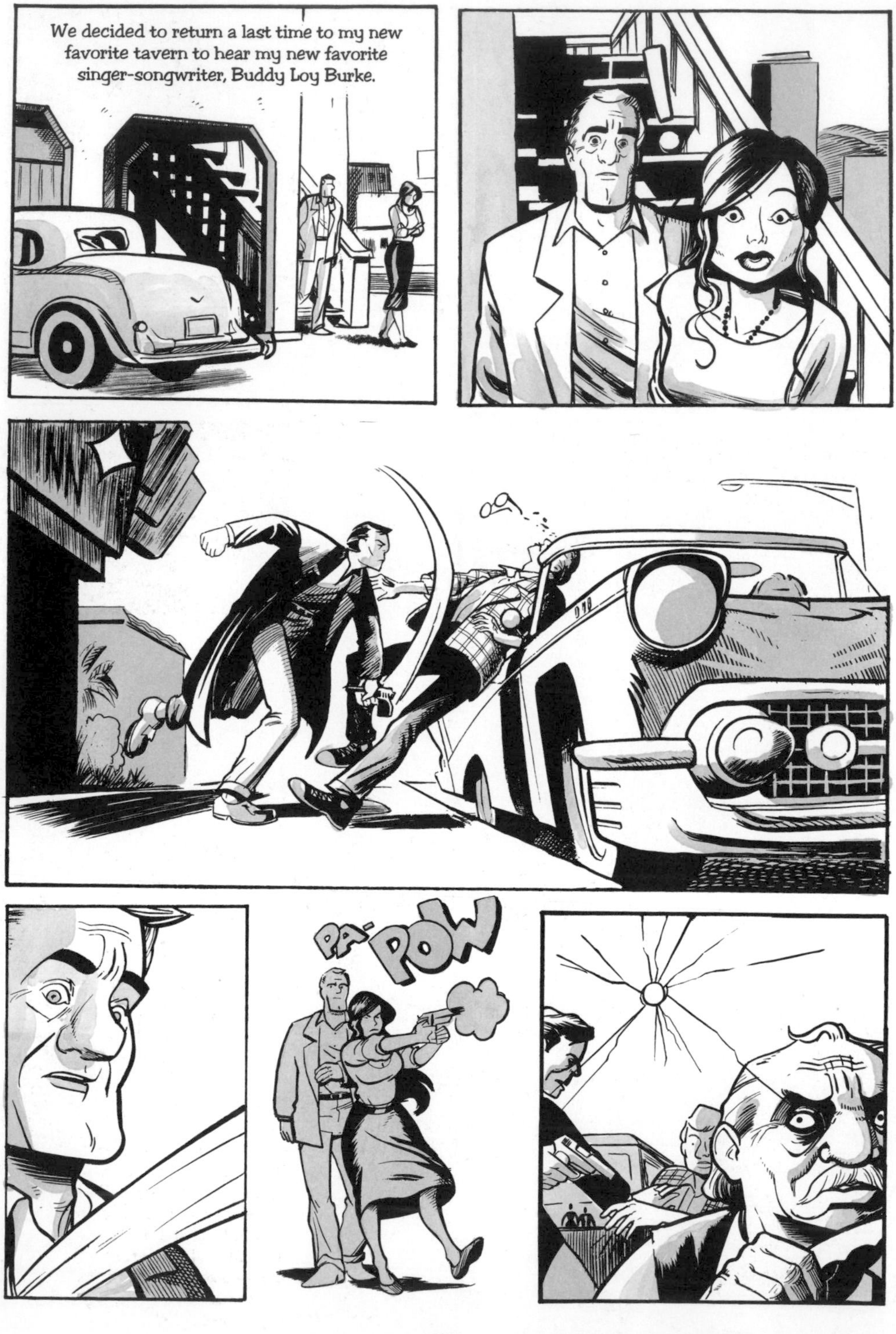
We decided to return a last time to my new favorite tavern to hear my new favorite singer-songwriter, Buddy Loy Burke.
PA-POW

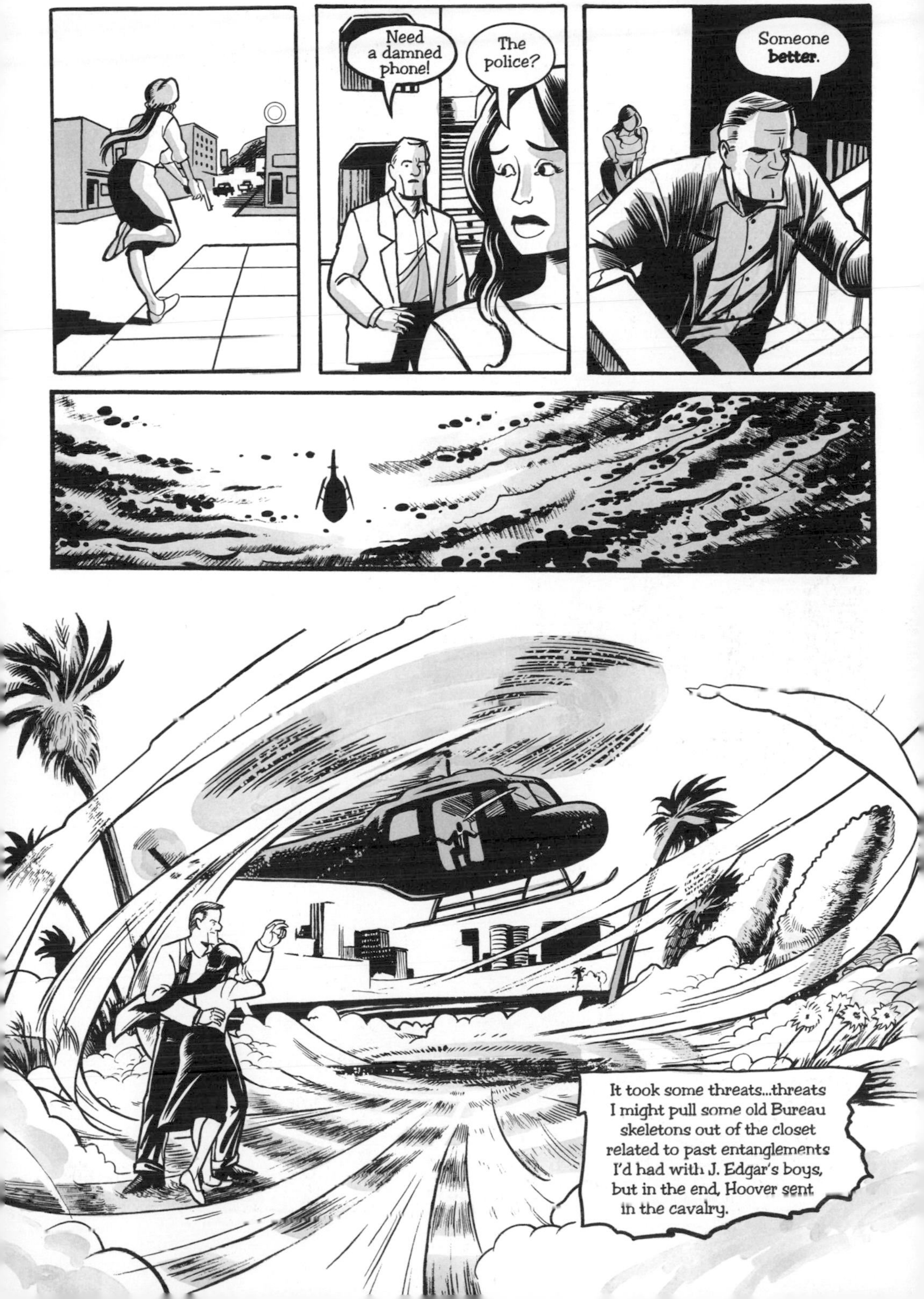
Need a damned phone!
The police?
Someone **better**.
It took some threats...threats I might pull some old Bureau skeletons out of the closet related to past entanglements I'd had with J. Edgar's boys, but in the end, Hoover sent in the cavalry.

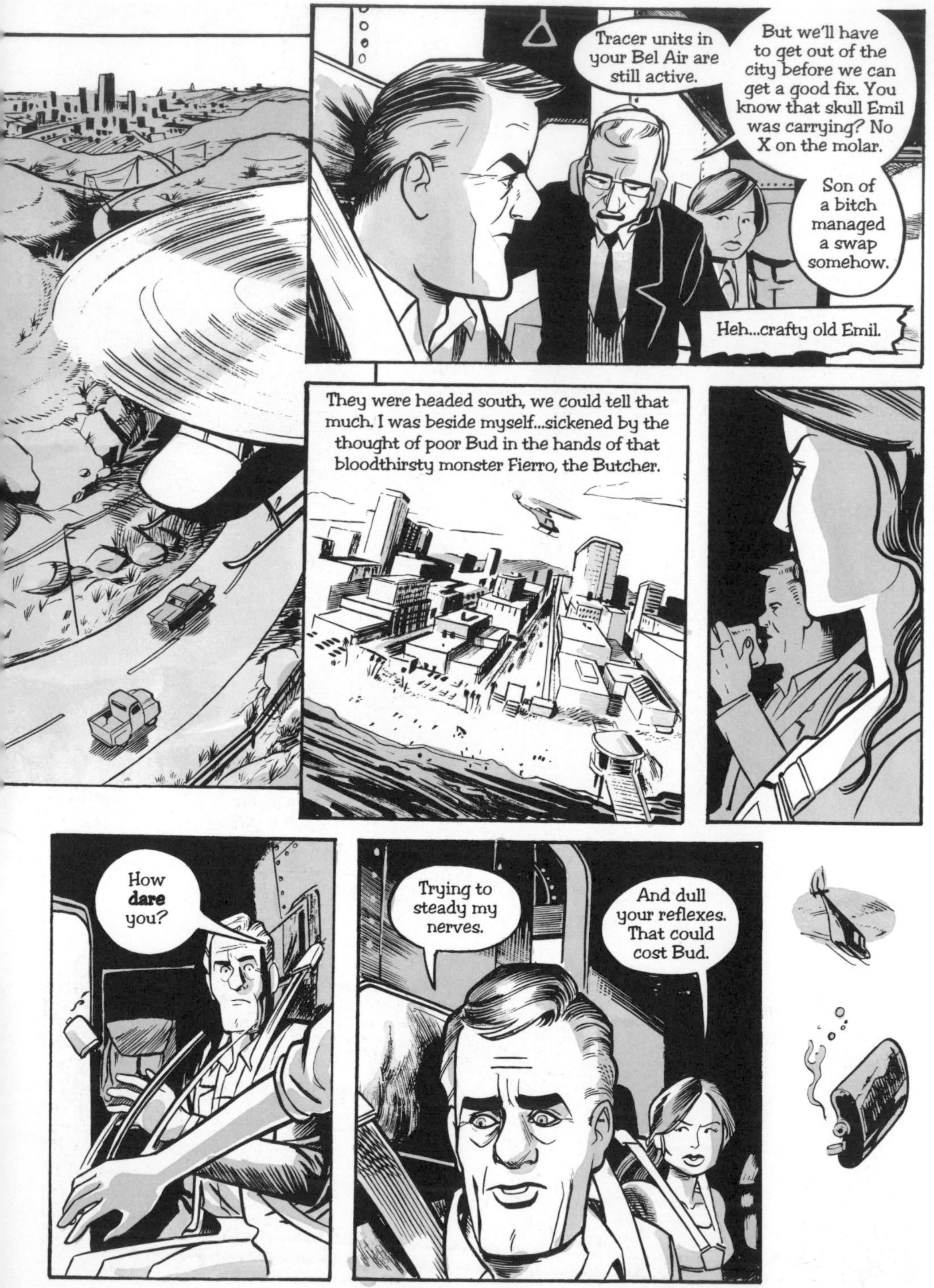
Tracer units in your Bel Air are still active.
But we'll have to get out of the city before we can get a good fix. You know that skull Emil was carrying? No X on the molar.
Son of a bitch managed a swap somehow.
Heh...crafty old Emil.
They were headed south, we could tell that much. I was beside myself...sickened by the thought of poor Bud in the hands of that bloodthirsty monster Fierro, the Butcher.
How **dare** you?
Trying to steady my nerves.
And dull your reflexes. That could cost Bud.

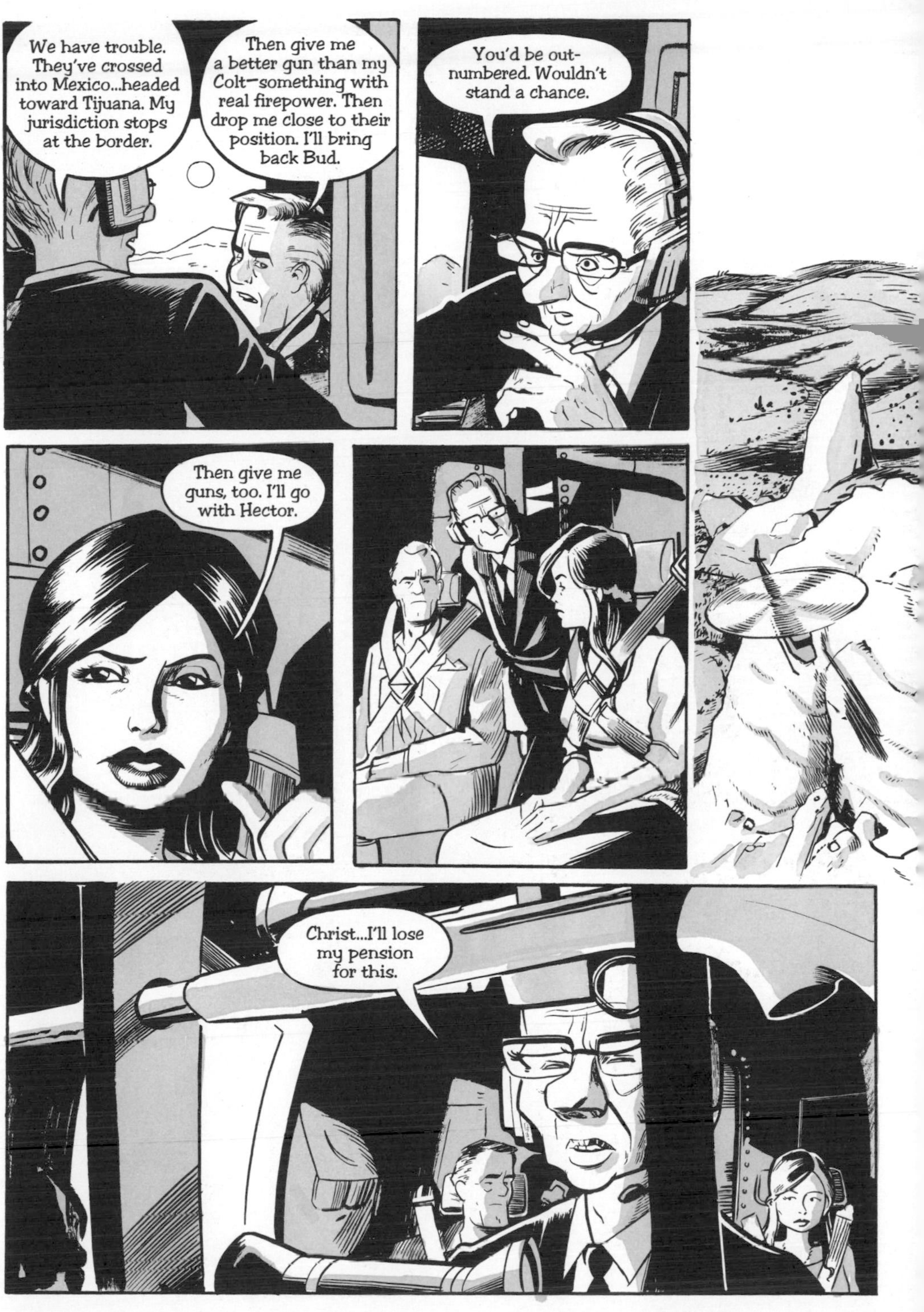

We have trouble. They've crossed into Mexico...headed toward Tijuana. My jurisdiction stops at the border.
Then give me a better gun than my Colt—something with real firepower. Then drop me close to their position. I'll bring back Bud.
You'd be out-numbered. Wouldn't stand a chance.
Then give me guns, too. I'll go with Hector.
Christ...I'll lose my pension for this.

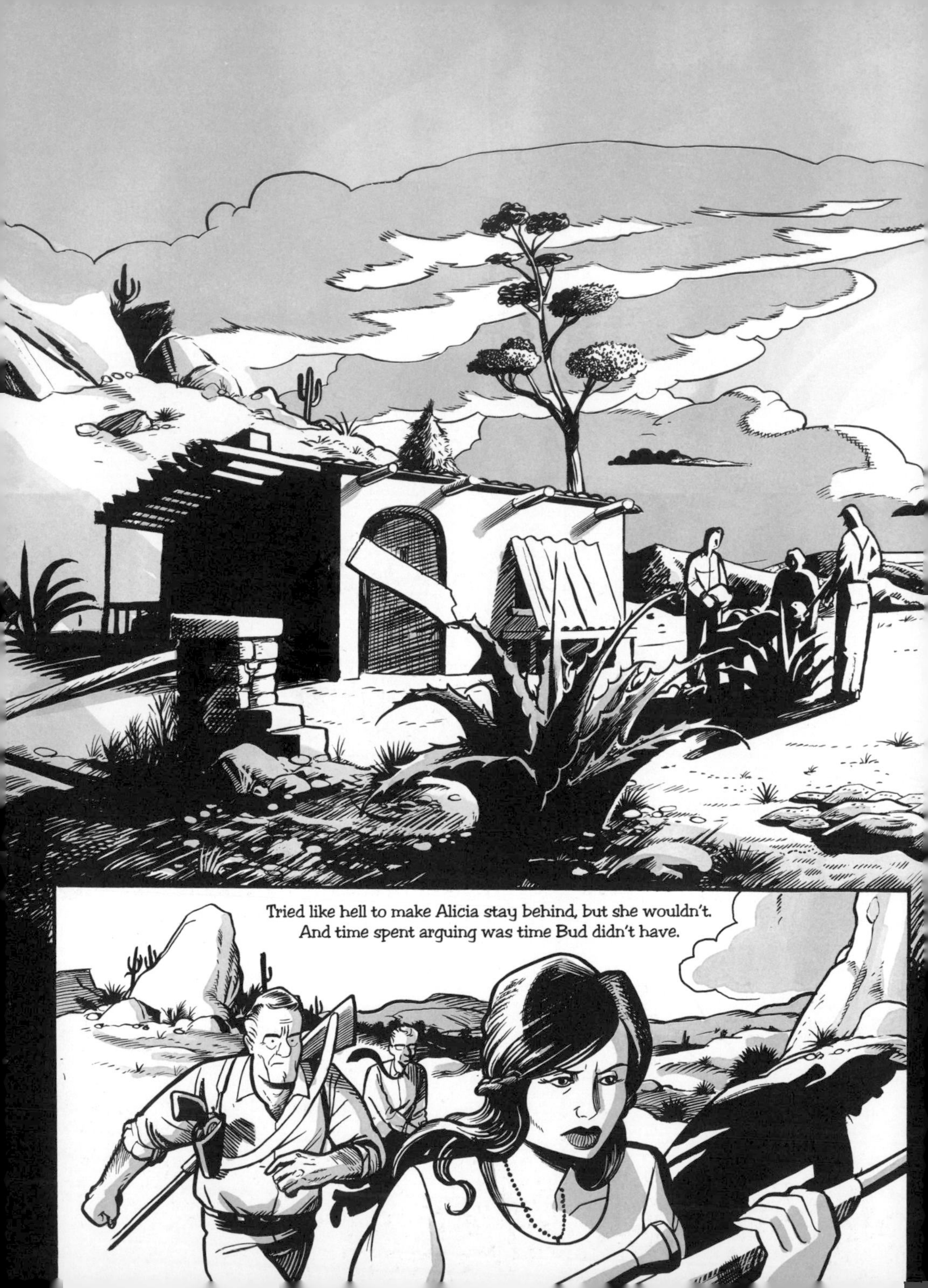
Tried like hell to make Alicia stay behind, but she wouldn't. And time spent arguing was time Bud didn't have.

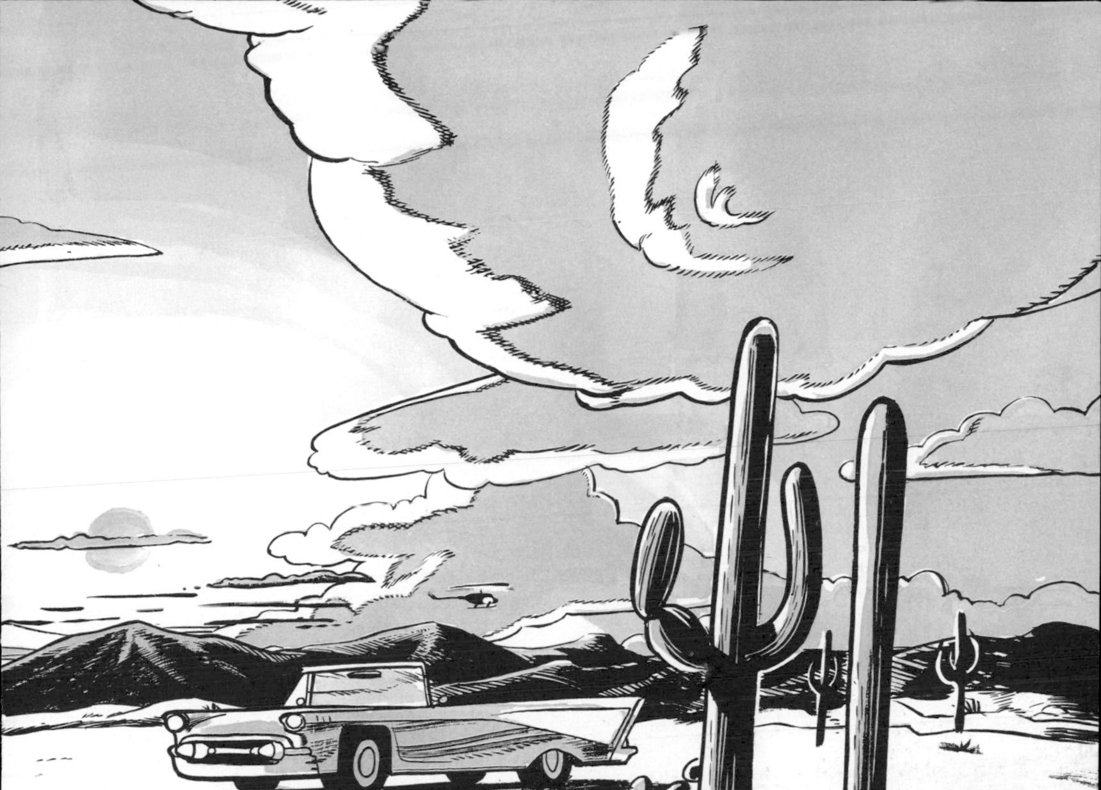

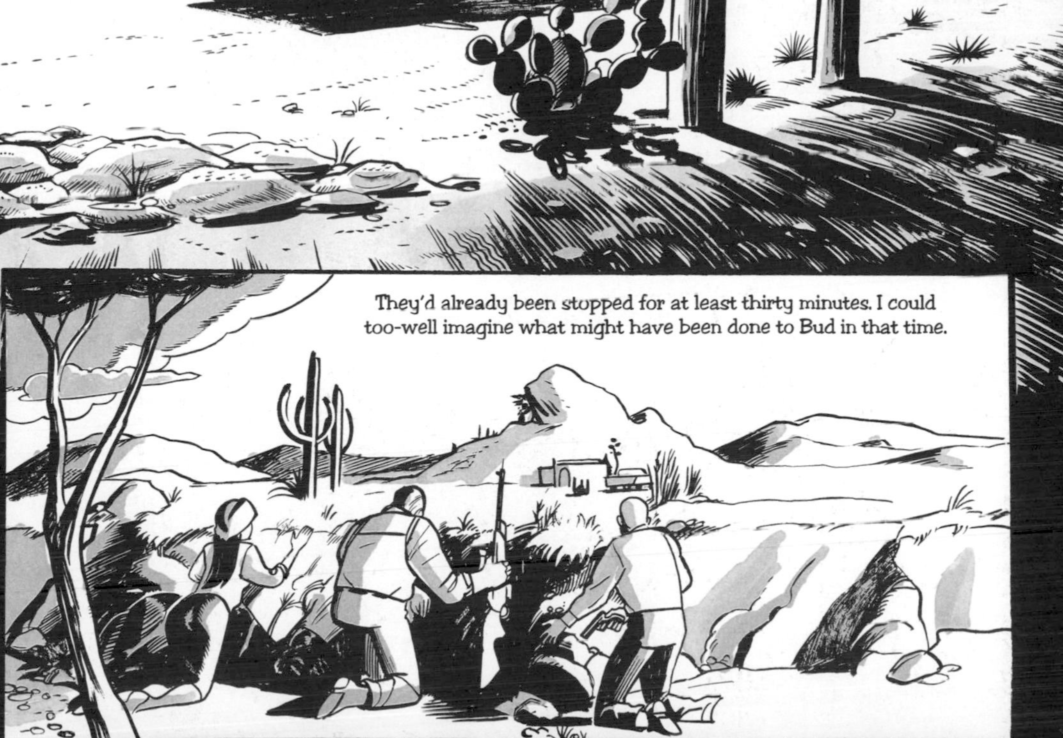
They'd already been stopped for at least thirty minutes. I could too-well imagine what might have been done to Bud in that time.

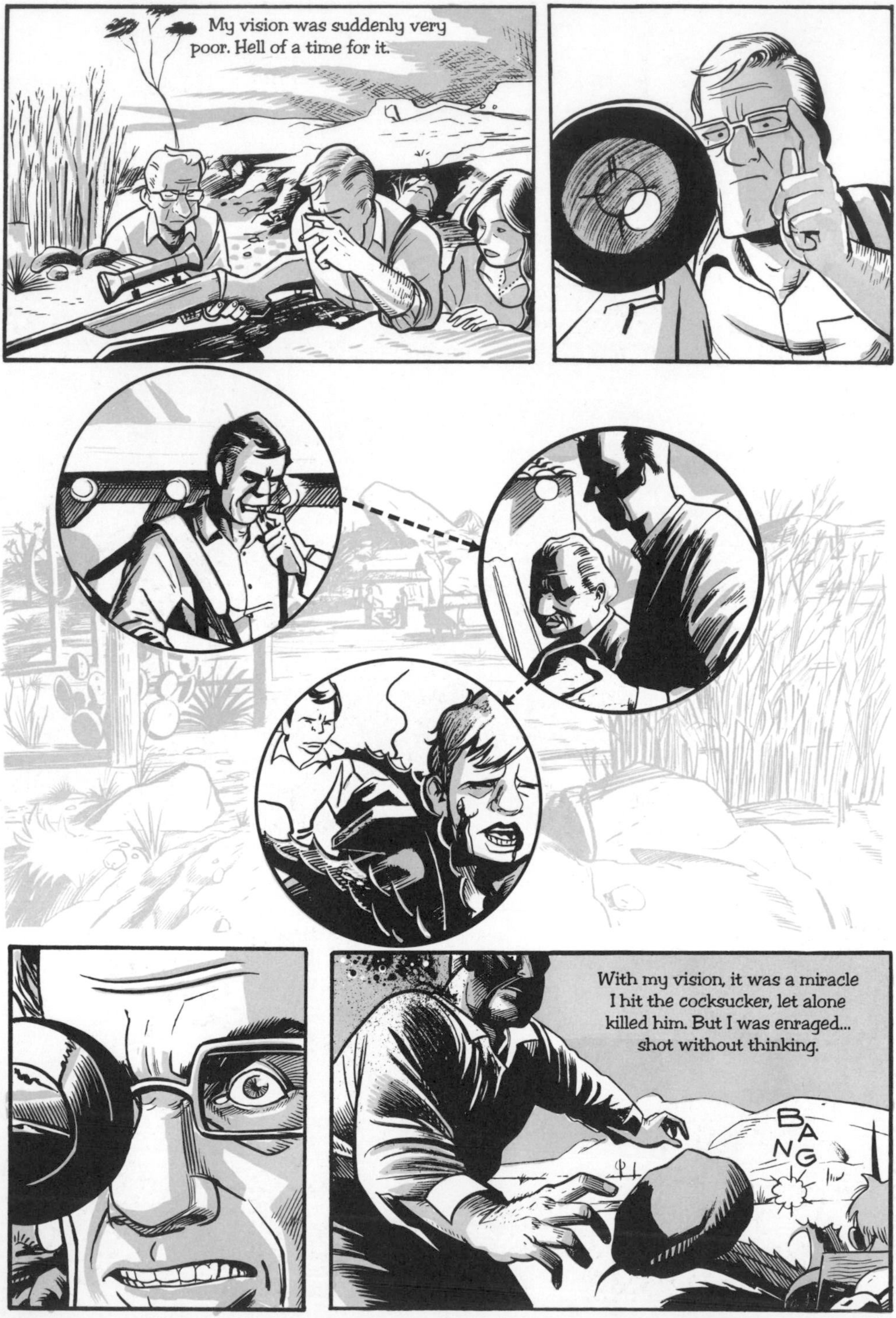
My vision was suddenly very poor. Hell of a time for it.
With my vision, it was a miracle I hit the cocksucker, let alone killed him. But I was enraged... shot without thinking.
BANG

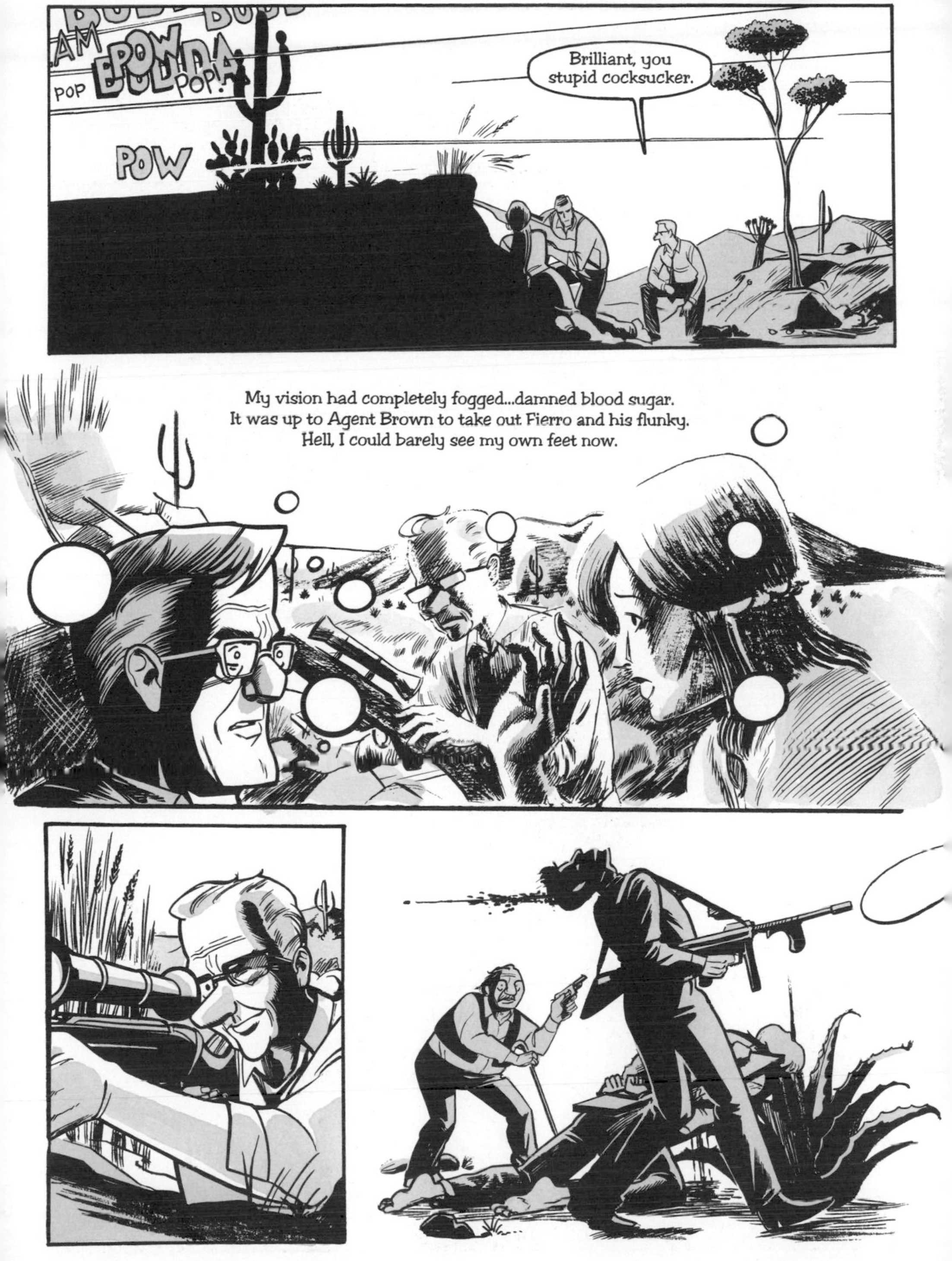
POW
POP
POP!
POW
Brilliant, you stupid cocksucker.
My vision had completely fogged...damned blood sugar.
It was up to Agent Brown to take out Fierro and his flunky.
Hell, I could barely see my own feet now.

Brown was trying to sound angry at me for shooting the first one, but the agent couldn't quite get there. He was exhilarated in that way we get with bullets flying.

That just leaves Fierro.

KAFF

POP
POP
POP

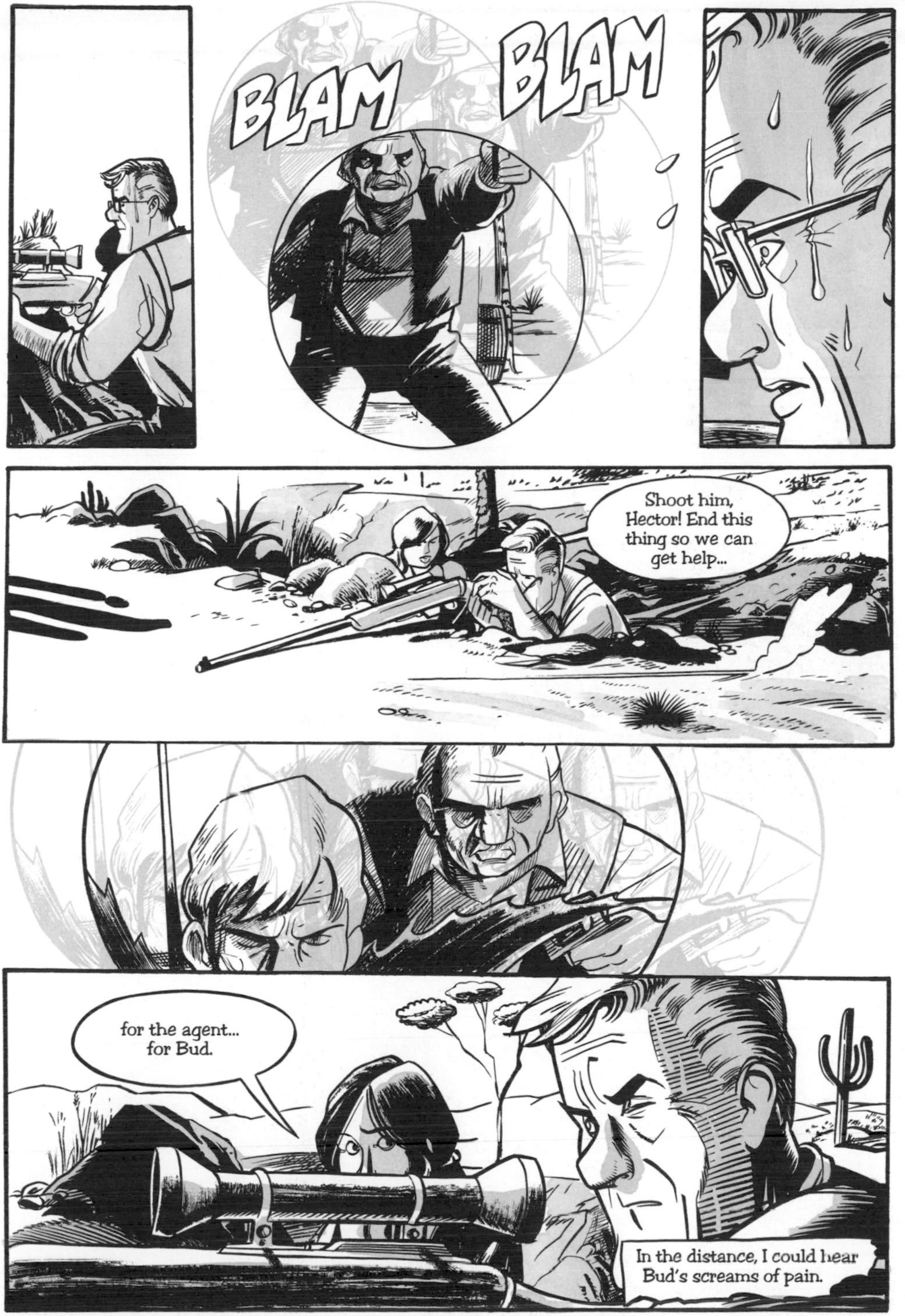
BLAM
BLAM
Shoot him, Hector! End this thing so we can get help...
for the agent... for Bud.
In the distance, I could hear Bud's screams of pain.

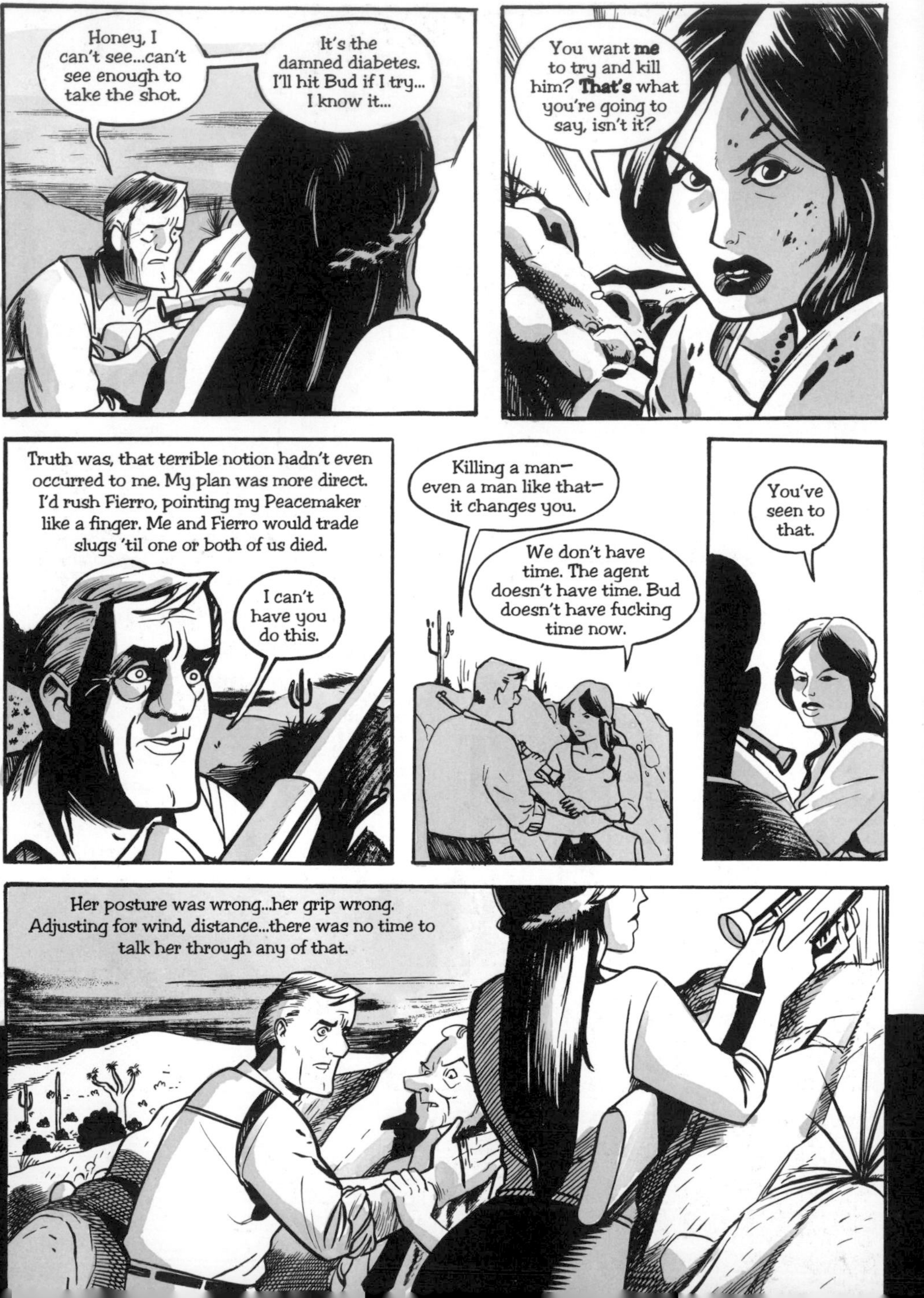
Honey, I can't see...can't see enough to take the shot.
It's the damned diabetes. I'll hit Bud if I try... I know it...
You want me to try and kill him? That's what you're going to say, isn't it?
Truth was, that terrible notion hadn't even occurred to me. My plan was more direct. I'd rush Fierro, pointing my Peacemaker like a finger. Me and Fierro would trade slugs 'til one or both of us died.
I can't have you do this.
Killing a man—even a man like that—it changes you.
We don't have time. The agent doesn't have time. Bud doesn't have fucking time now.
You've seen to that.
Her posture was wrong...her grip wrong. Adjusting for wind, distance...there was no time to talk her through any of that.

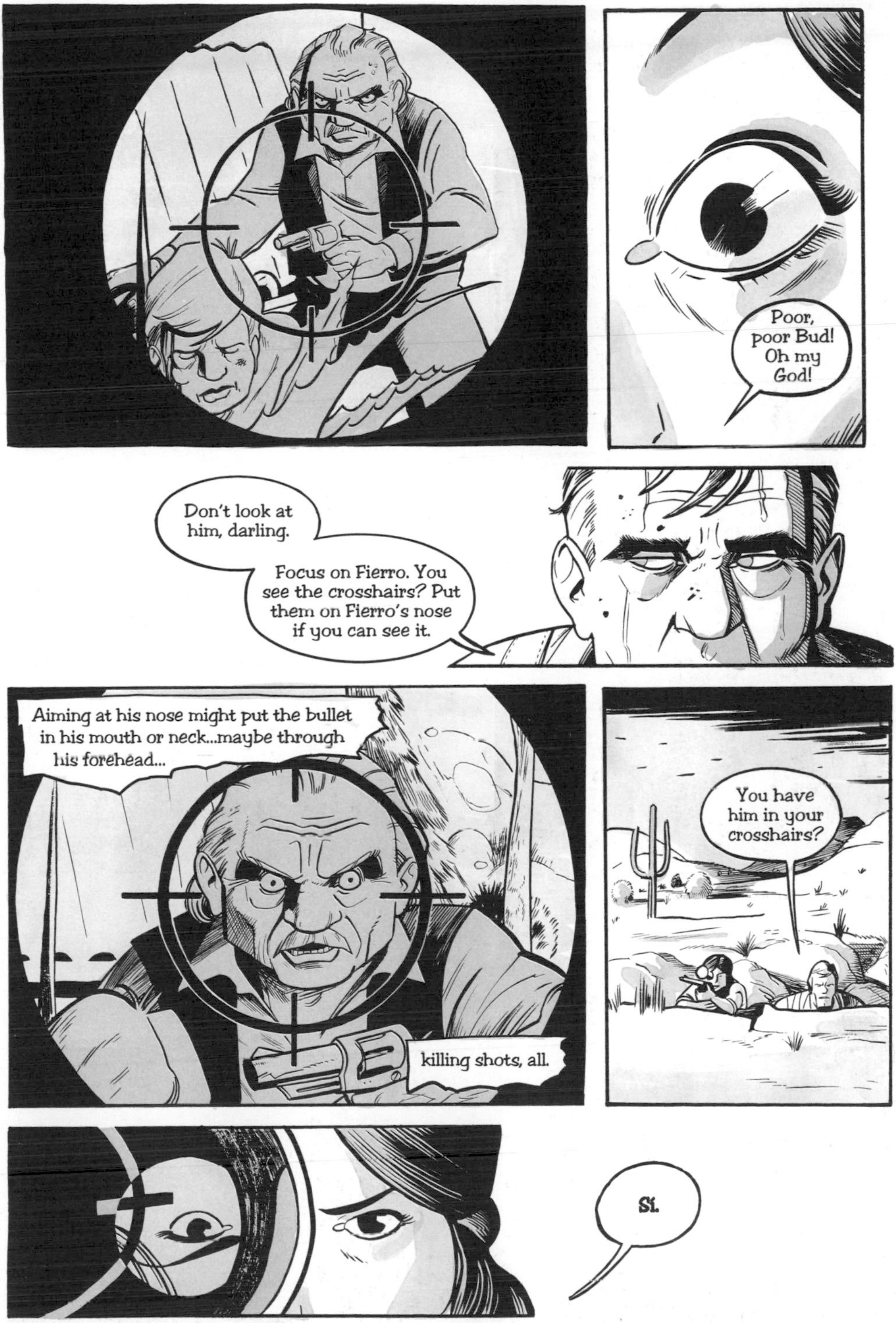
Poor, poor Bud! Oh my God!
Don't look at him, darling.
Focus on Fierro. You see the crosshairs? Put them on Fierro's nose if you can see it.
Aiming at his nose might put the bullet in his mouth or neck...maybe through his forehead...
killing shots, all.
You have him in your crosshairs?
Sí.

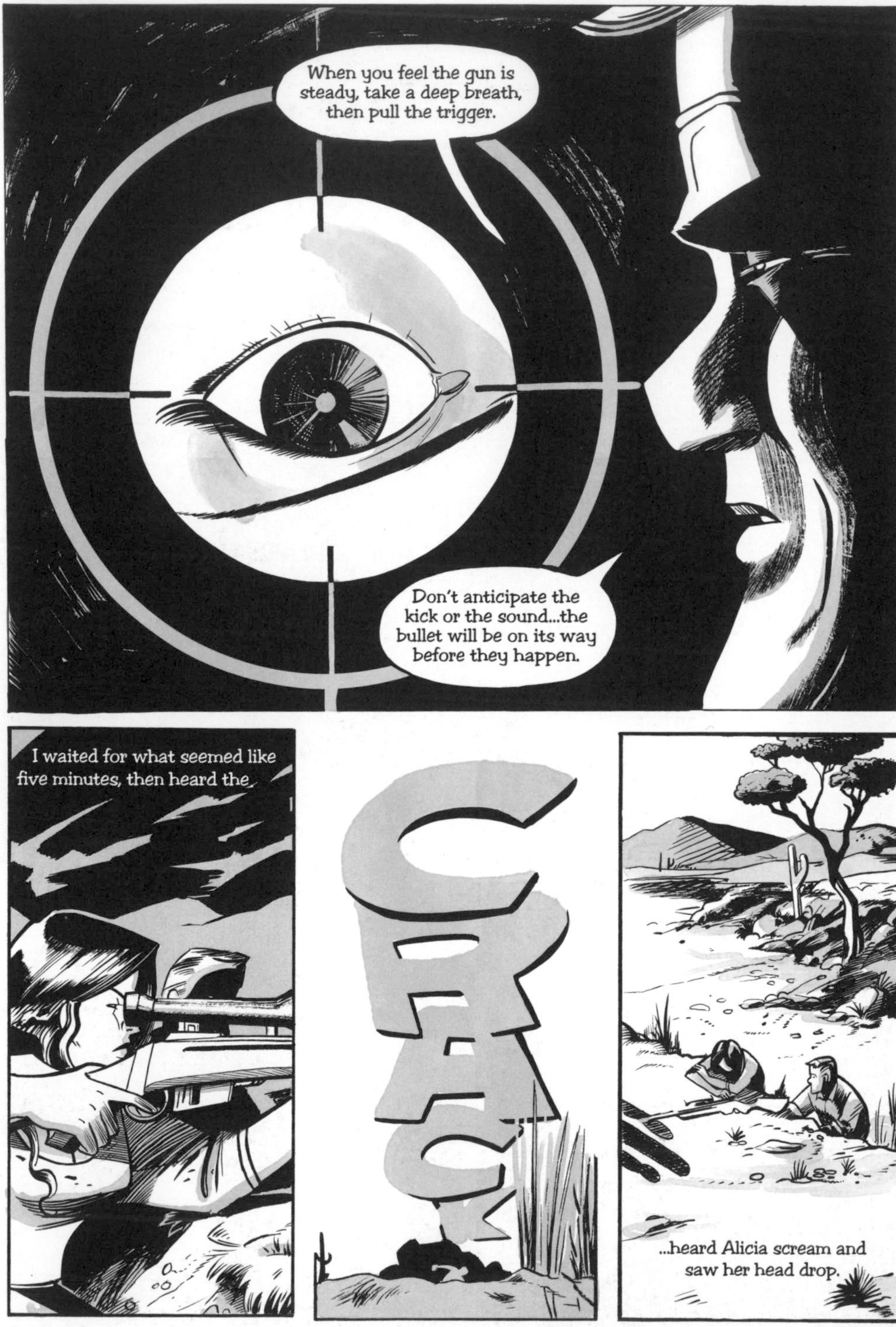
When you feel the gun is steady, take a deep breath, then pull the trigger.
Don't anticipate the kick or the sound...the bullet will be on its way before they happen.
I waited for what seemed like five minutes, then heard the
CRACK
...heard Alicia scream and saw her head drop.

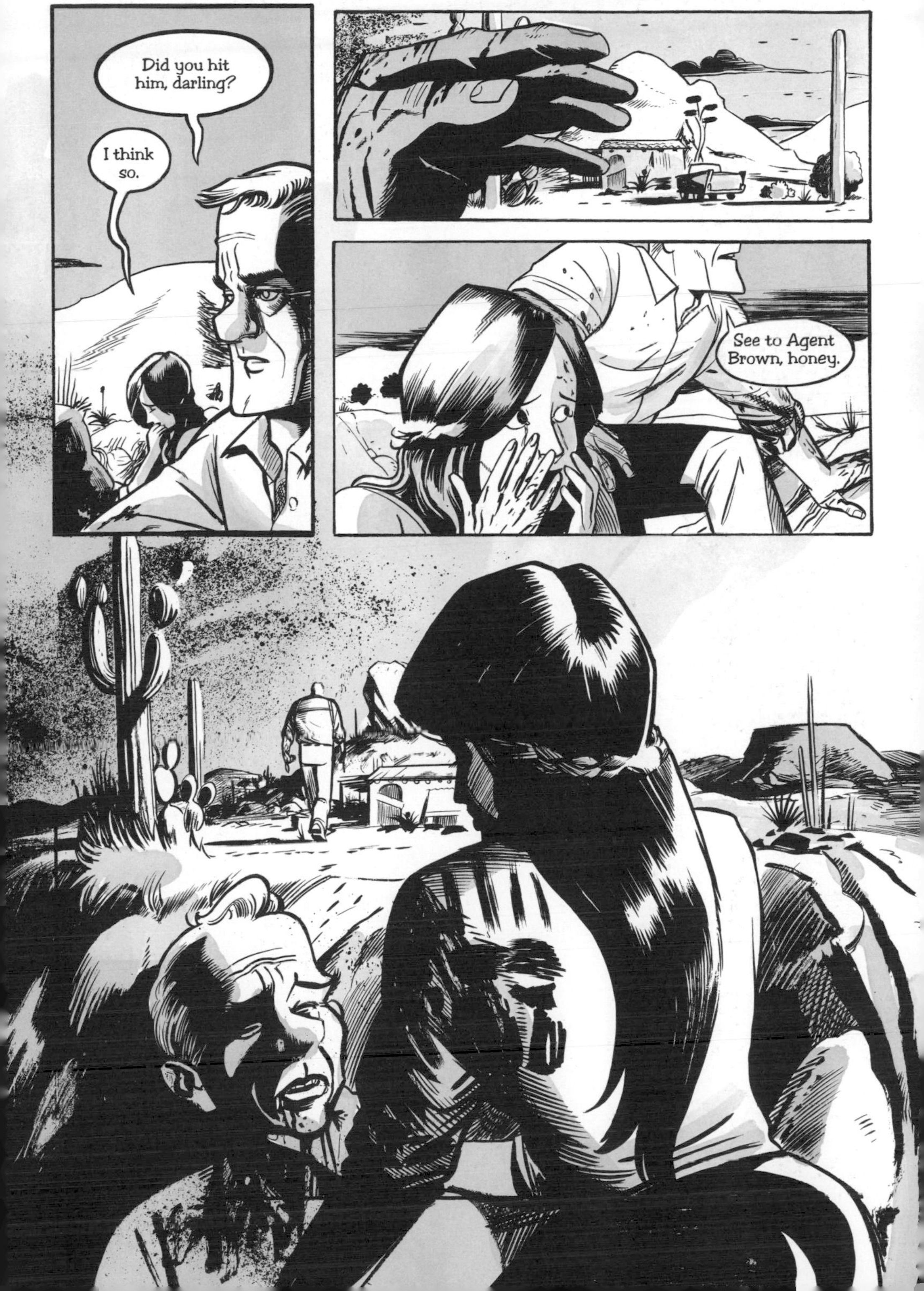
Did you hit him, darling?
I think so.
See to Agent Brown, honey.

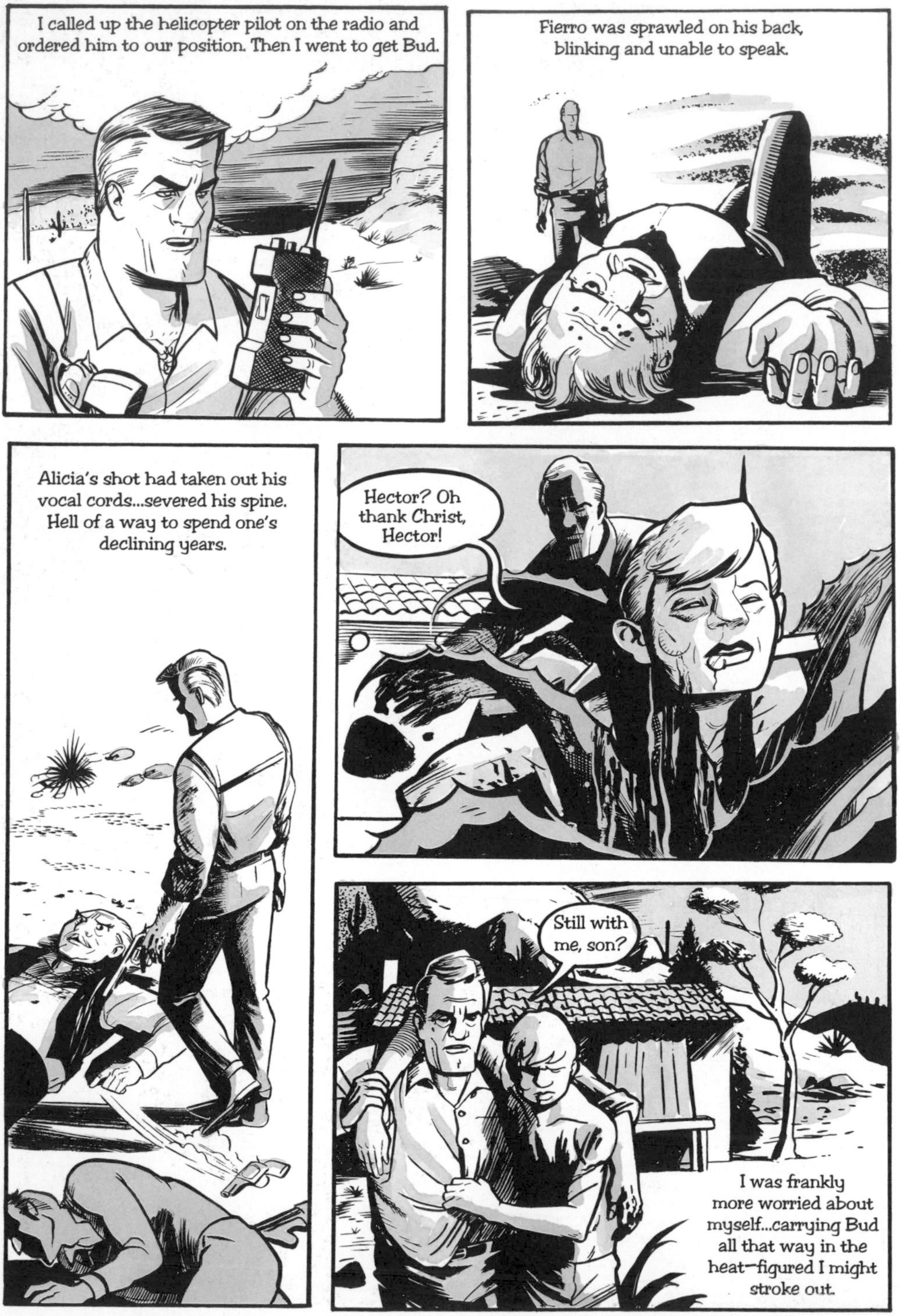
I called up the helicopter pilot on the radio and ordered him to our position. Then I went to get Bud.
Fierro was sprawled on his back, blinking and unable to speak.
Alicia's shot had taken out his vocal cords...severed his spine. Hell of a way to spend one's declining years.
Hector? Oh thank Christ, Hector!
Still with me, son?
I was frankly more worried about myself...carrying Bud all that way in the heat—figured I might stroke out.

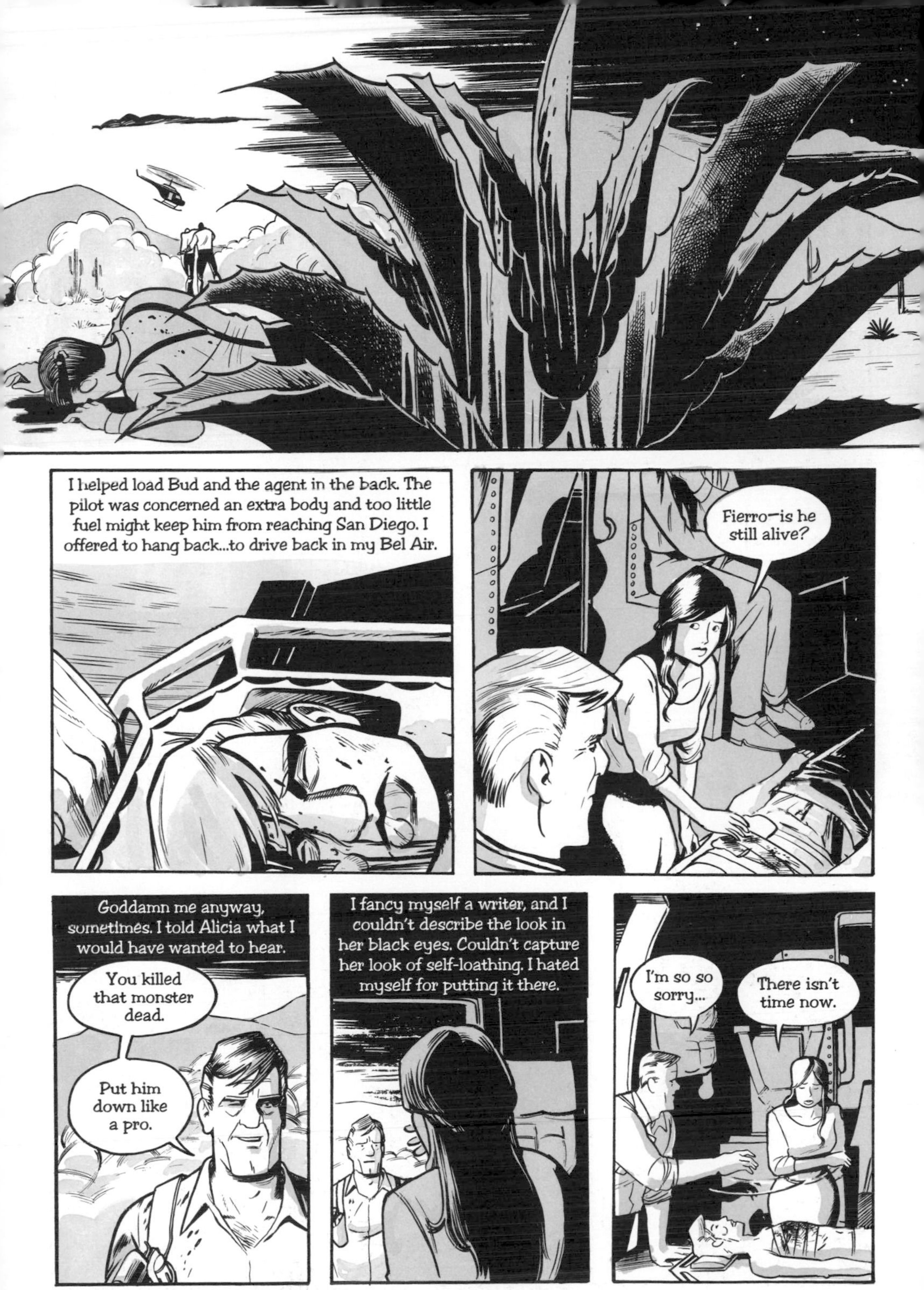
I helped load Bud and the agent in the back. The pilot was concerned an extra body and too little fuel might keep him from reaching San Diego. I offered to hang back...to drive back in my Bel Air.
Fierro—is he still alive?
Goddamn me anyway, sometimes. I told Alicia what I would have wanted to hear.
You killed that monster dead.
Put him down like a pro.
I fancy myself a writer, and I couldn't describe the look in her black eyes. Couldn't capture her look of self-loathing. I hated myself for putting it there.
I'm so so sorry...
There isn't time now.

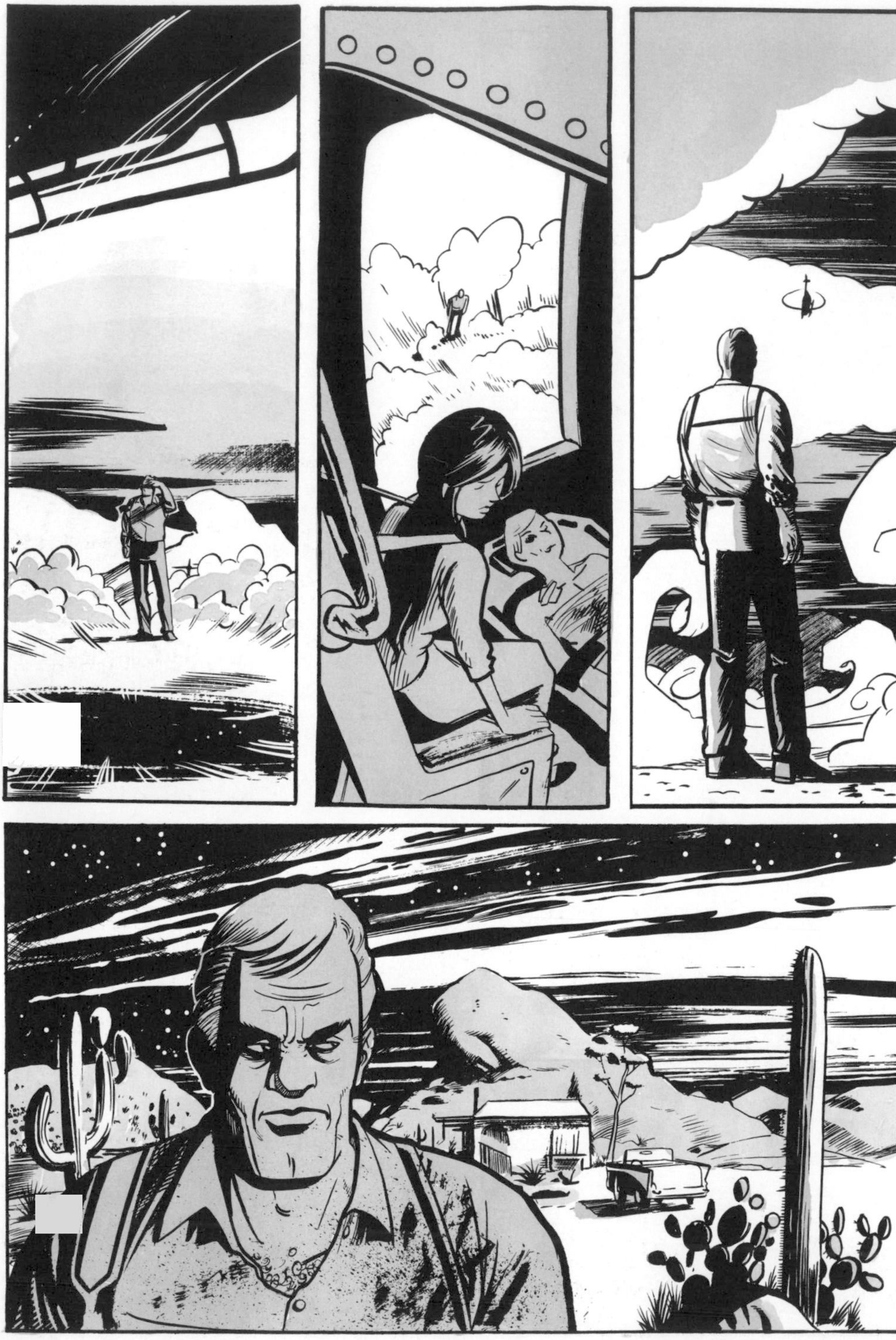

I wolfed down a couple of melting candy bars I found in the glove compartment. Then I found Alicia's honey bottle.

Fierro probably intended to use those ants against Bud if the plant didn't break him.

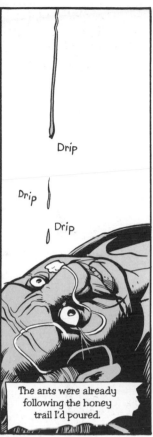

Drip

Drip

Drip

The ants were already following the honey trail I'd poured.

Viva Villa.

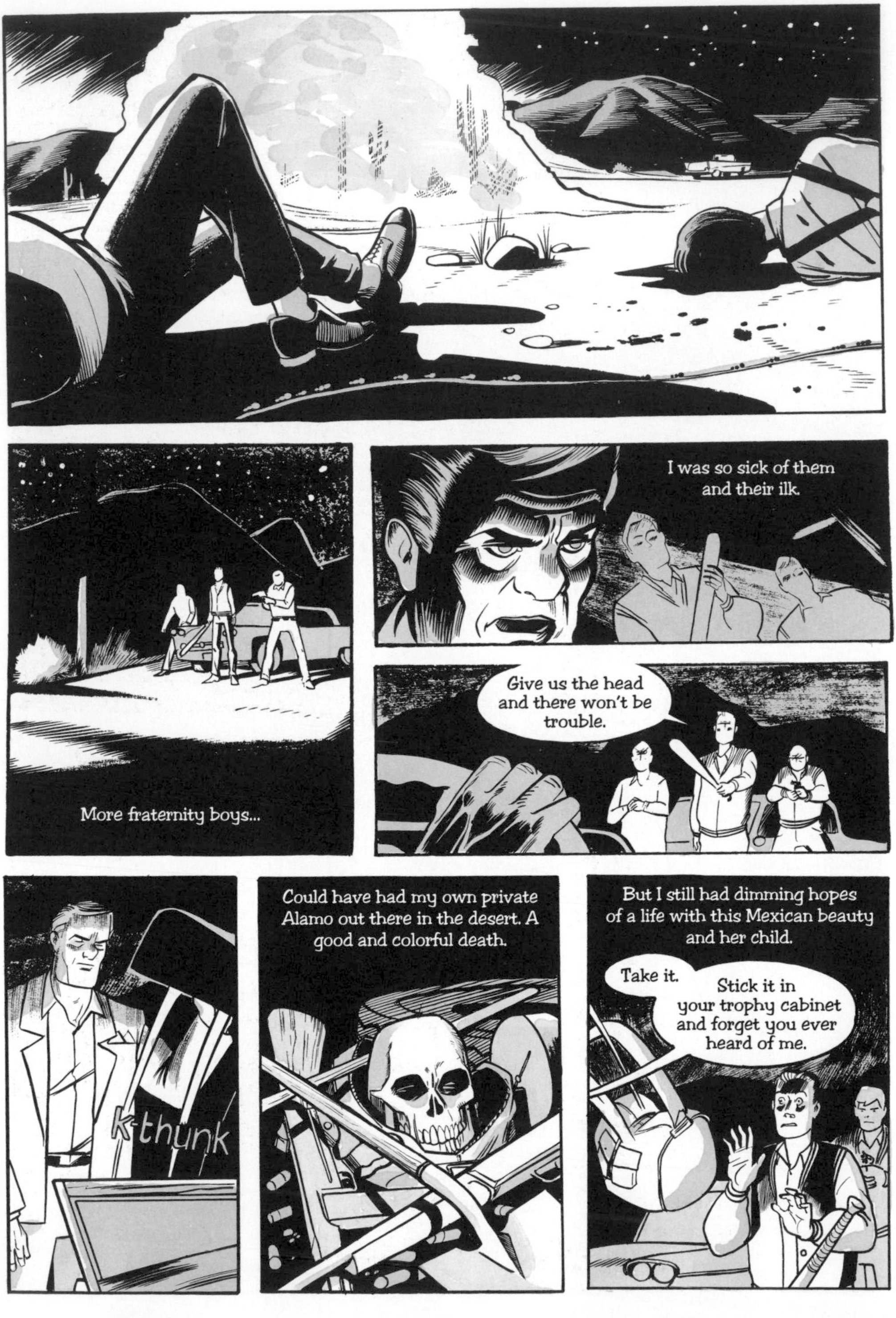
More fraternity boys...
I was so sick of them and their ilk.
Give us the head and there won't be trouble.
k-thunk
Could have had my own private Alamo out there in the desert. A good and colorful death.
But I still had dimming hopes of a life with this Mexican beauty and her child.
Take it.
Stick it in your trophy cabinet and forget you ever heard of me.

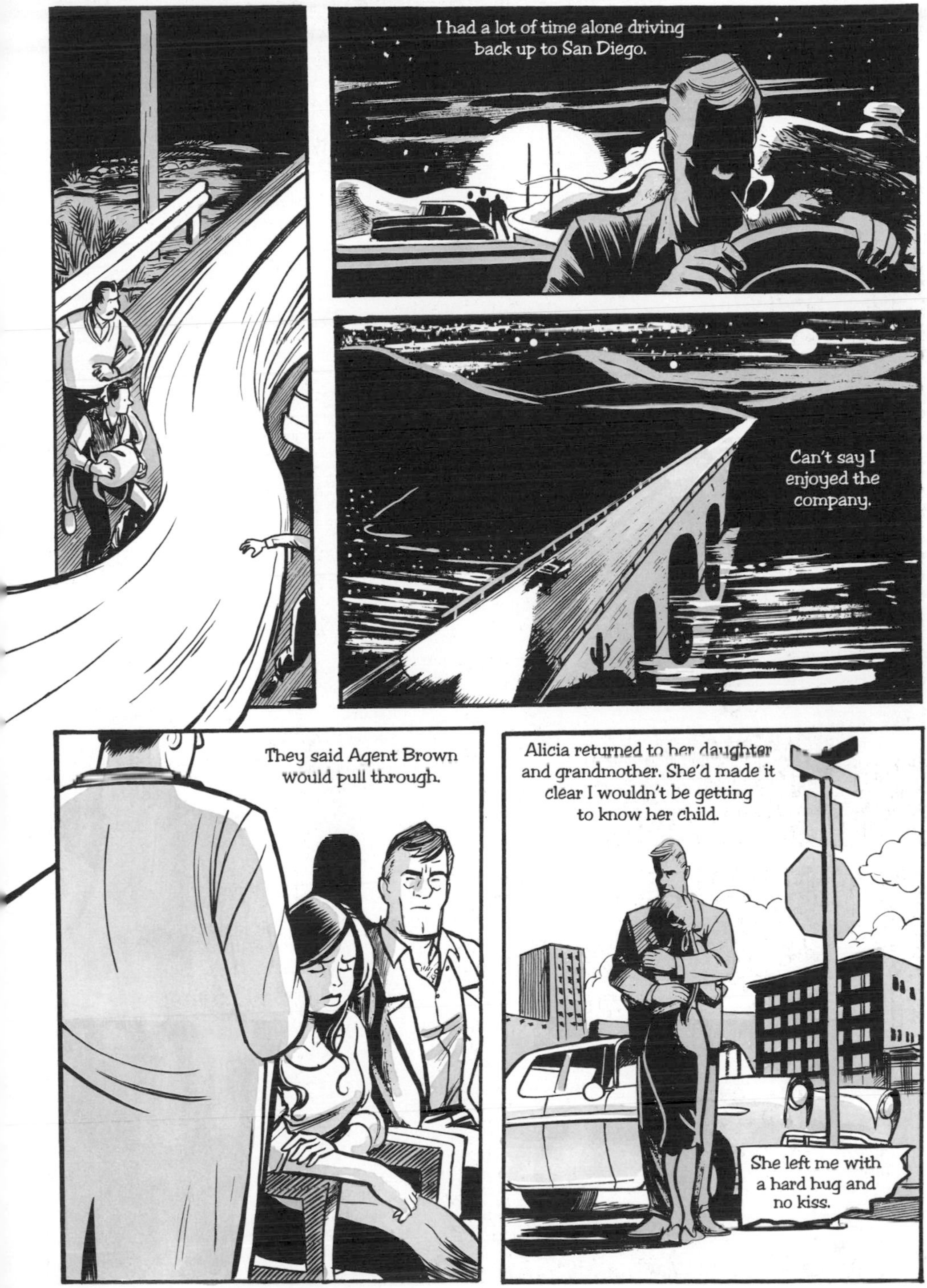
I had a lot of time alone driving back up to San Diego.
Can't say I enjoyed the company.
They said Agent Brown would pull through.
Alicia returned to her daughter and grandmother. She'd made it clear I wouldn't be getting to know her child.
She left me with a hard hug and no kiss.

Bud was working on his profile of me. He was having trouble getting it going.

I do it every day. Make it up, like I do.

Make it up. Build a legend around me. **Lie.**

I can't do that. **You** wouldn't do that.

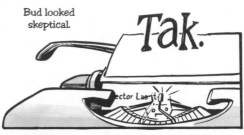

Bud looked skeptical.

Tak.

Tak.
tak Tak.
Tak.

At ends, always a dangerous way for me to be, I returned to Orson's film set.

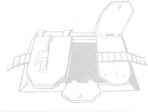

Next time you watch **Touch of Evil**, notice how you never see Marlene and Orson in frame together.

When Marlene is talking to "Hank," that's actually **me** she's speaking to.

Those are **my** hands drunkenly spreading those tarot cards. And I **was** drunk...flying on mescal.

I want to stay the night.

Tonight you can.

She was humming some tune I half-recognized. I asked her what it was.

A tune Papa taught me. **Canción Mixteca.**

I sing it with German lyrics.

I felt the hairs rise on the back of my neck.

115

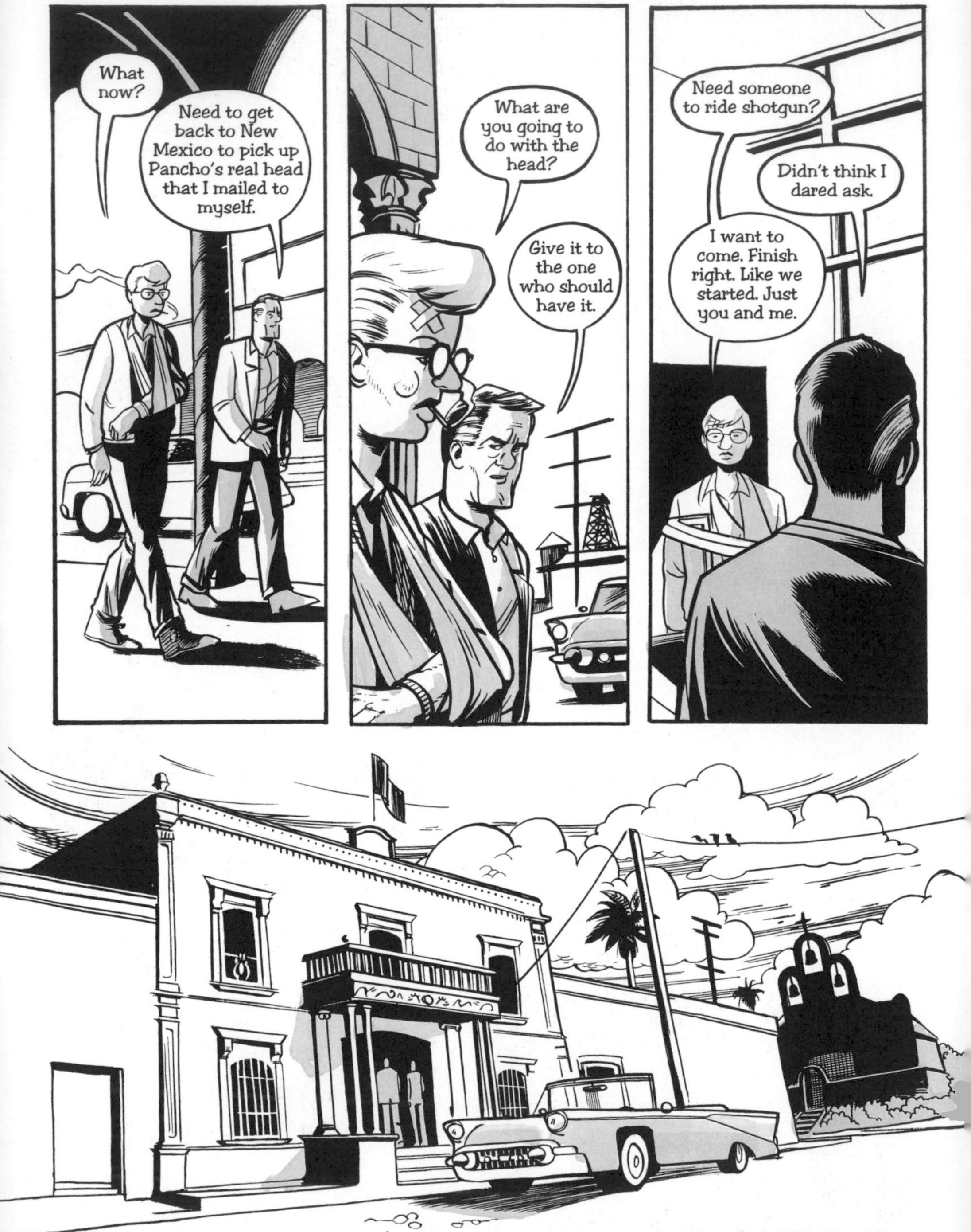
What now?
Need to get back to New Mexico to pick up Pancho's real head that I mailed to myself.
What are you going to do with the head?
Give it to the one who should have it.
Need someone to ride shotgun?
Didn't think I dared ask.
I want to come. Finish right. Like we started. Just you and me.

Pancho's widow, **Luz Corral Vda. De Villa** met us at the door...led us inside.

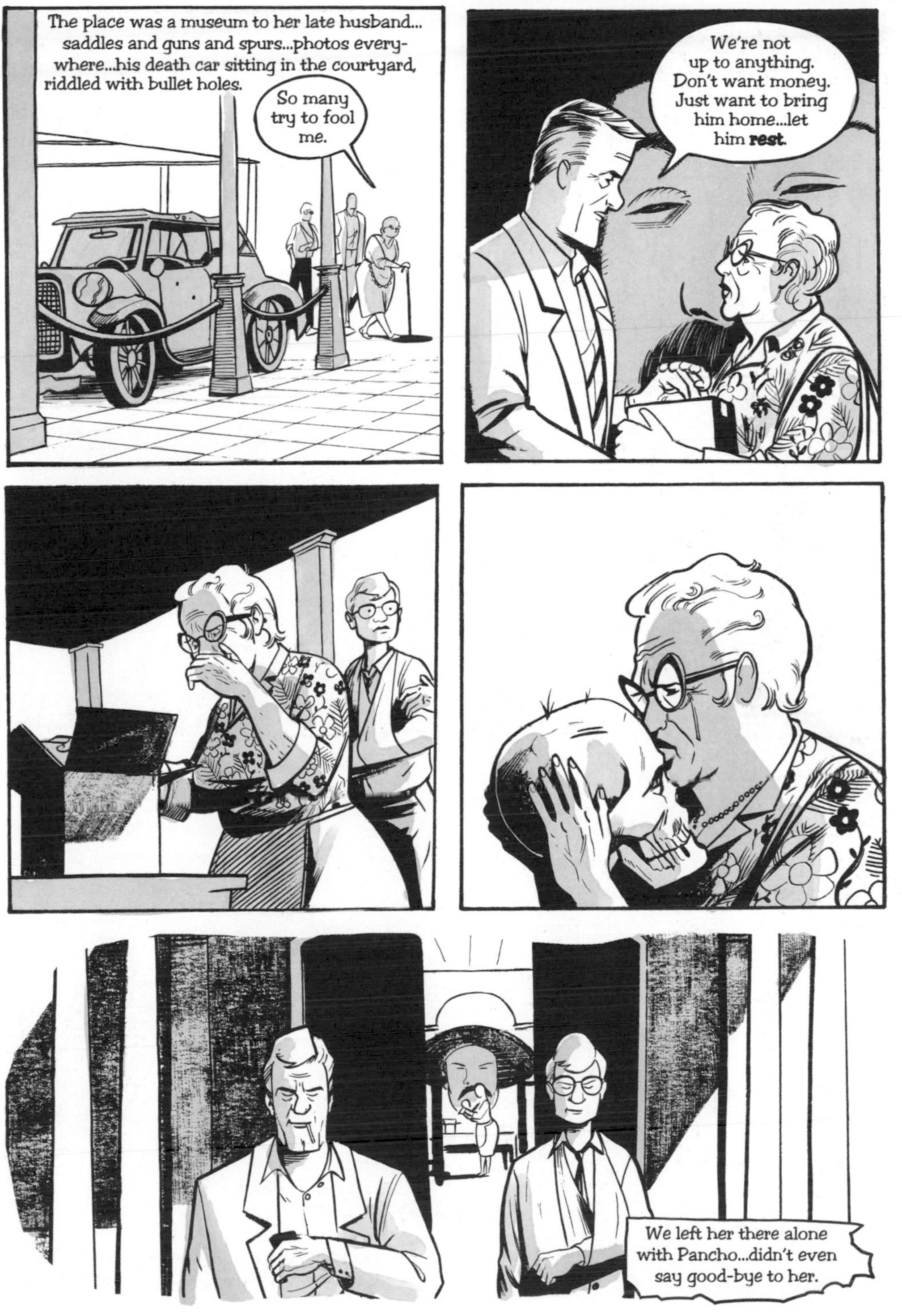
The place was a museum to her late husband... saddles and guns and spurs...photos everywhere...his death car sitting in the courtyard, riddled with bullet holes.
So many try to fool me.
We're not up to anything. Don't want money. Just want to bring him home...let him **rest**.
We left her there alone with Pancho...didn't even say good-bye to her.

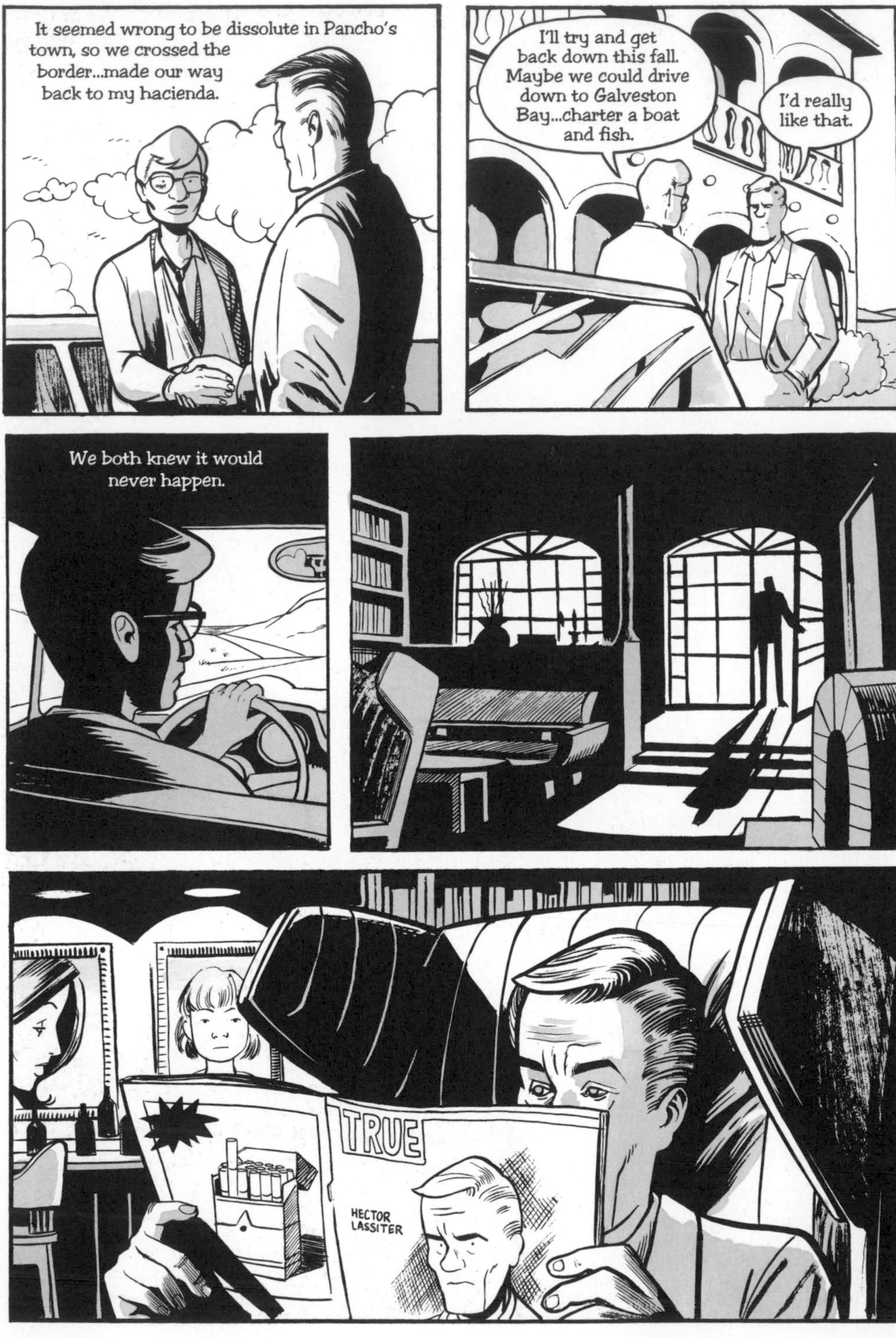
It seemed wrong to be dissolute in Pancho's town, so we crossed the border...made our way back to my hacienda.
I'll try and get back down this fall. Maybe we could drive down to Galveston Bay...charter a boat and fish.
I'd really like that.
We both knew it would never happen.
TRUE
HECTOR LASSITER

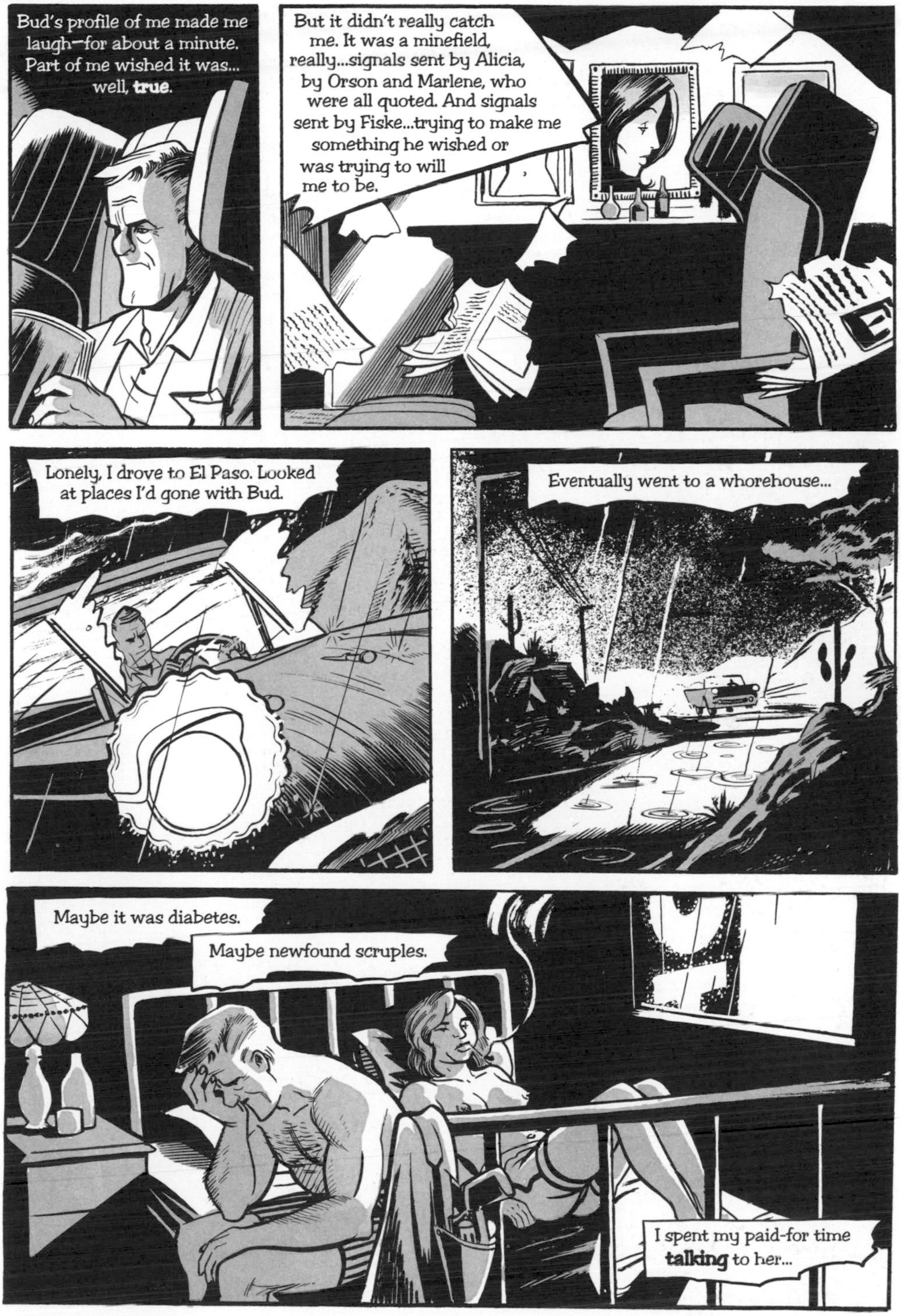
Bud's profile of me made me laugh—for about a minute. Part of me wished it was... well, **true**.
But it didn't really catch me. It was a minefield, really...signals sent by Alicia, by Orson and Marlene, who were all quoted. And signals sent by Fiske...trying to make me something he wished or was trying to will me to be.
Lonely, I drove to El Paso. Looked at places I'd gone with Bud.
Eventually went to a whorehouse...
Maybe it was diabetes.
Maybe newfound scruples.
I spent my paid-for time **talking** to her...

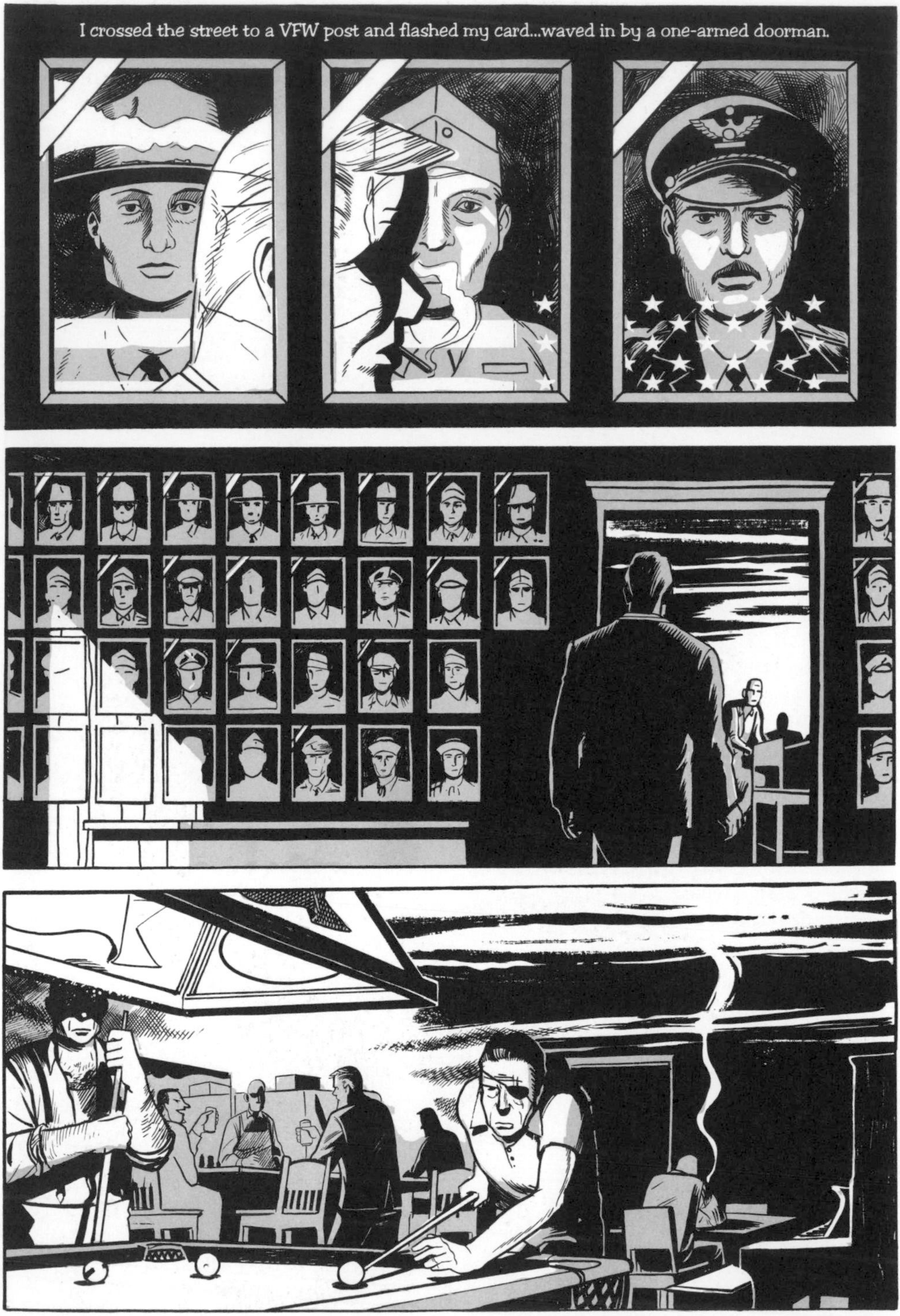
I crossed the street to a VFW post and flashed my card...waved in by a one-armed doorman.

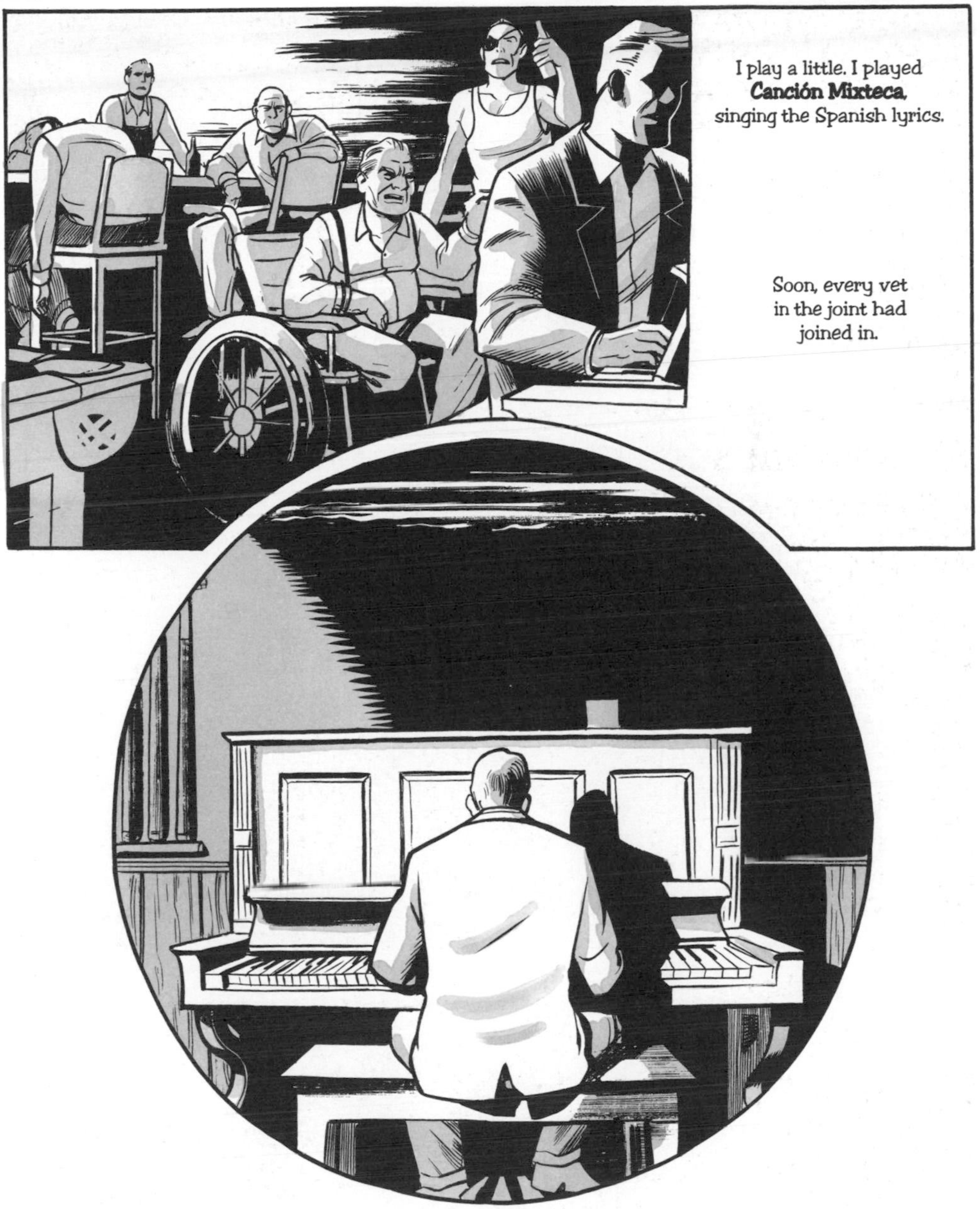
I play a little. I played **Canción Mixteca**, singing the Spanish lyrics.
Soon, every vet in the joint had joined in.

I'd reached the end of the song before I realized I was crying.

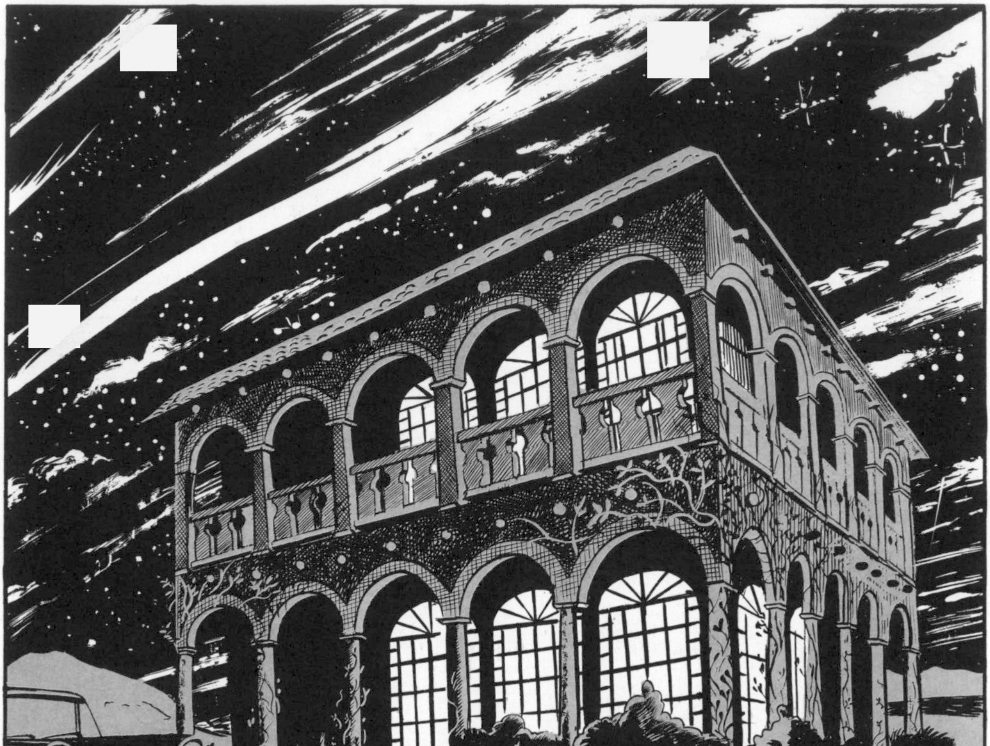
Part II: 1967—The Land of Dread and Fear

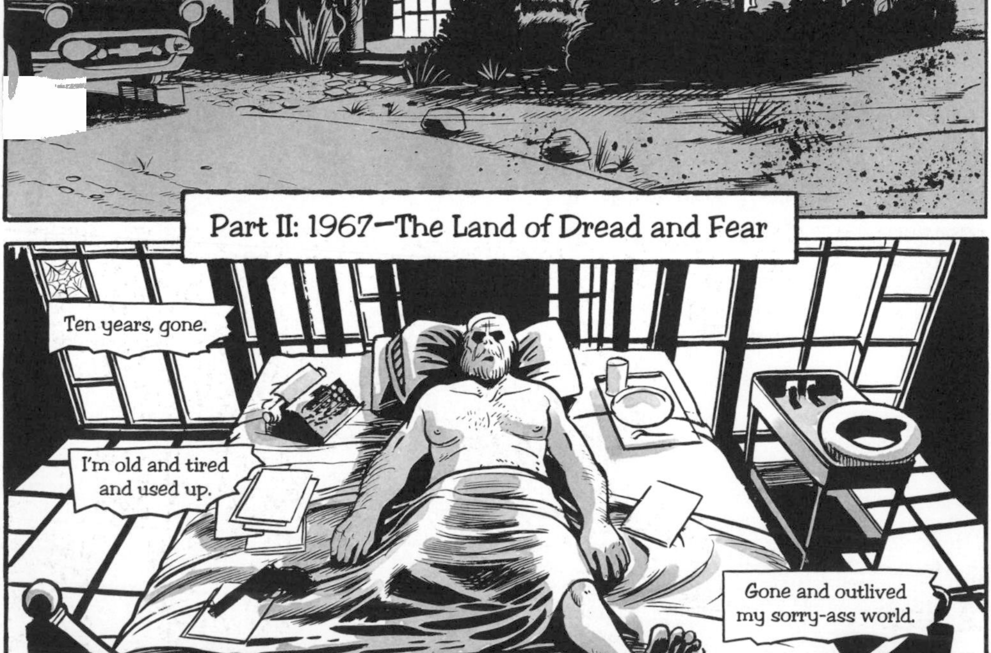
Ten years, gone.
I'm old and tired and used up.
Gone and outlived my sorry-ass world.

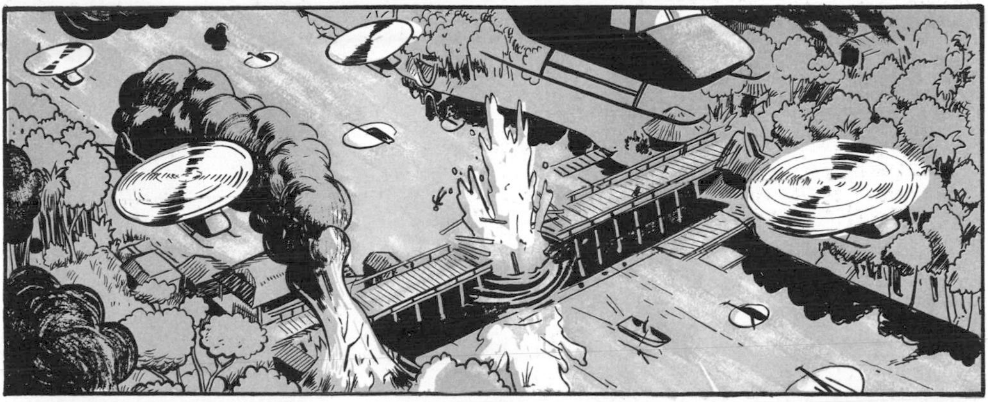

Our last two presidents have led us into another war, but not the kind of conflict a crafty mercenary like old Emil could turn a buck on. Only the industrial military complex profits from war now.

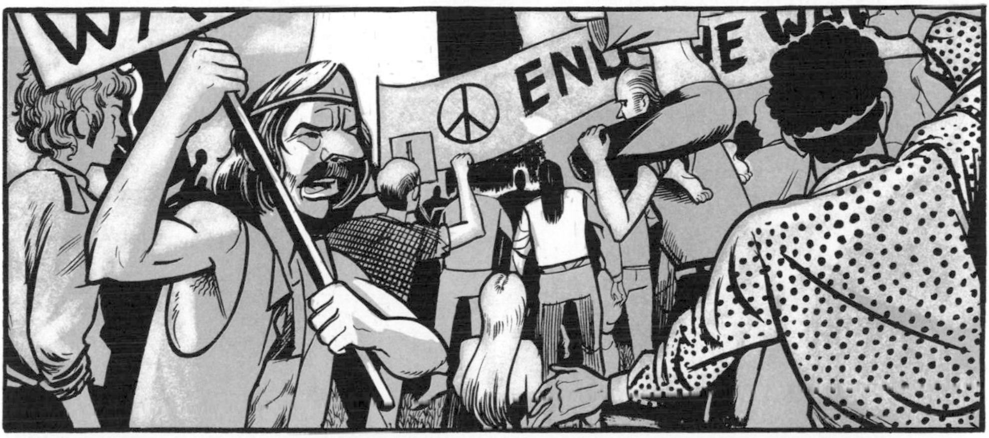

Kids are growing their hair long and burning the flag and blowing up their schools.

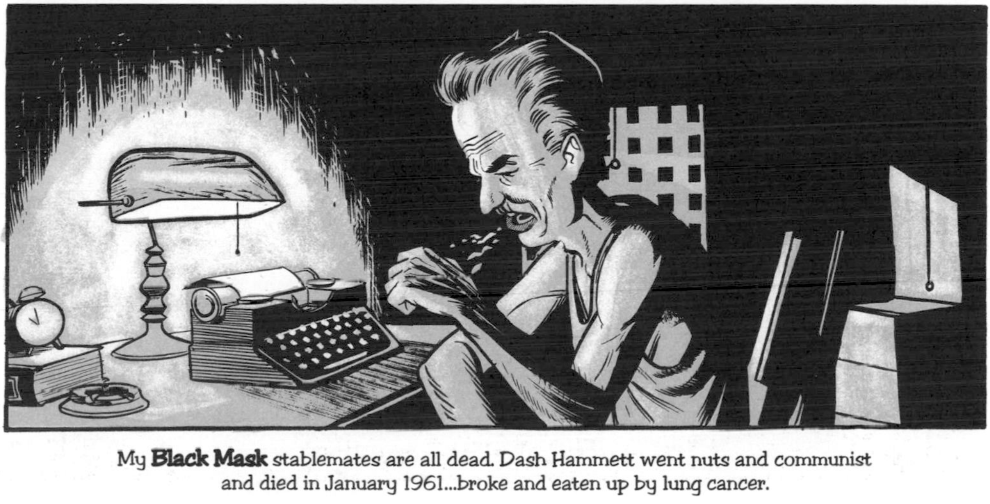

My **Black Mask** stablemates are all dead. Dash Hammett went nuts and communist and died in January 1961...broke and eaten up by lung cancer.

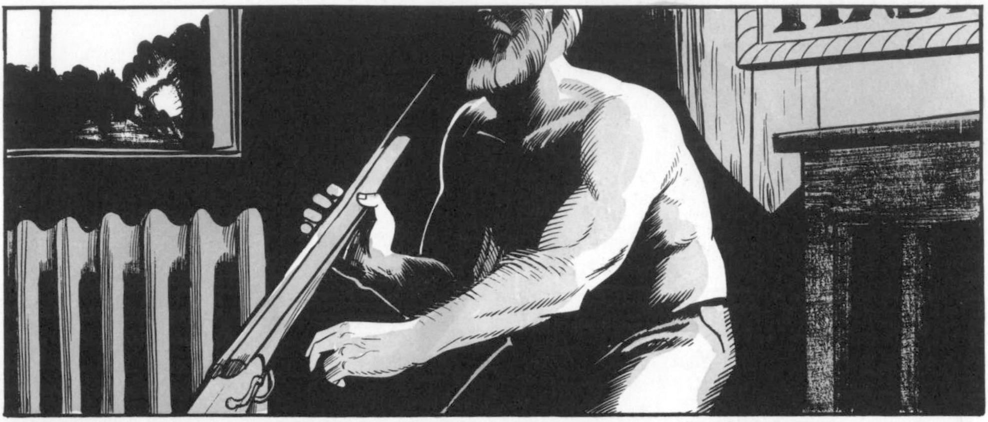

Hemingway, the Great Ape of American letters, shot himself in Idaho in 1961, old and sick and deprived of everything he loved. Especially the writing.

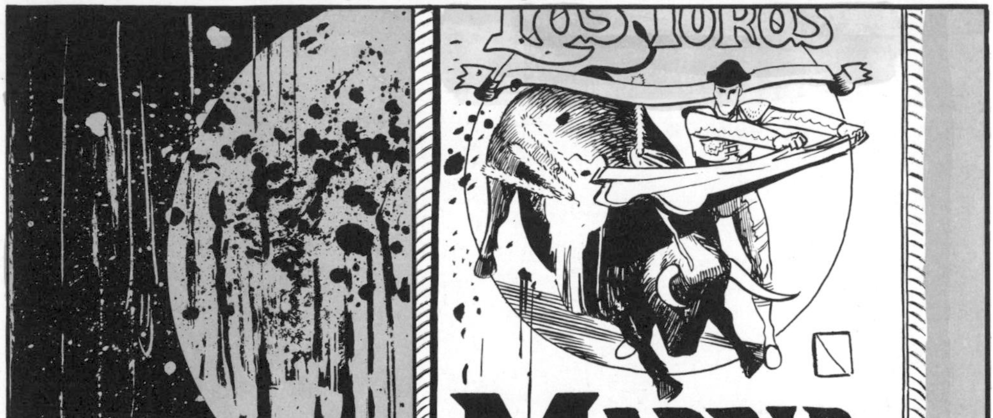

Thank God we patched it up first. When I got word, I poured a glass of Rioja Alta for Hem's maybe thirsty spirit. He wasn't thirsty, so I drank it for him.

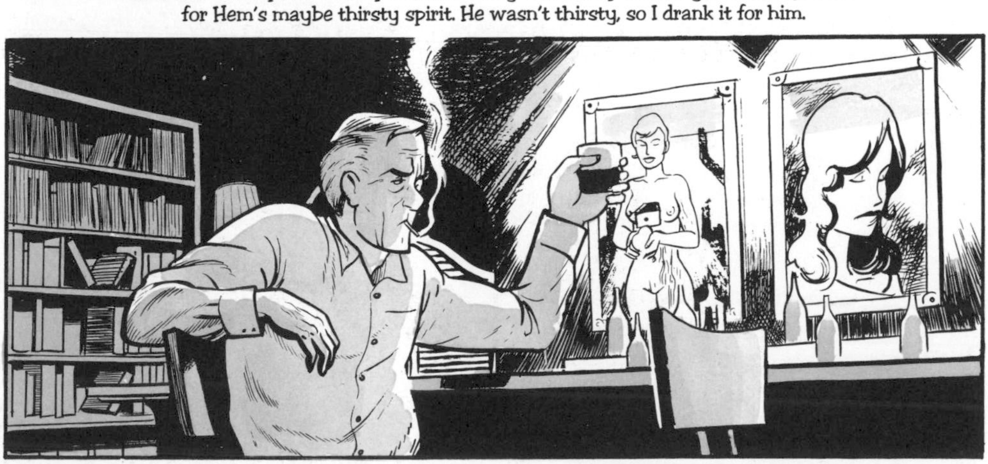

I understand why Papa took himself out. I understand it more every day. A terrible kind of wisdom... come too late to use. Diabetes and cataracts—an unbeatable tag team.

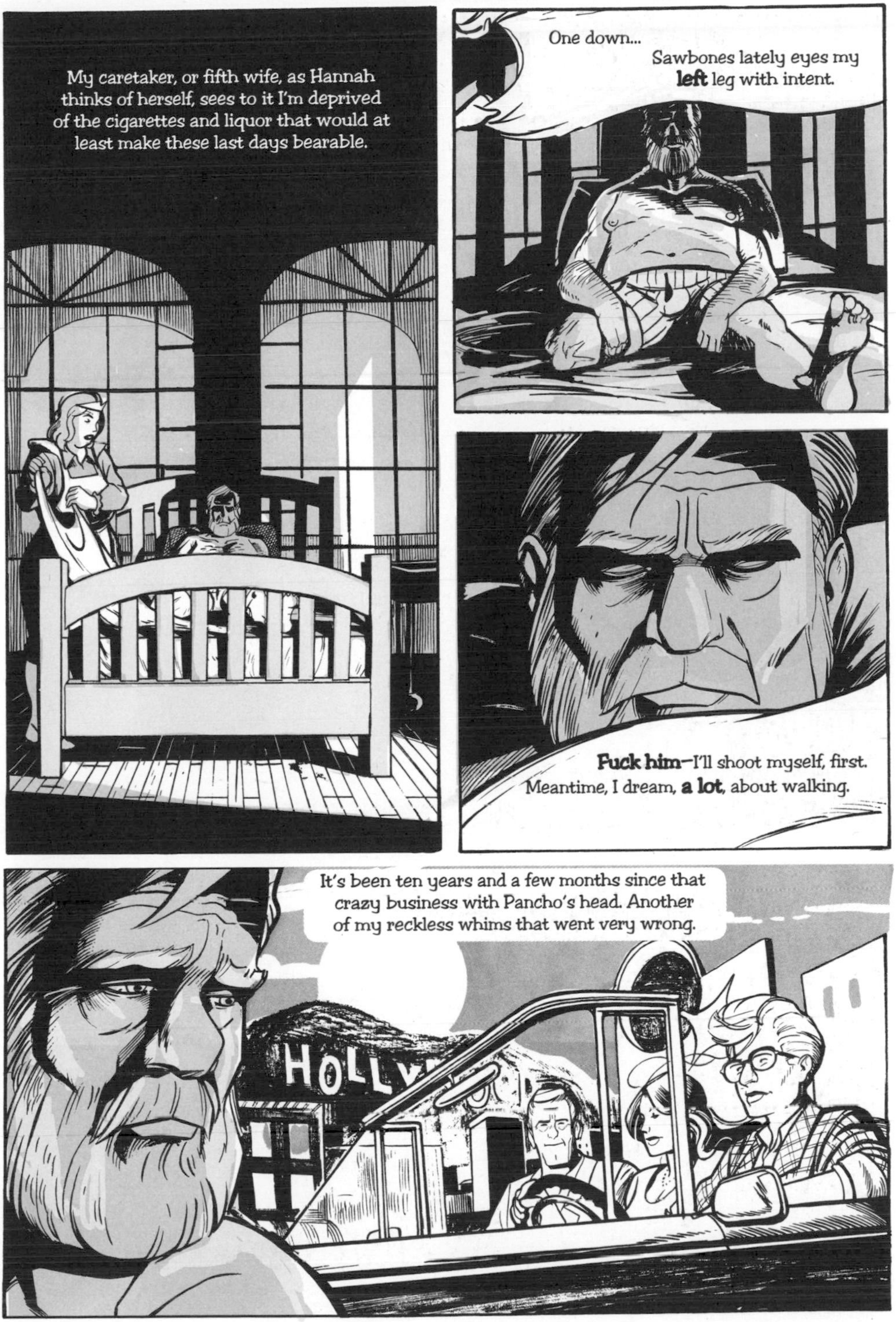
My caretaker, or fifth wife, as Hannah thinks of herself, sees to it I'm deprived of the cigarettes and liquor that would at least make these last days bearable.
One down...
Sawbones lately eyes my **left** leg with intent.
Fuck him—I'll shoot myself, first. Meantime, I dream, **a lot**, about walking.
It's been ten years and a few months since that crazy business with Pancho's head. Another of my reckless whims that went very wrong.
HOLLY

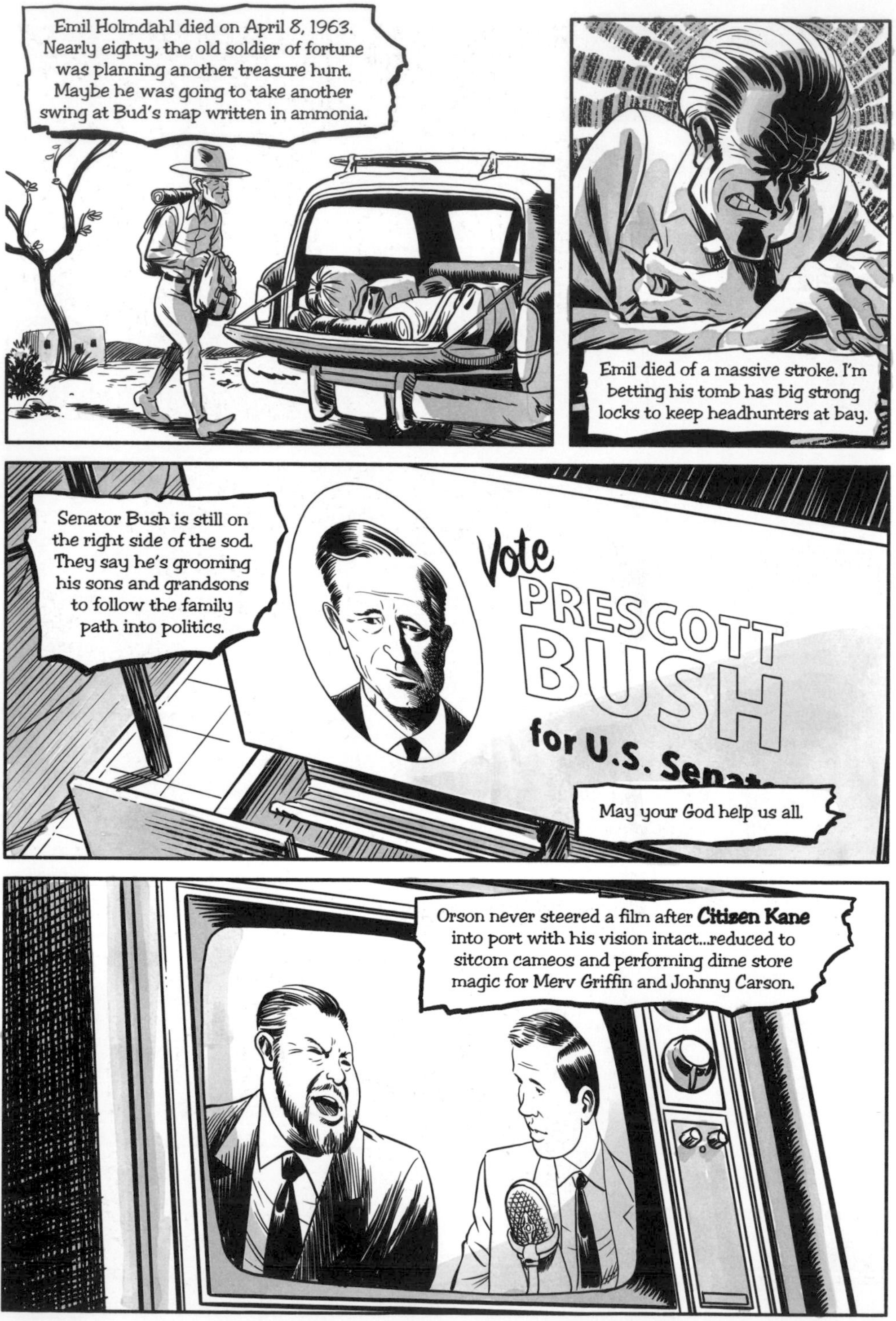
Emil Holmdahl died on April 8, 1963. Nearly eighty, the old soldier of fortune was planning another treasure hunt. Maybe he was going to take another swing at Bud's map written in ammonia.
Emil died of a massive stroke. I'm betting his tomb has big strong locks to keep headhunters at bay.
Senator Bush is still on the right side of the sod. They say he's grooming his sons and grandsons to follow the family path into politics.
Vote
PRESCOTT
BUSH
for U.S. Senat
May your God help us all.
Orson never steered a film after **Citizen Kane** into port with his vision intact...reduced to sitcom cameos and performing dime store magic for Merv Griffin and Johnny Carson.

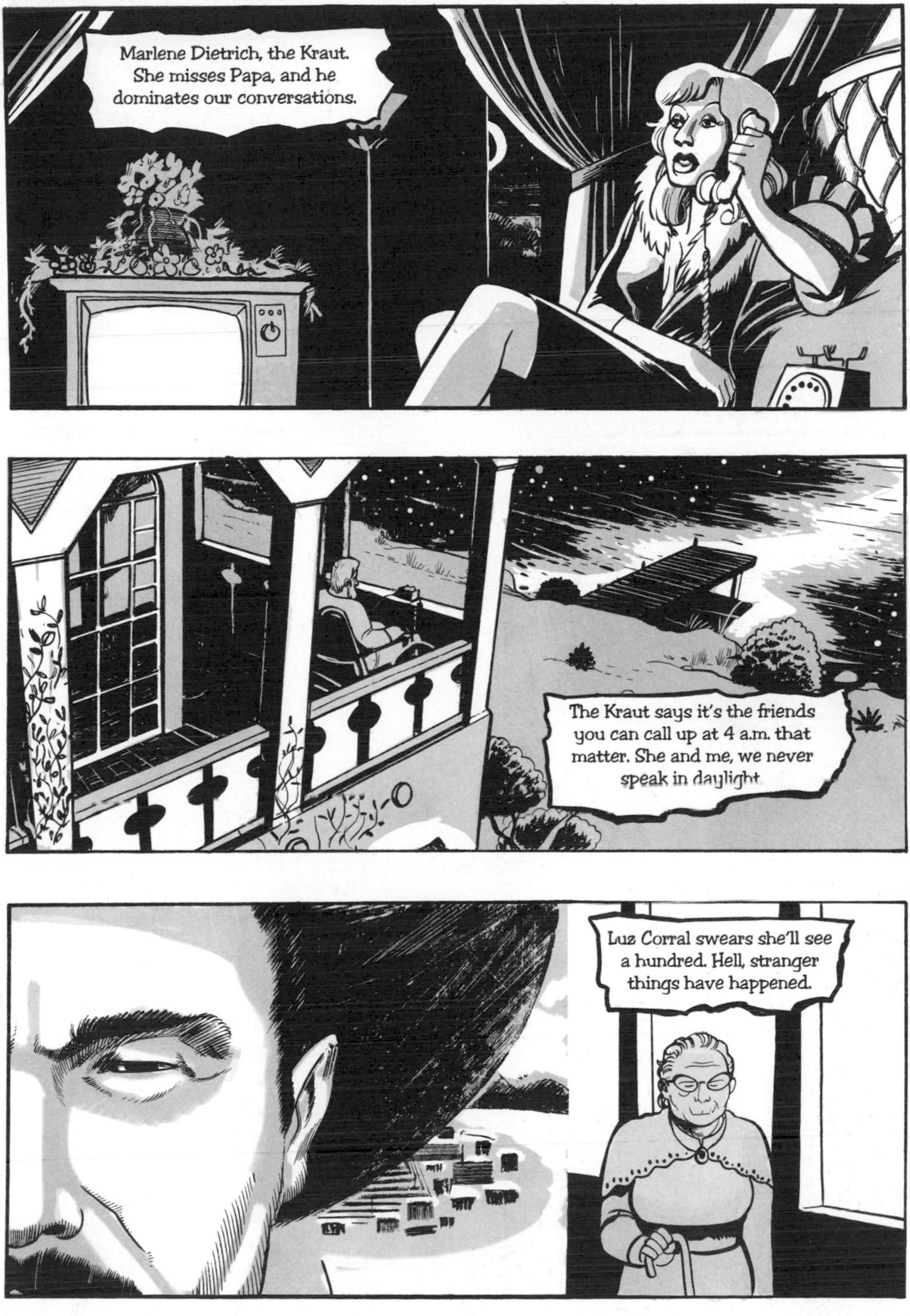
Marlene Dietrich, the Kraut. She misses Papa, and he dominates our conversations.
The Kraut says it's the friends you can call up at 4 a.m. that matter. She and me, we never speak in daylight.
Luz Corral swears she'll see a hundred. Hell, stranger things have happened.

Bud Fiske, poet, sometimes country music lyricist...screenwriter, busker, and pop culture celebrity.

Caught a glimpse of Bud on that loopy Bob Conrad Western the other night...with some of his Rat Pack buddies.

Good ol' Bud—can still turn a hell of a phrase when he's pressed to.

Alicia...

I sometimes lose an evening staring at the one photo I have of her...

...her, and her **children**.

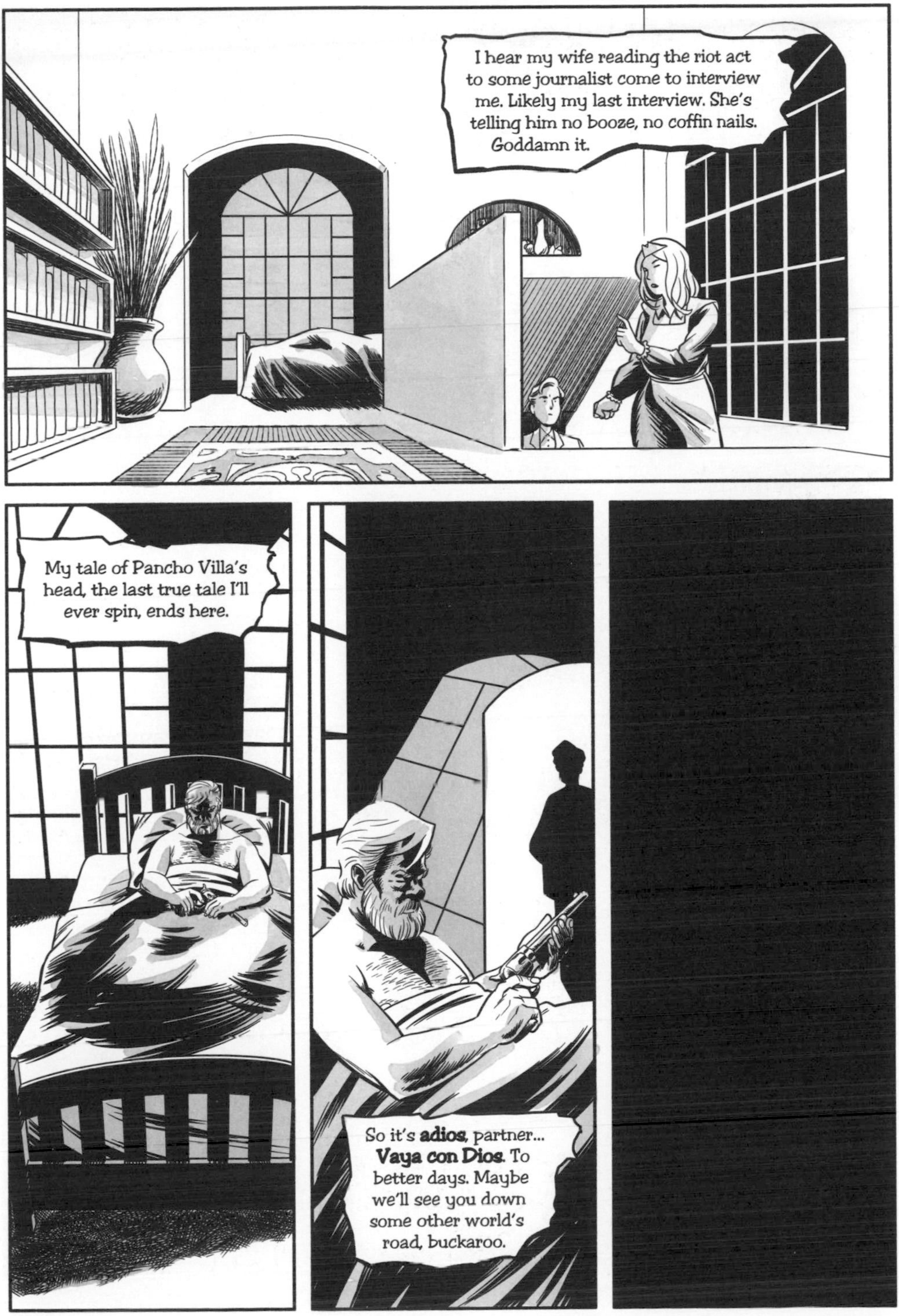
I hear my wife reading the riot act to some journalist come to interview me. Likely my last interview. She's telling him no booze, no coffin nails. Goddamn it.
My tale of Pancho Villa's head, the last true tale I'll ever spin, ends here.
So it's **adios**, partner... **Vaya con Dios**. To better days. Maybe we'll see you down some other world's road, buckaroo.

EARLY EDITION

El Paso H

Vol. 86, No. 306 EL PASO, TEX. THUR

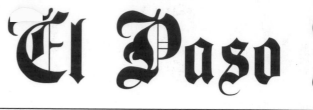

MYSTERY AUTHOR FOUND DEAD IN BIZARRE MURDER - SUICIDE

Journalist Suspected of Slaying Last of the Great Pulp Writers

By RUSSELL HARDIN
Herald Staff Writer

Celebrated crime novelist Hector Mason Lassiter was found shot to death in his own bed yesterday afternoon.

Lassiter's presumed killer is Andrew Nagel, a Chicago-based freelance journalist who'd driven cross-country to interview the famous mystery writer.

Sheriff Dave Duhan said Lassiter was found dead as the result of a single gunshot wound to the stomach.

Lassiter's suspected slayer, Nagel, age 22, apparently killed himself with a single shot to the head from the same weapon: a vintage, 1873-model Colt Peacemaker.

"It's a real museum piece," Sheriff Duhan said. "The gun belonged to Hector Lassiter, who often slept with the revolver under his pillow for security, according to his widow. We suspect Nagel wrestled the gun from Lassiter and gut shot him with it, then turned the Colt on himself."

The sheriff said there were signs of a fierce struggle; the remnants of several broken cosmetic bottles were scattered across the bed and an adjacent nightstand.

"It's frustrating," Duhan said, "because there are some tantalizing potential clues that have been lost to us." Those clues, he elaborated, would likely have come from a tape recorder found with the two bodies. The reel-to-reel recording machine belonged to the journalist and appeared to have been running for some time.

But the gun was twice turned on the tape machine, the sheriff said.

Despite doctor's orders to the contrary, and strict instructions from Mrs. Lassiter, the journalist appears to have shared several cigarettes and a bottle of liquor with the ailing author.

The door to the bedroom/murder scene was found locked from the inside when Mrs. Lassiter and her housekeeper returned home.

Two mysterious initials were also scrawled in blood above the author's bed: "E.Q."

Sheriff Duhan said that several handwritten letters sent to Lassiter by fellow author Estelle Quartermain — a British mystery author, who, ironically enough, is famed for her own so-called "locked-room" mysteries — were found by the victim's bedside. Perhaps significantly, Nagel had interviewed Dame Estelle Quartermain several weeks before soliciting the interview with Hector Lassiter.

Sheriff Duhan refused to comment on any possible connection, or to divulge the contents of the letters. Repeated calls to Dame Quartermain went unreturned.

Mrs. Lassiter also refused to speak with the *Herald*. There are as-yet-unconfirmed reports that she is engaged in a bitter legal dispute concerning her late husband's estate. Lassiter's will, according to attorney Hobie Meed, left the bulk of his estate, including the home in La Mesilla, to his client, former actress Alicia Vicente, and her three children. A second home, located in Key West, Florida, was left to Hannah Lassiter.

When contacted for a comment about his death, longtime Lassiter friend Marlene Dietrich, famed German-born actress and chanteuse, said simply, "He was a hell of a man. What more than that can I say that would matter a damn? When you're dead, you're dead. End of your story."

Another longtime friend, noir poet and *Hollywood Squares* regular Eskin "Bud" Fiske said, "Hec was the last great one...the last true writer of the old *Black Mask*

erald Post

TODAY'S WEATHER
from the U.S. Weather Office

Fair, 60°
cooler tomorrow

, NOVEMBER 2, 1967 **SEVEN CENTS** **FORTY PAGES**

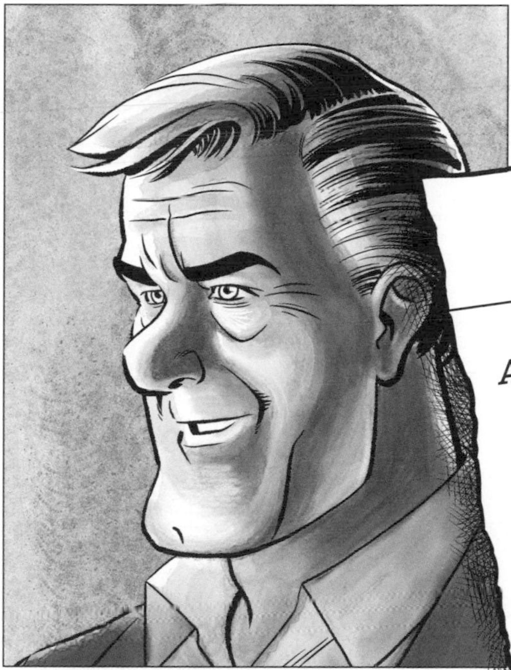

Hector Lassiter in 1959 *(Photo courtesy Mrs. Lassiter)*

school...I hope they have enough room in Valhalla for the magnificent (expletive deleted)." Fiske then added, somewhat cryptically, "And I find it *very* significant that some hophead from Yale took Hector out. That doesn't go unnoticed by me. And I mean to look into that a bit more myself. 'Prescott' will know what I mean."

Fiske resisted repeated requests by this reporter to elaborate on his rather bizarre statement, or to explain to whom the name "Prescott" referred.

Sheriff Duhan, however, did confirm that a syringe and heroin were indeed found among Nagel's personal effects recovered from the Lassiters' guest room. He also confirmed that both of Nagel's forearms were covered with old and new needle scars. "He was a longtime and frequent heroin abuser," Duhan said. The sheriff also confirmed that Nagel was indeed a Yale graduate, "Although I frankly fail to see what that has to do with anything," Duhan said.

President Johnson Expected to Announce Solicitor

EL PASO HERALD POST
SUNDAY, NOVEMBER 1, 1970

Author's Grave Robbed and Corpse Mutilated

Local authorities are continuing the investigation into the robbing of crime novelist/screenwriter Hector Lassiter's grave on Halloween night.

The grave was found uncovered and the coffin pried open. The body of Lassiter was found partially exposed and decapitated. The head of the famed author—the victim of a bizarre murder three years ago to the day—remains missing.

Authorities say they are baffled.

Mayor Announces ... to Address Youth ... State College

enue...
he is prep...
advances to his wo...
sistence; so he advances
manner, his own subsistence ... order which reigns
suitable to the profit which he ... effect of govern-
expect from the sale of his goods. U... e principles of
him this profit, therefore, they do ... stitution of
what they may very properly be said to ... ment, and
cost him. ... ment

Though the price, therefore, which leaves ... nce
this profit is not always the lowest at which a dealer
may sometimes sell his goods, it is the lowest at

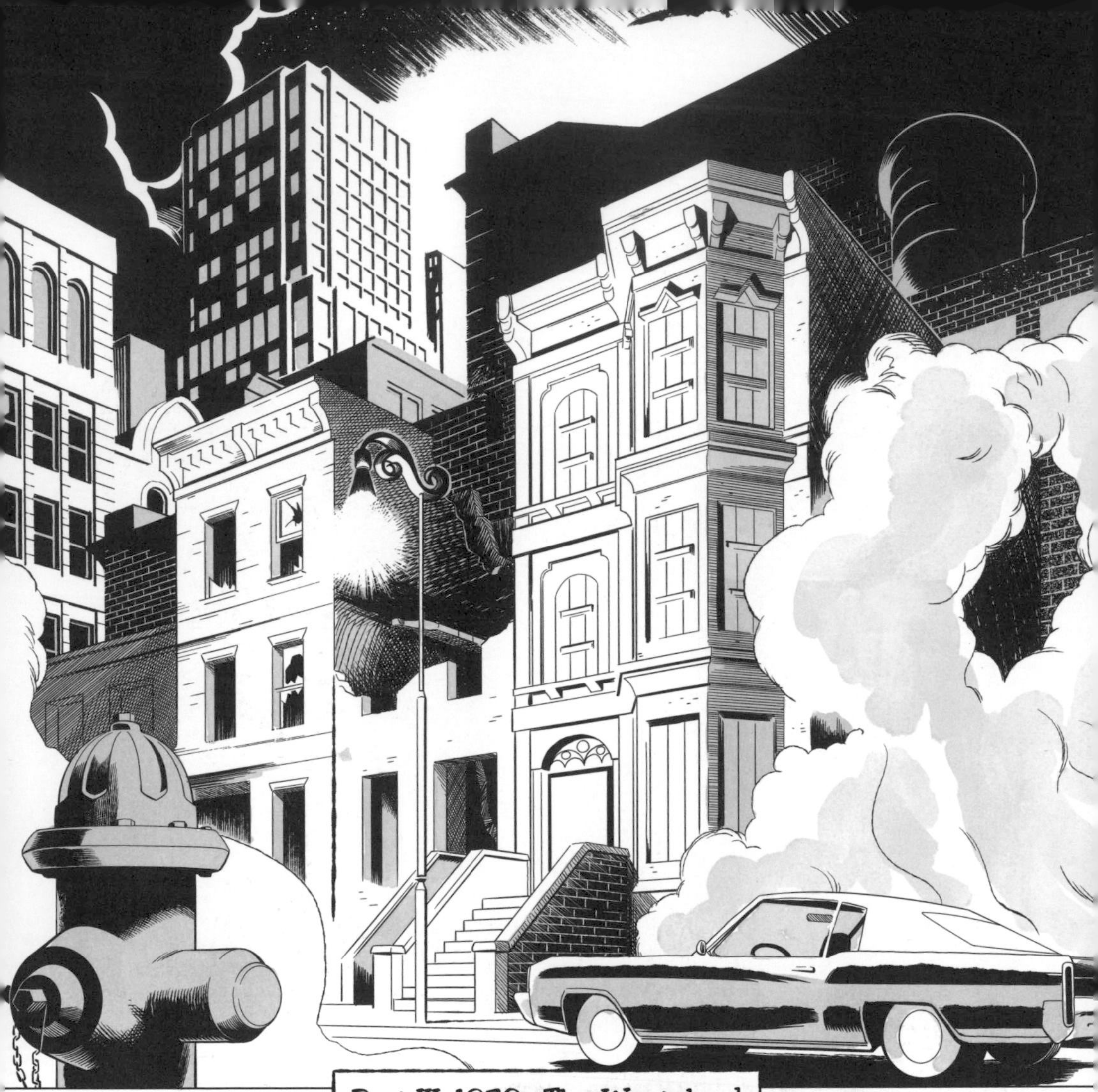
Part III: 1970—The Wasteland

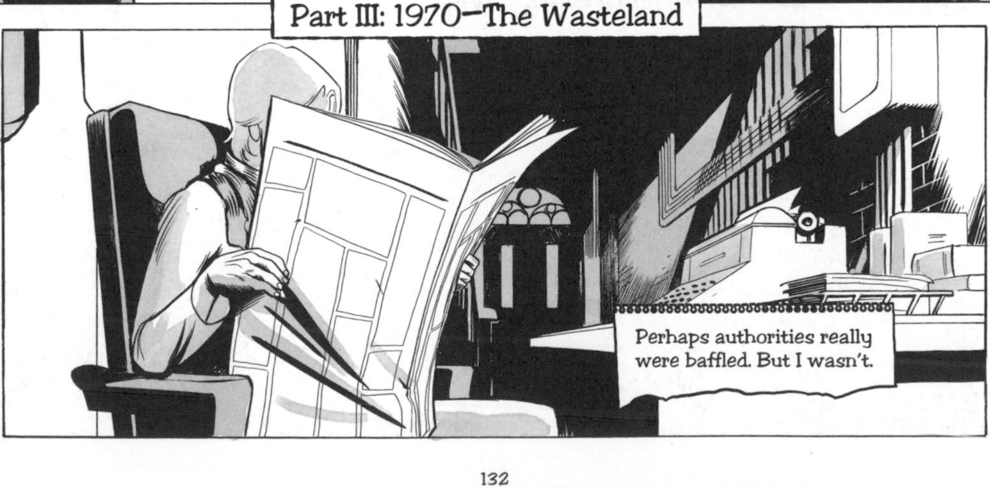
Perhaps authorities really
were baffled. But I wasn't.

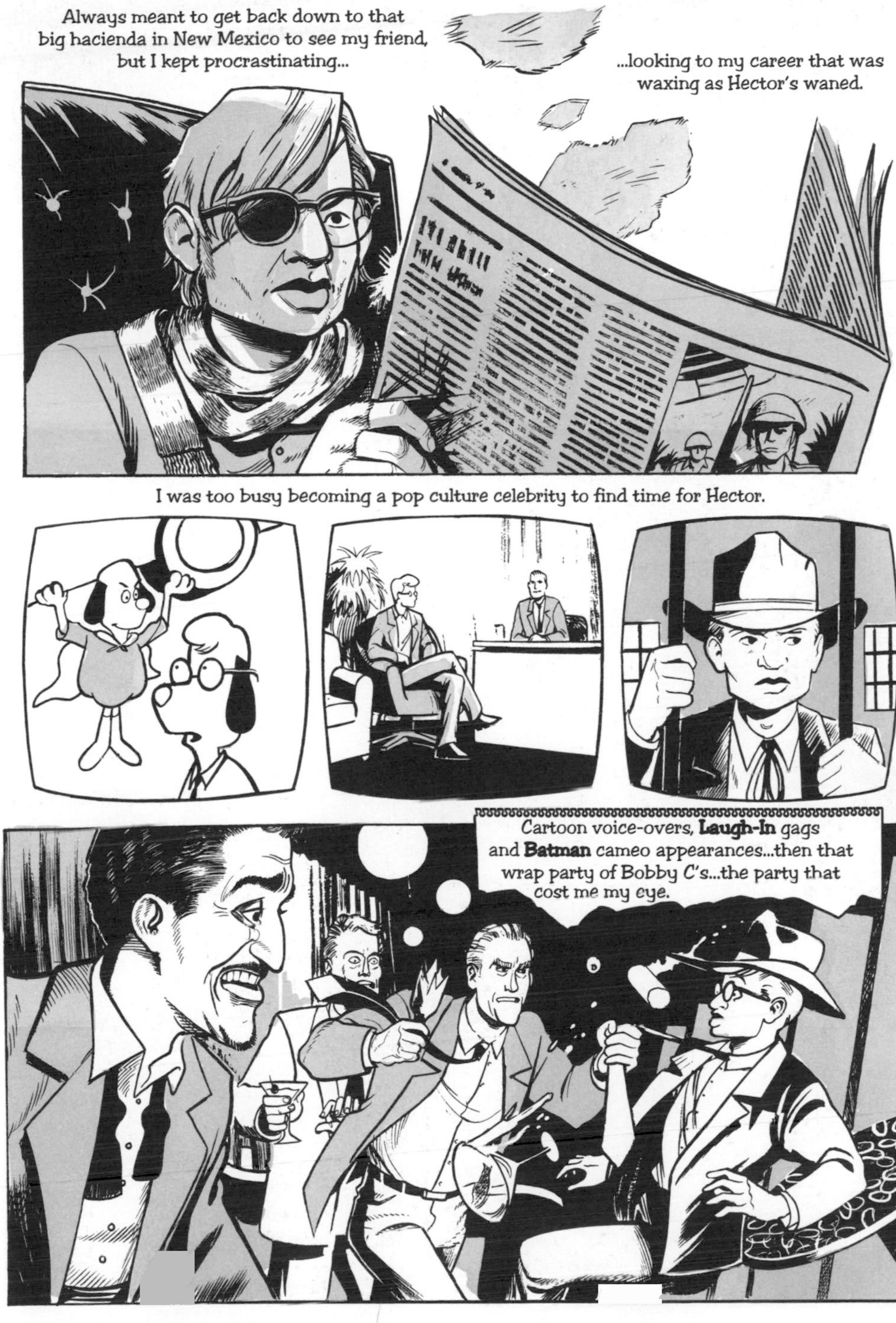
Always meant to get back down to that big hacienda in New Mexico to see my friend, but I kept procrastinating...
...looking to my career that was waxing as Hector's waned.
I was too busy becoming a pop culture celebrity to find time for Hector.
Cartoon voice-overs, **Laugh-In** gags and **Batman** cameo appearances...then that wrap party of Bobby C's...the party that cost me my eye.

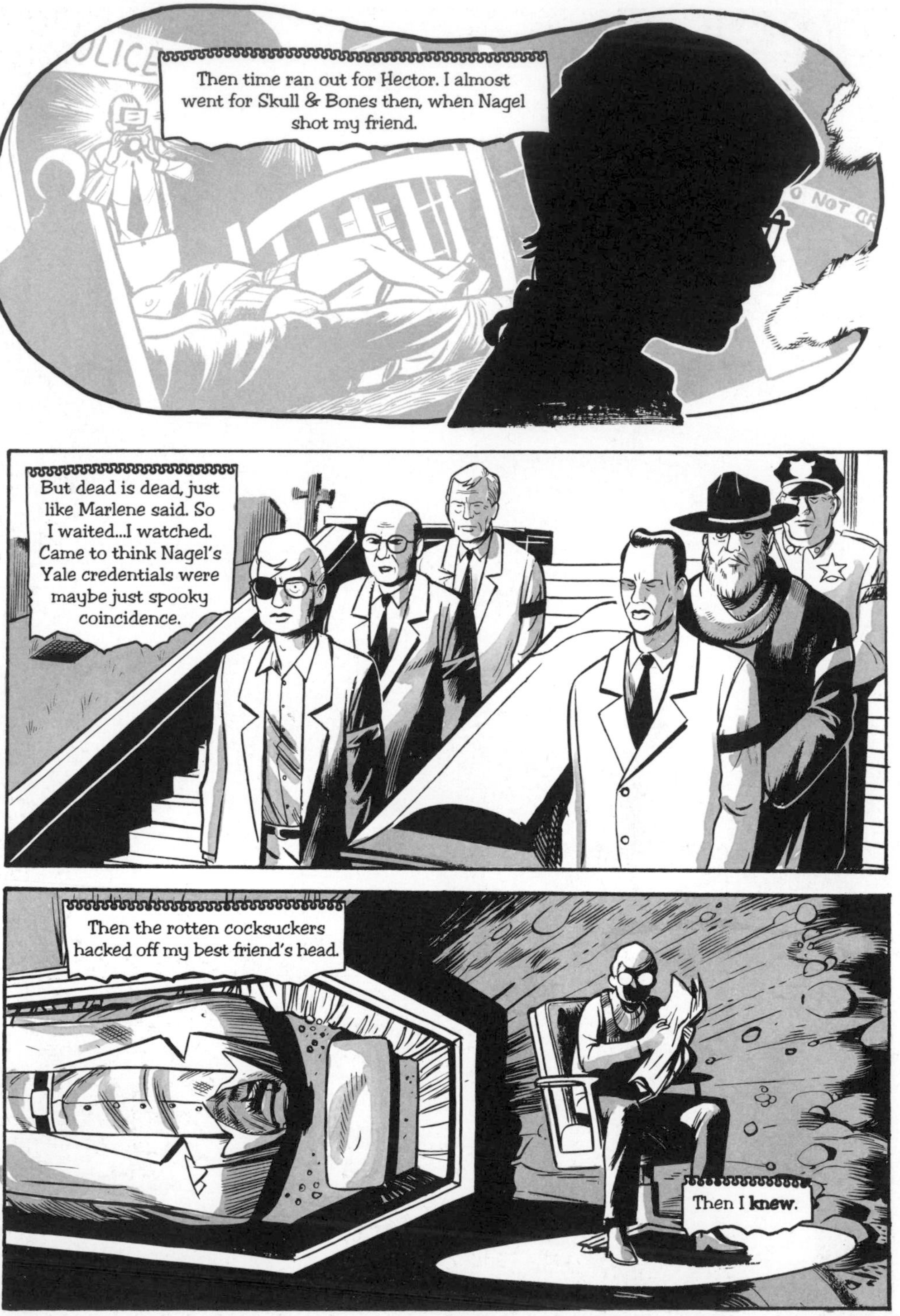
Then time ran out for Hector. I almost went for Skull & Bones then, when Nagel shot my friend.
POLICE
DO NOT CR
But dead is dead, just like Marlene said. So I waited...I watched. Came to think Nagel's Yale credentials were maybe just spooky coincidence.
Then the rotten cocksuckers hacked off my best friend's head.
Then I **knew**.

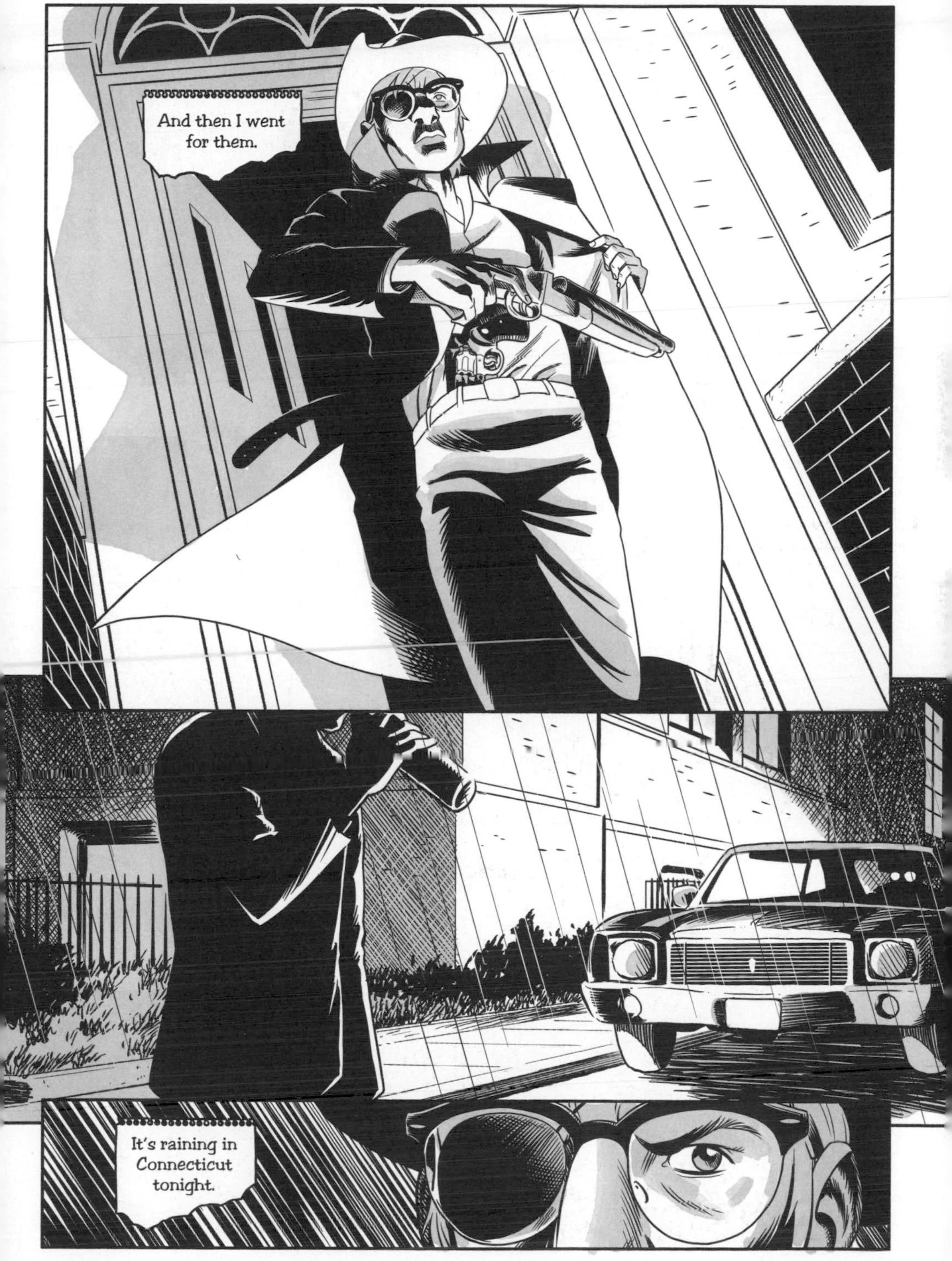

And then I went for them.
It's raining in Connecticut tonight.

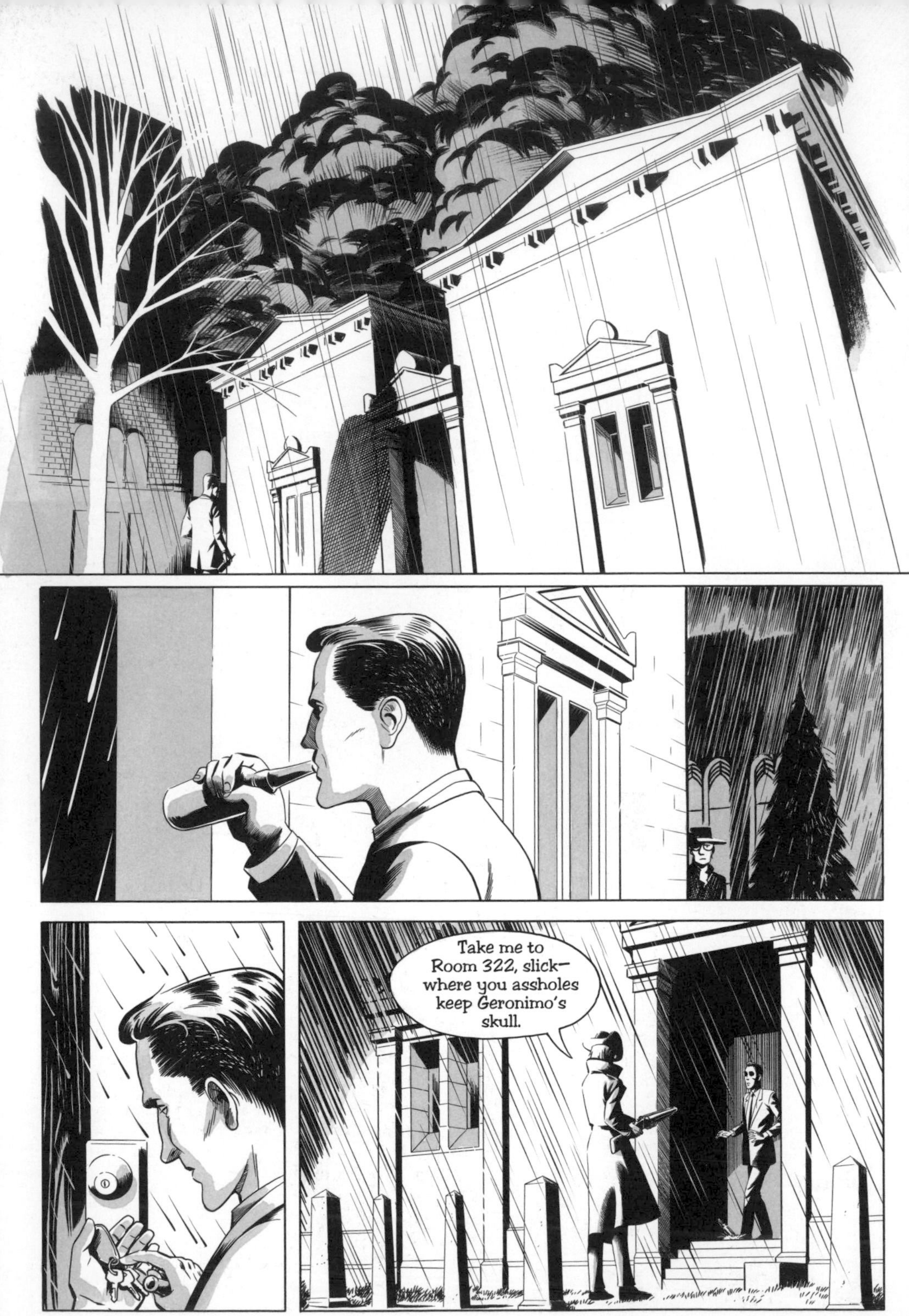
Take me to Room 322, slick— where you assholes keep Geronimo's skull.

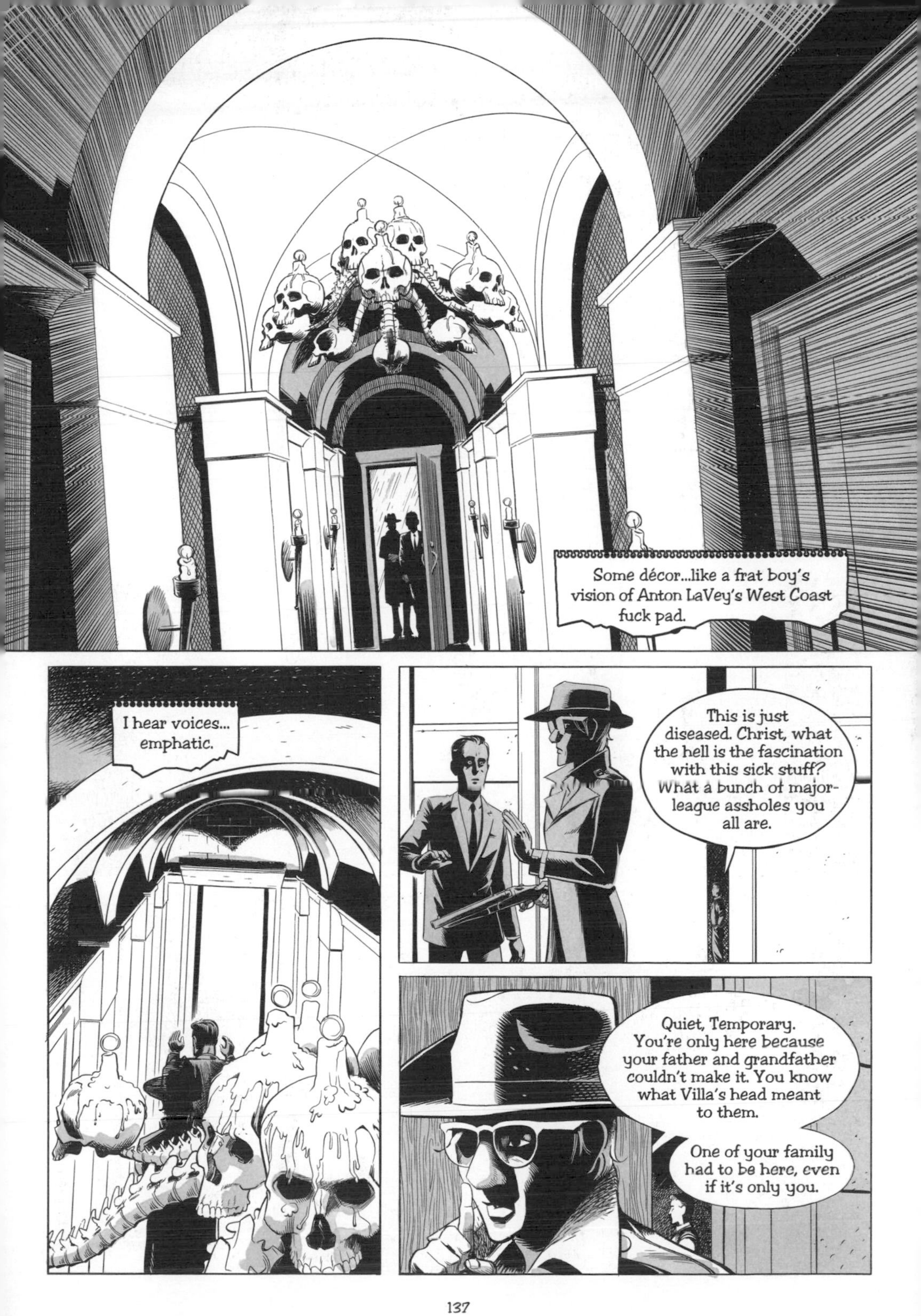
Some décor...like a frat boy's vision of Anton LaVey's West Coast fuck pad.
I hear voices... emphatic.
This is just diseased. Christ, what the hell is the fascination with this sick stuff? What a bunch of major-league assholes you all are.
Quiet, Temporary. You're only here because your father and grandfather couldn't make it. You know what Villa's head meant to them.
One of your family had to be here, even if it's only you.

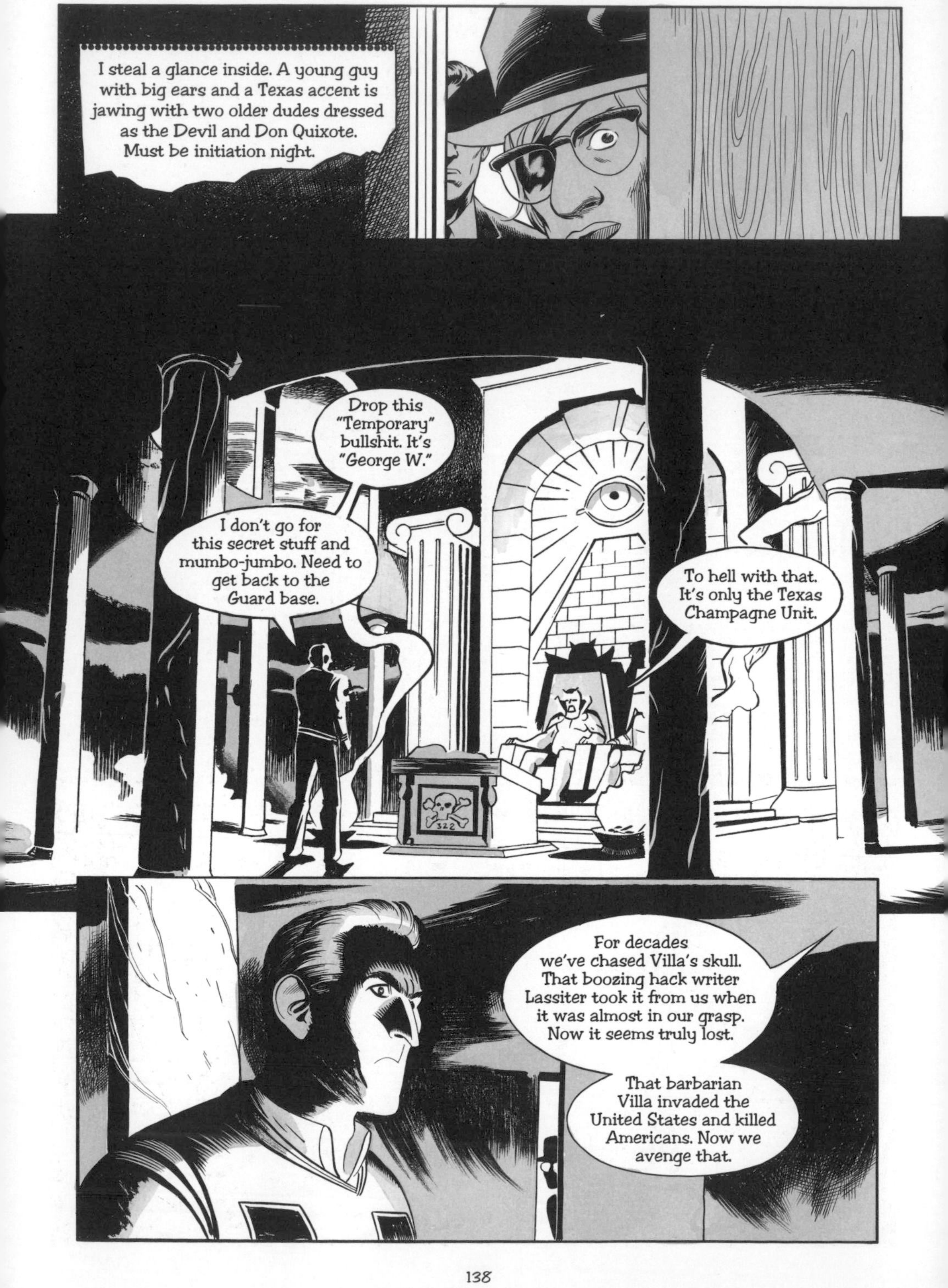
I steal a glance inside. A young guy with big ears and a Texas accent is jawing with two older dudes dressed as the Devil and Don Quixote. Must be initiation night.
Drop this "Temporary" bullshit. It's "George W."
I don't go for this secret stuff and mumbo-jumbo. Need to get back to the Guard base.
To hell with that. It's only the Texas Champagne Unit.
322
For decades we've chased Villa's skull. That boozing hack writer Lassiter took it from us when it was almost in our grasp. Now it seems truly lost.
That barbarian Villa invaded the United States and killed Americans. Now we avenge that.

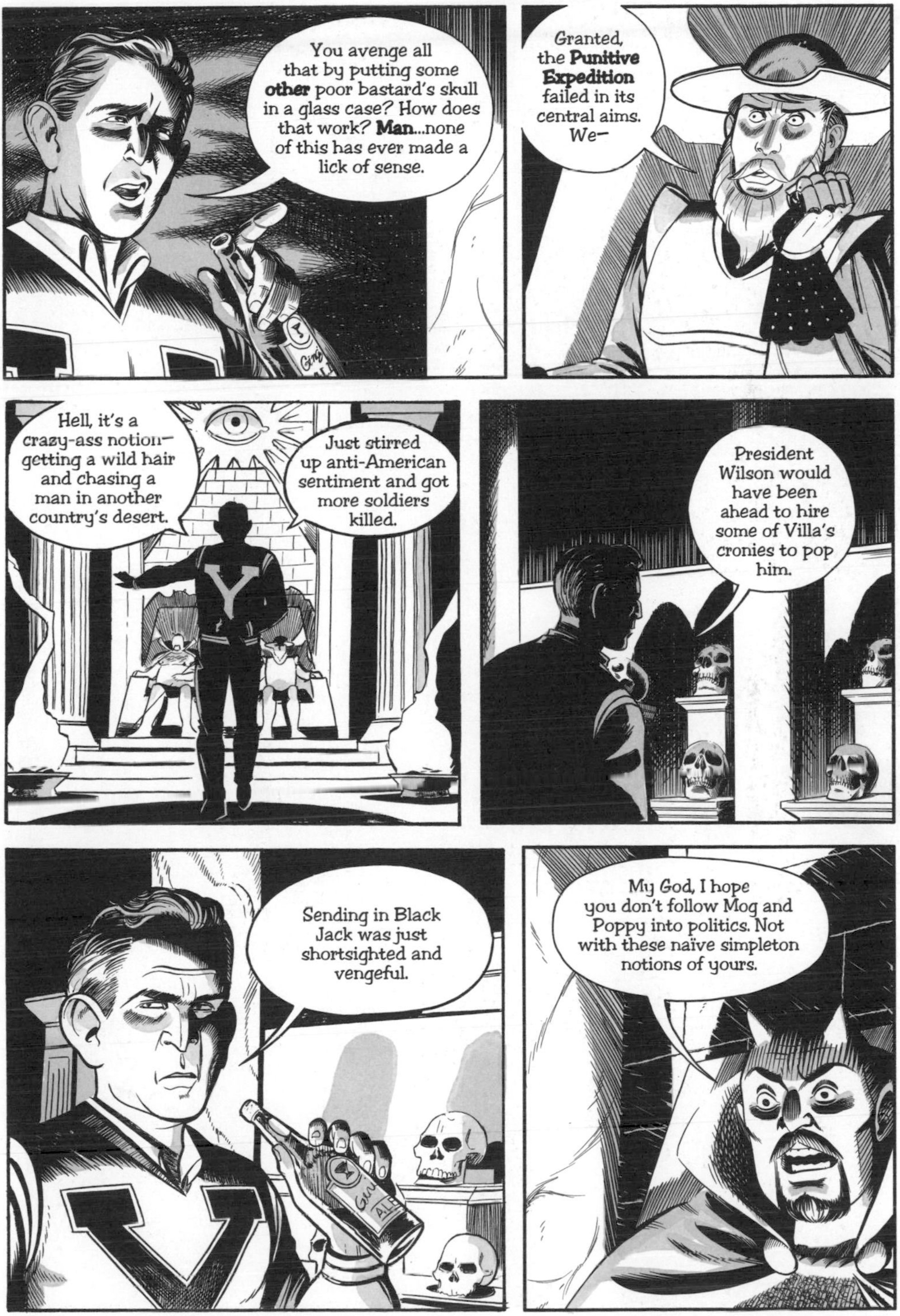

You avenge all that by putting some **other** poor bastard's skull in a glass case? How does that work? **Man**...none of this has ever made a lick of sense.
Granted, the **Punitive Expedition** failed in its central aims. We—
Hell, it's a crazy-ass notion—getting a wild hair and chasing a man in another country's desert.
Just stirred up anti-American sentiment and got more soldiers killed.
President Wilson would have been ahead to hire some of Villa's cronies to pop him.
Sending in Black Jack was just shortsighted and vengeful.
My God, I hope you don't follow Mog and Poppy into politics. Not with these naïve simpleton notions of yours.

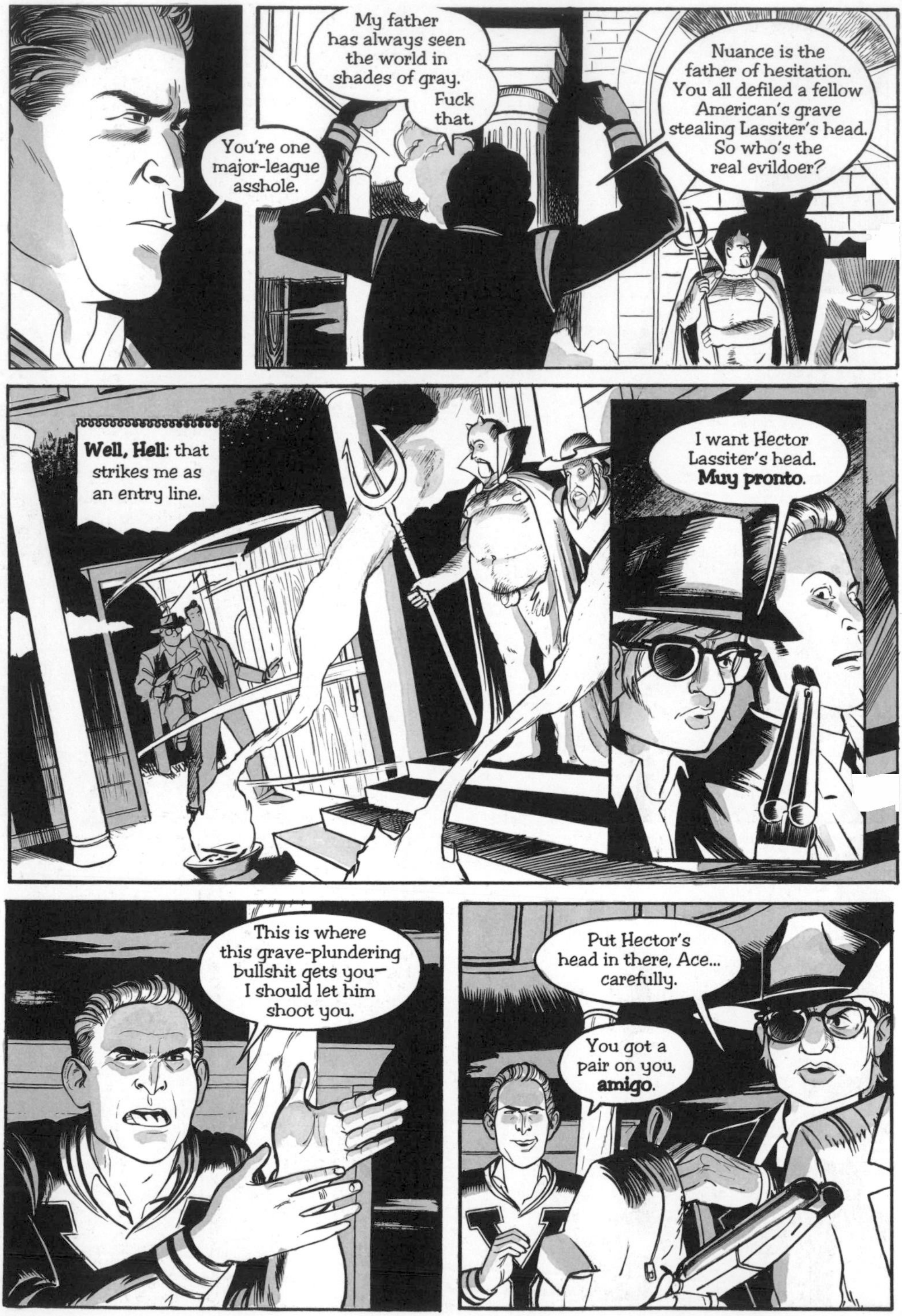

You're one major-league asshole.
My father has always seen the world in shades of gray.
Fuck that.
Nuance is the father of hesitation. You all defiled a fellow American's grave stealing Lassiter's head. So who's the real evildoer?
Well, Hell: that strikes me as an entry line.
I want Hector Lassiter's head. **Muy pronto**.
This is where this grave-plundering bullshit gets you— I should let him shoot you.
Put Hector's head in there, Ace... carefully.
You got a pair on you, **amigo**.

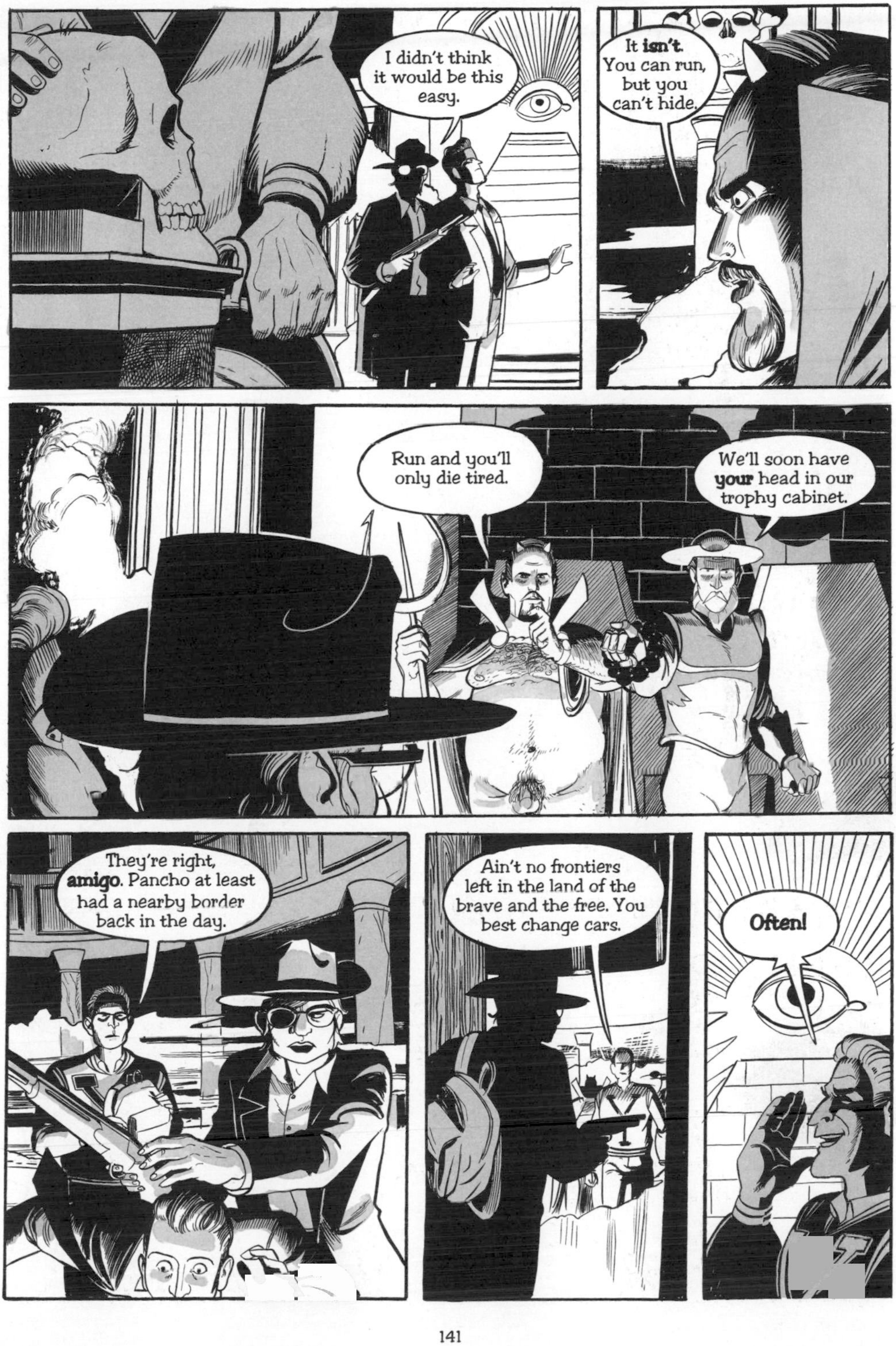
I didn't think it would be this easy.
It **isn't.** You can run, but you can't hide.
Run and you'll only die tired.
We'll soon have **your** head in our trophy cabinet.
They're right, **amigo**. Pancho at least had a nearby border back in the day.
Ain't no frontiers left in the land of the brave and the free. You best change cars.
Often!

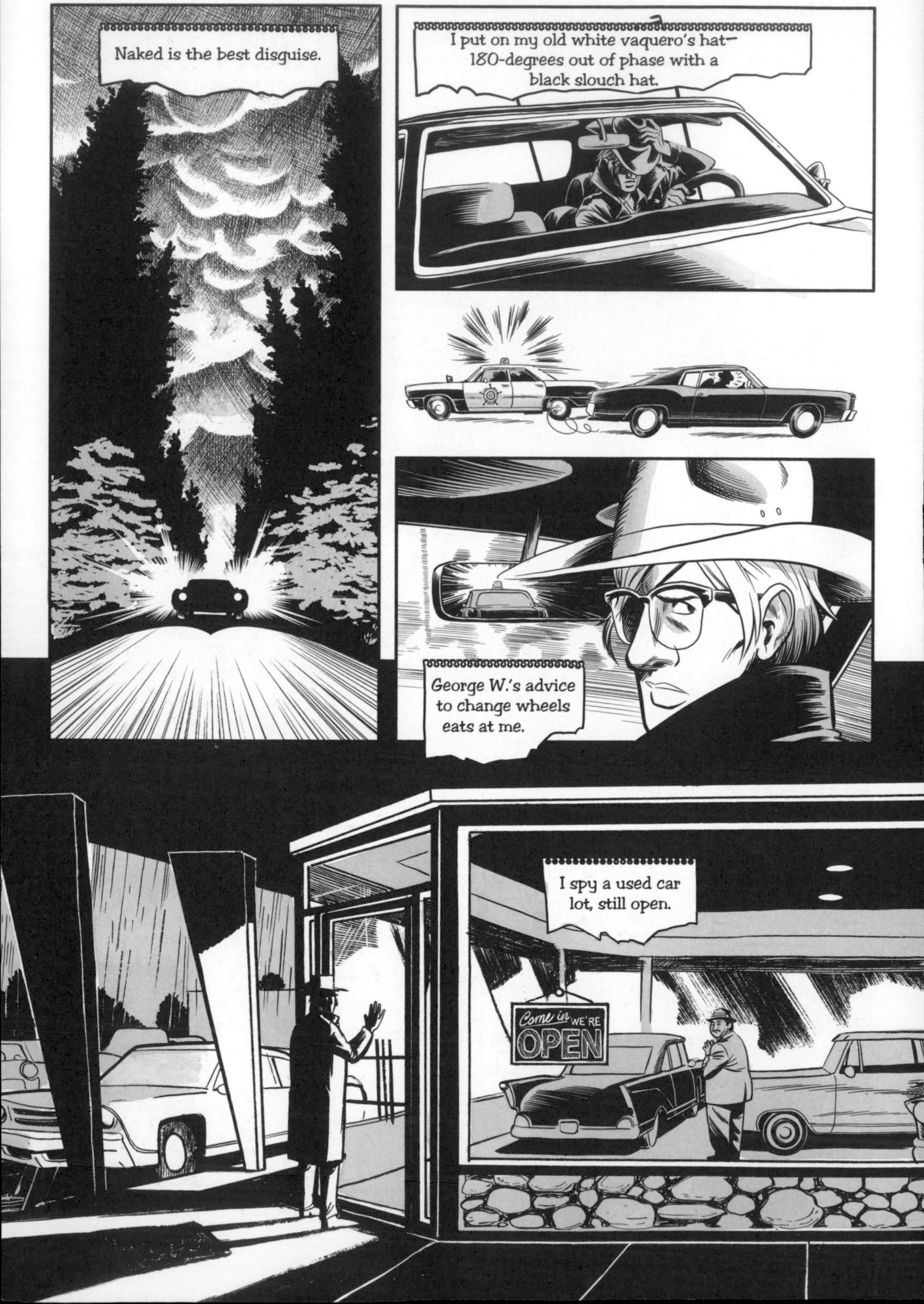
Naked is the best disguise.
I put on my old white vaquero's hat—180-degrees out of phase with a black slouch hat.
George W.'s advice to change wheels eats at me.
I spy a used car lot, still open.
Come in WE'RE OPEN

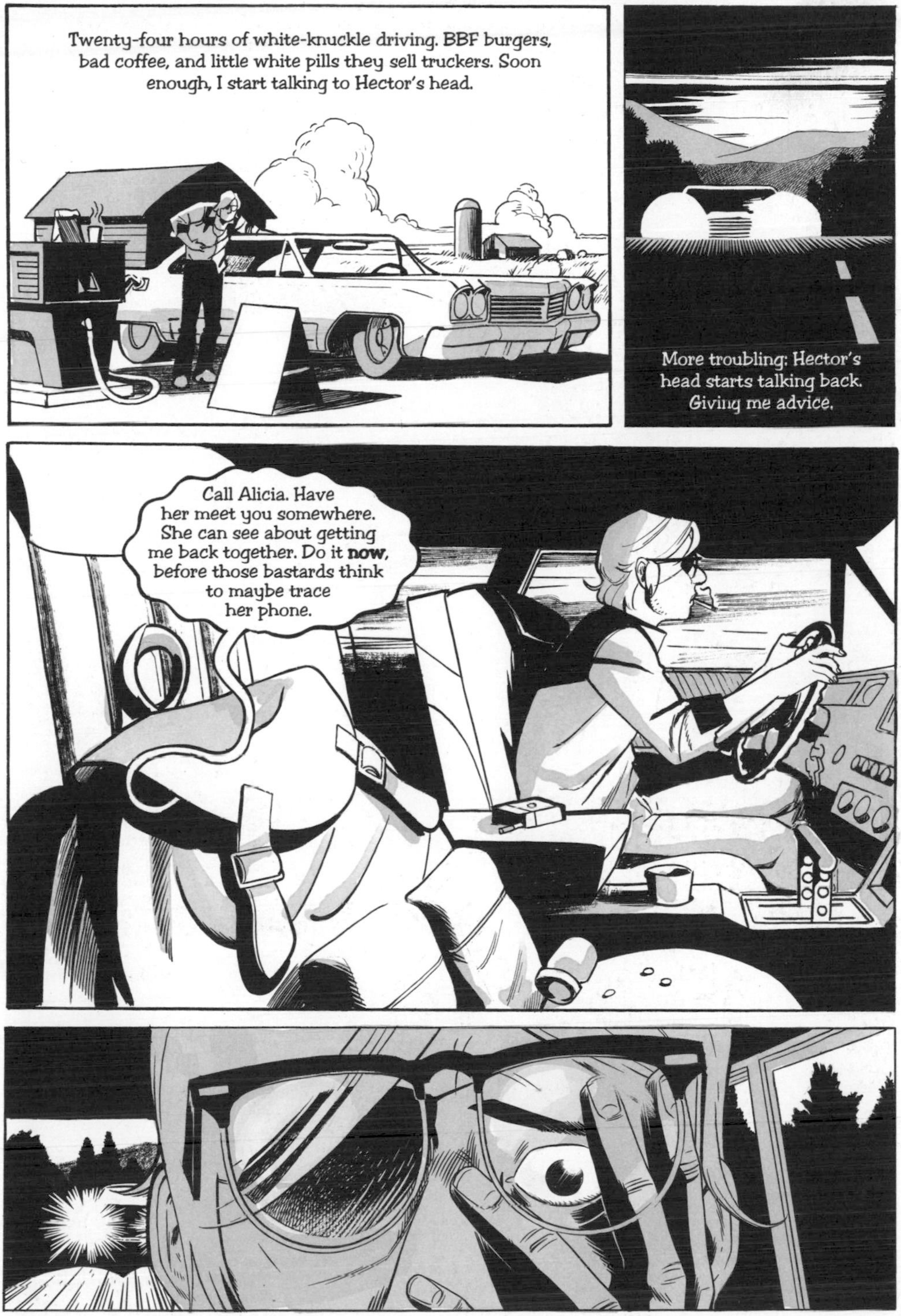
Twenty-four hours of white-knuckle driving. BBF burgers, bad coffee, and little white pills they sell truckers. Soon enough, I start talking to Hector's head.
More troubling: Hector's head starts talking back. Giving me advice.
Call Alicia. Have her meet you somewhere. She can see about getting me back together. Do it **now**, before those bastards think to maybe trace her phone.

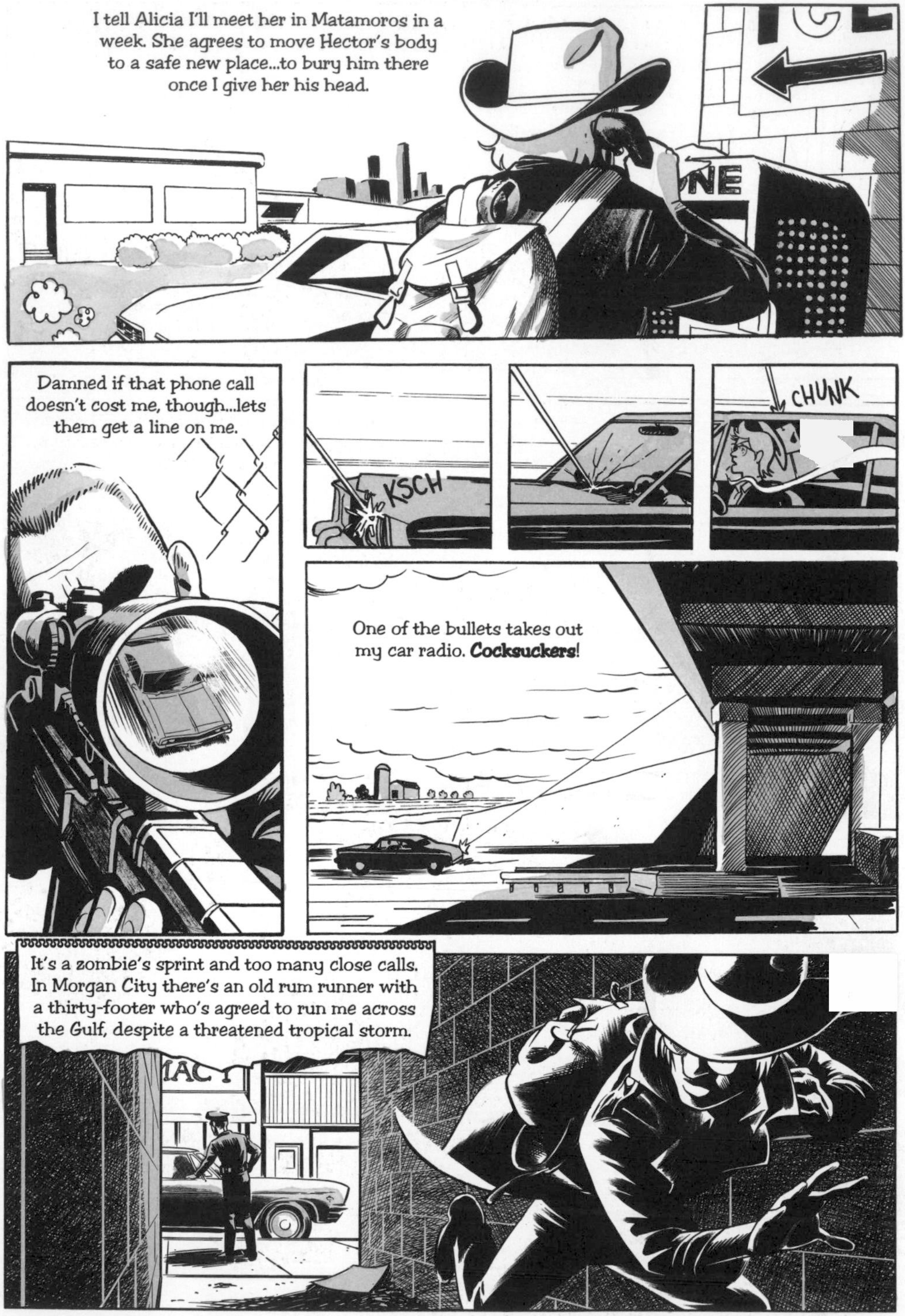
I tell Alicia I'll meet her in Matamoros in a week. She agrees to move Hector's body to a safe new place...to bury him there once I give her his head.
NE
Damned if that phone call doesn't cost me, though...lets them get a line on me.
KSCH
CHUNK
One of the bullets takes out my car radio. **Cocksuckers**!
It's a zombie's sprint and too many close calls. In Morgan City there's an old rum runner with a thirty-footer who's agreed to run me across the Gulf, despite a threatened tropical storm.
MACY

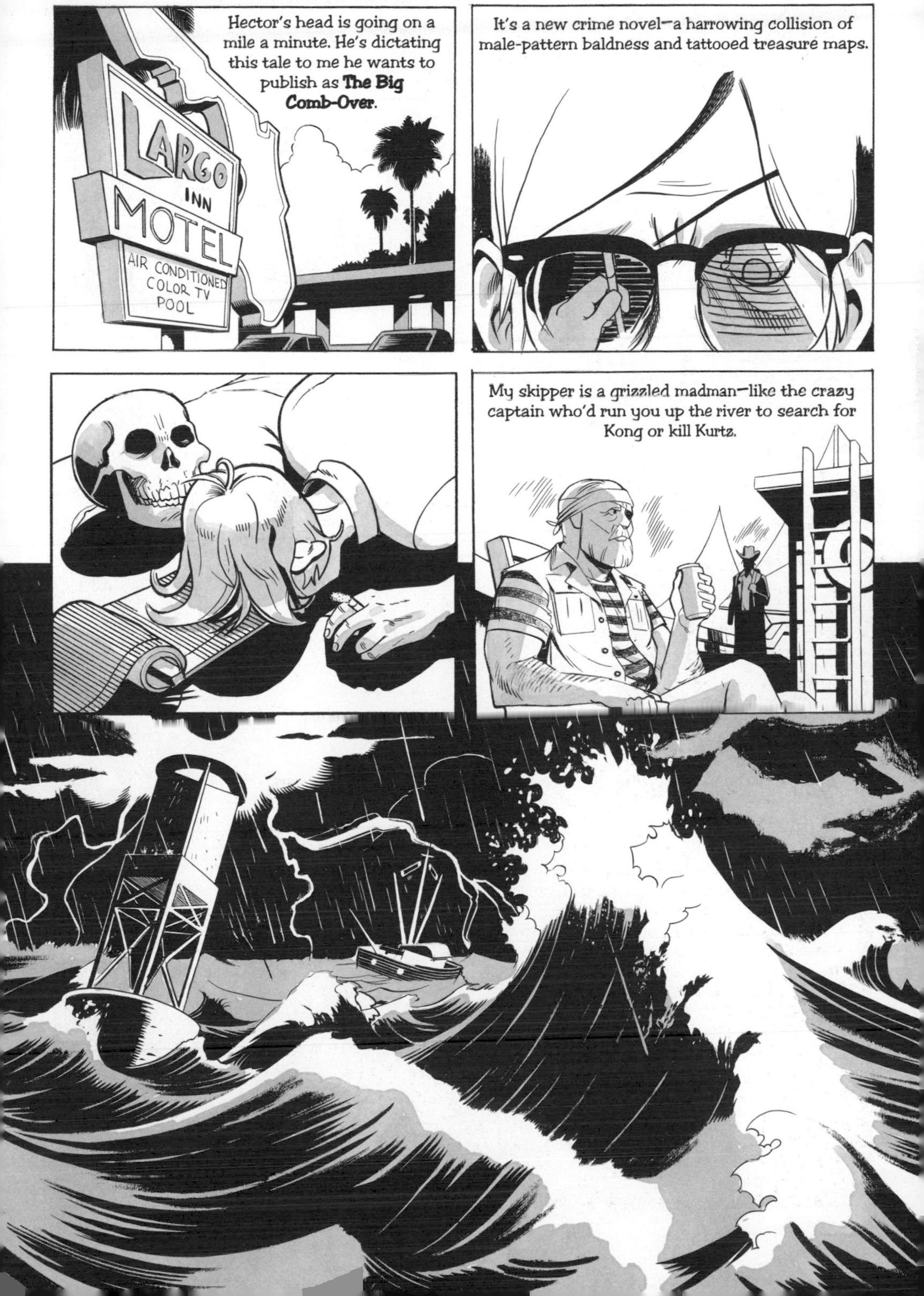
Hector's head is going on a mile a minute. He's dictating this tale to me he wants to publish as **The Big Comb-Over**.
LARGO
INN
MOTEL
AIR CONDITIONED
COLOR TV
POOL
It's a new crime novel—a harrowing collision of male-pattern baldness and tattooed treasure maps.
My skipper is a grizzled madman—like the crazy captain who'd run you up the river to search for Kong or kill Kurtz.

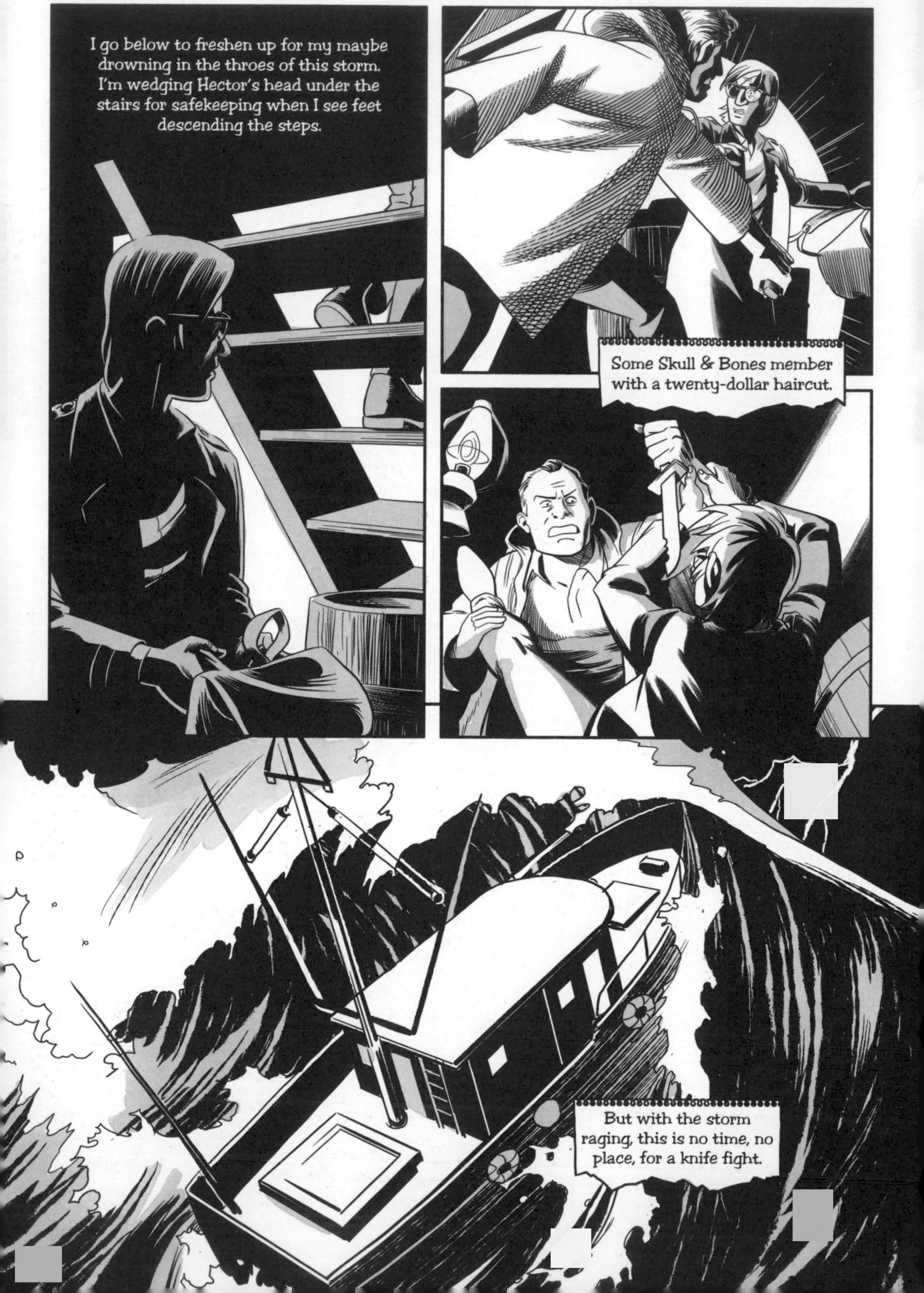
I go below to freshen up for my maybe drowning in the throes of this storm. I'm wedging Hector's head under the stairs for safekeeping when I see feet descending the steps.
Some Skull & Bones member with a twenty-dollar haircut.
But with the storm raging, this is no time, no place, for a knife fight.

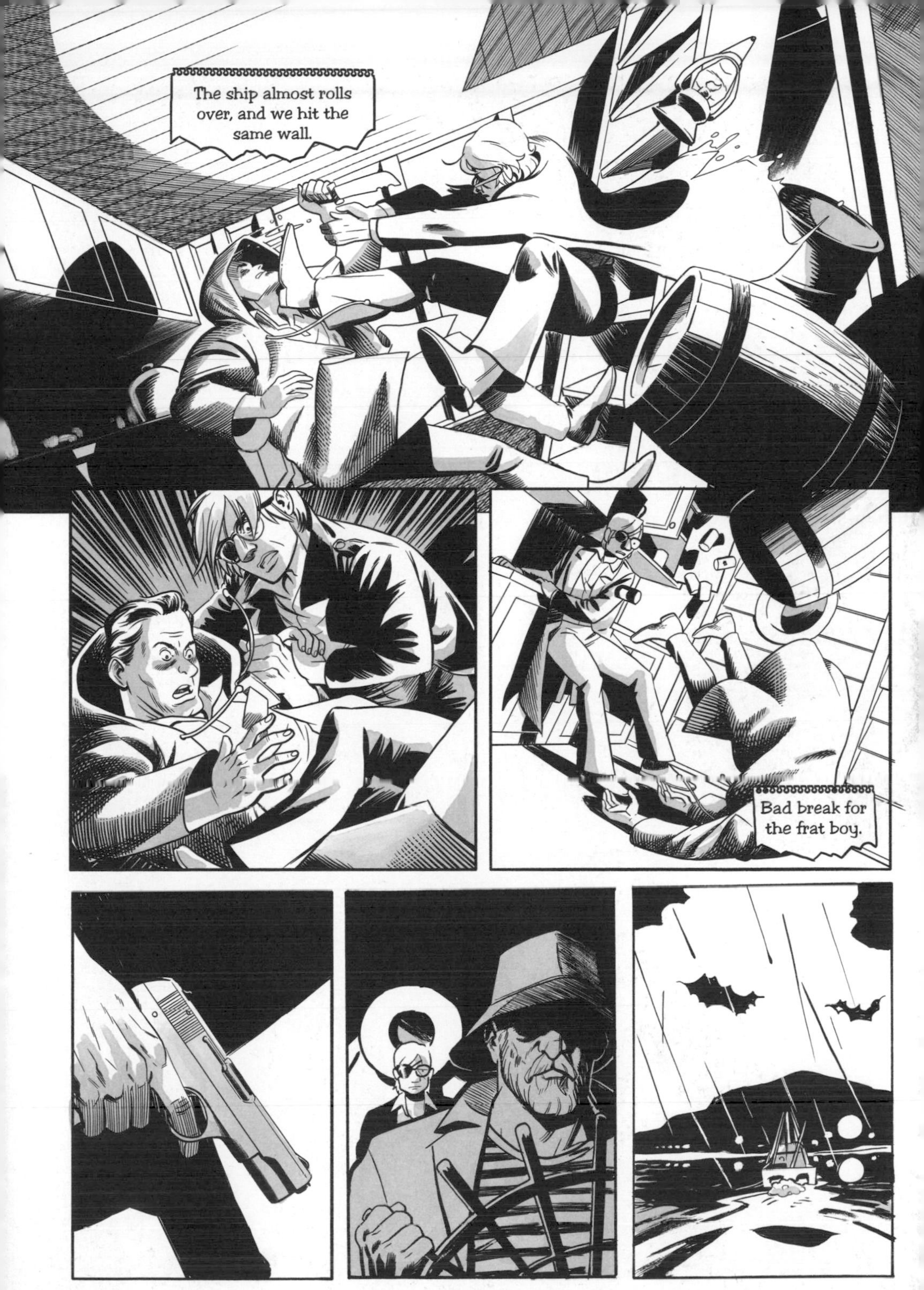
The ship almost rolls over, and we hit the same wall.
Bad break for the frat boy.

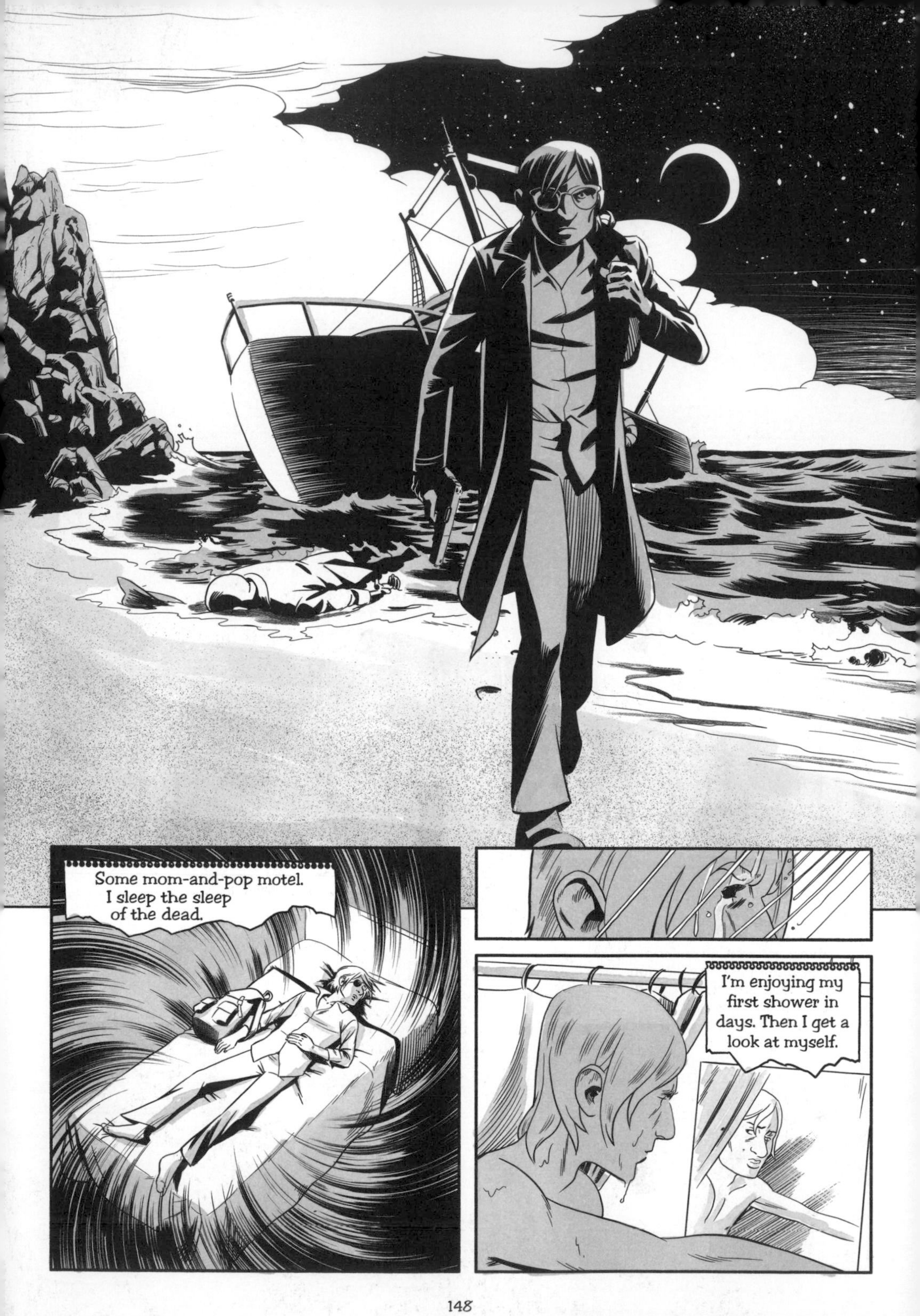

Some mom-and-pop motel. I sleep the sleep of the dead.
I'm enjoying my first shower in days. Then I get a look at myself.

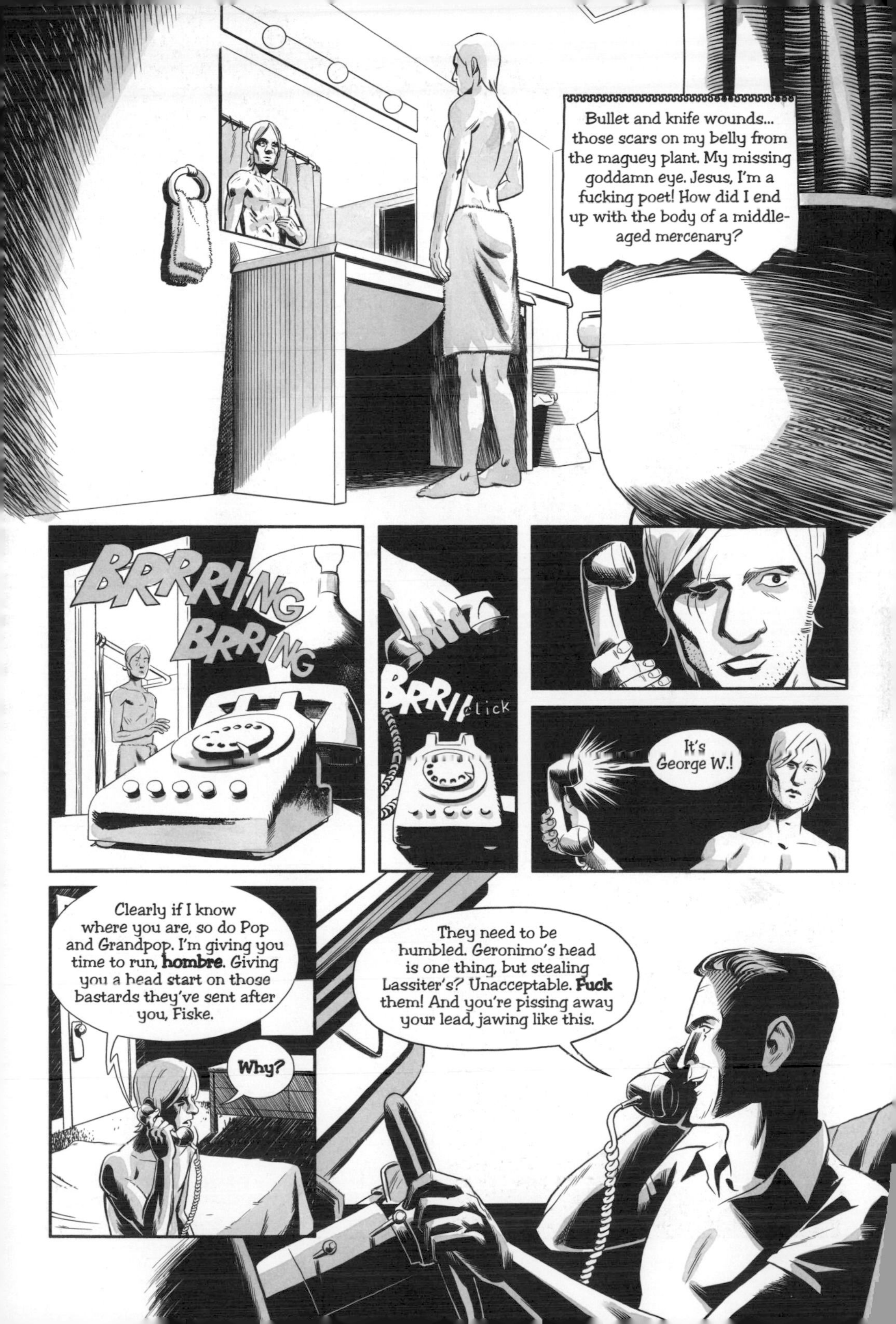
Bullet and knife wounds... those scars on my belly from the maguey plant. My missing goddamn eye. Jesus, I'm a fucking poet! How did I end up with the body of a middle-aged mercenary?
BRRRIIING
BRRRING
BRR//click
It's George W.!
Clearly if I know where you are, so do Pop and Grandpop. I'm giving you time to run, **hombre**. Giving you a head start on those bastards they've sent after you, Fiske.
Why?
They need to be humbled. Geronimo's head is one thing, but stealing Lassiter's? Unacceptable. **Fuck** them! And you're pissing away your lead, jawing like this.

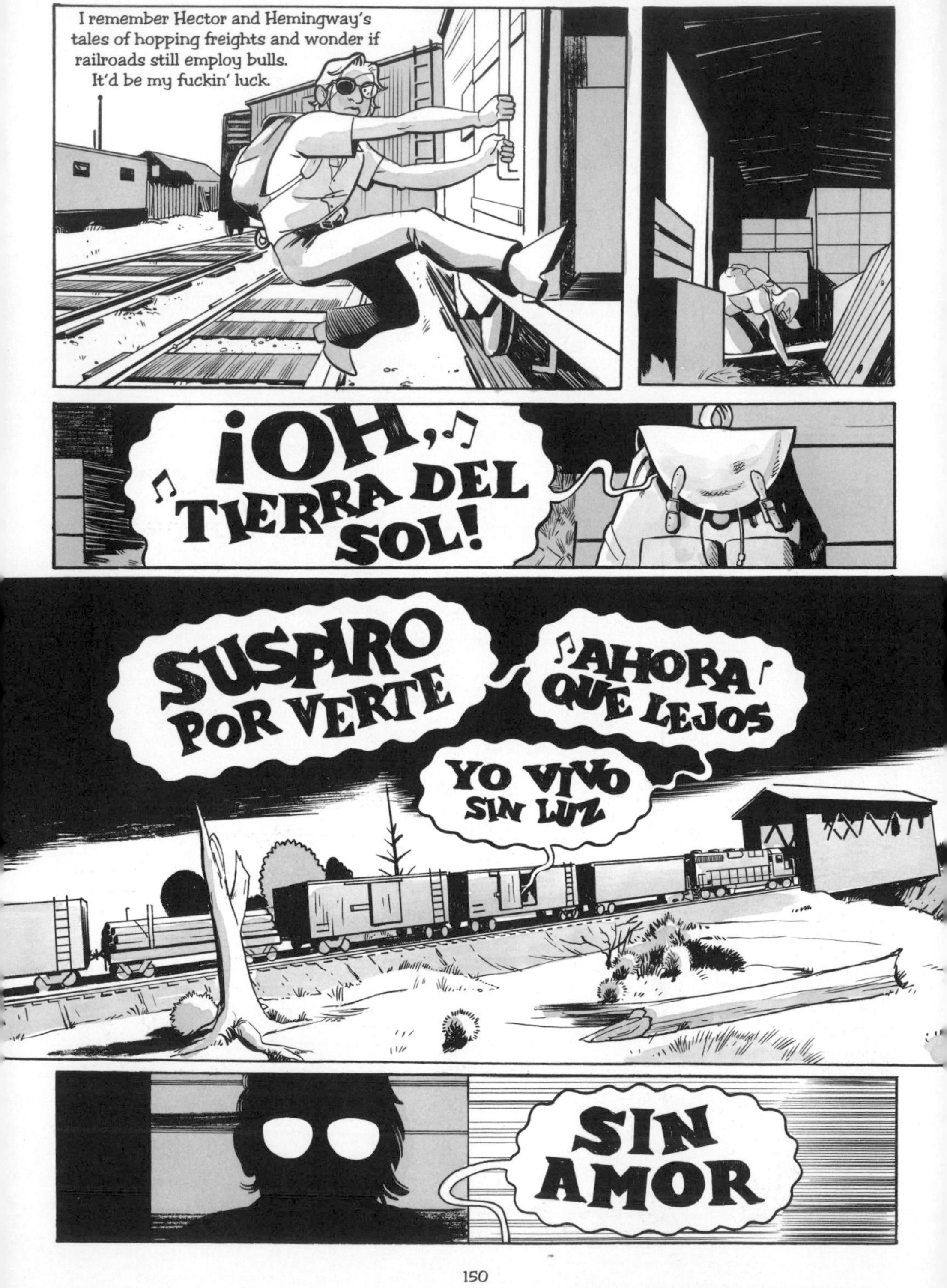
I remember Hector and Hemingway's tales of hopping freights and wonder if railroads still employ bulls. It'd be my fuckin' luck.
¡OH, TIERRA DEL SOL!
SUSPIRO POR VERTE
AHORA QUE LEJOS
YO VIVO SIN LUZ
SIN AMOR

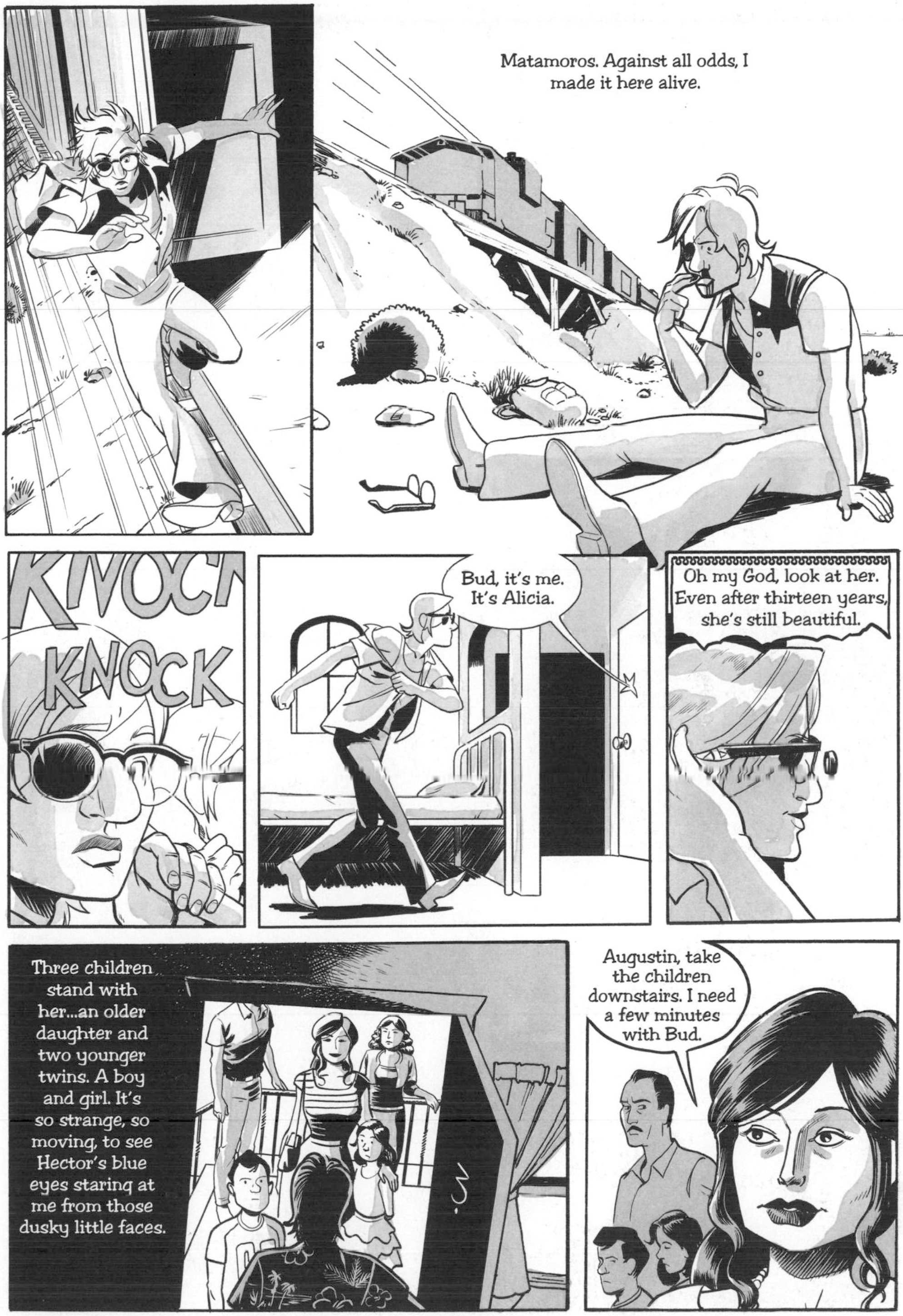
Matamoros. Against all odds, I made it here alive.
KNOCK
KNOCK
Bud, it's me. It's Alicia.
Oh my God, look at her. Even after thirteen years, she's still beautiful.
Three children stand with her...an older daughter and two younger twins. A boy and girl. It's so strange, so moving, to see Hector's blue eyes staring at me from those dusky little faces.
Augustin, take the children downstairs. I need a few minutes with Bud.

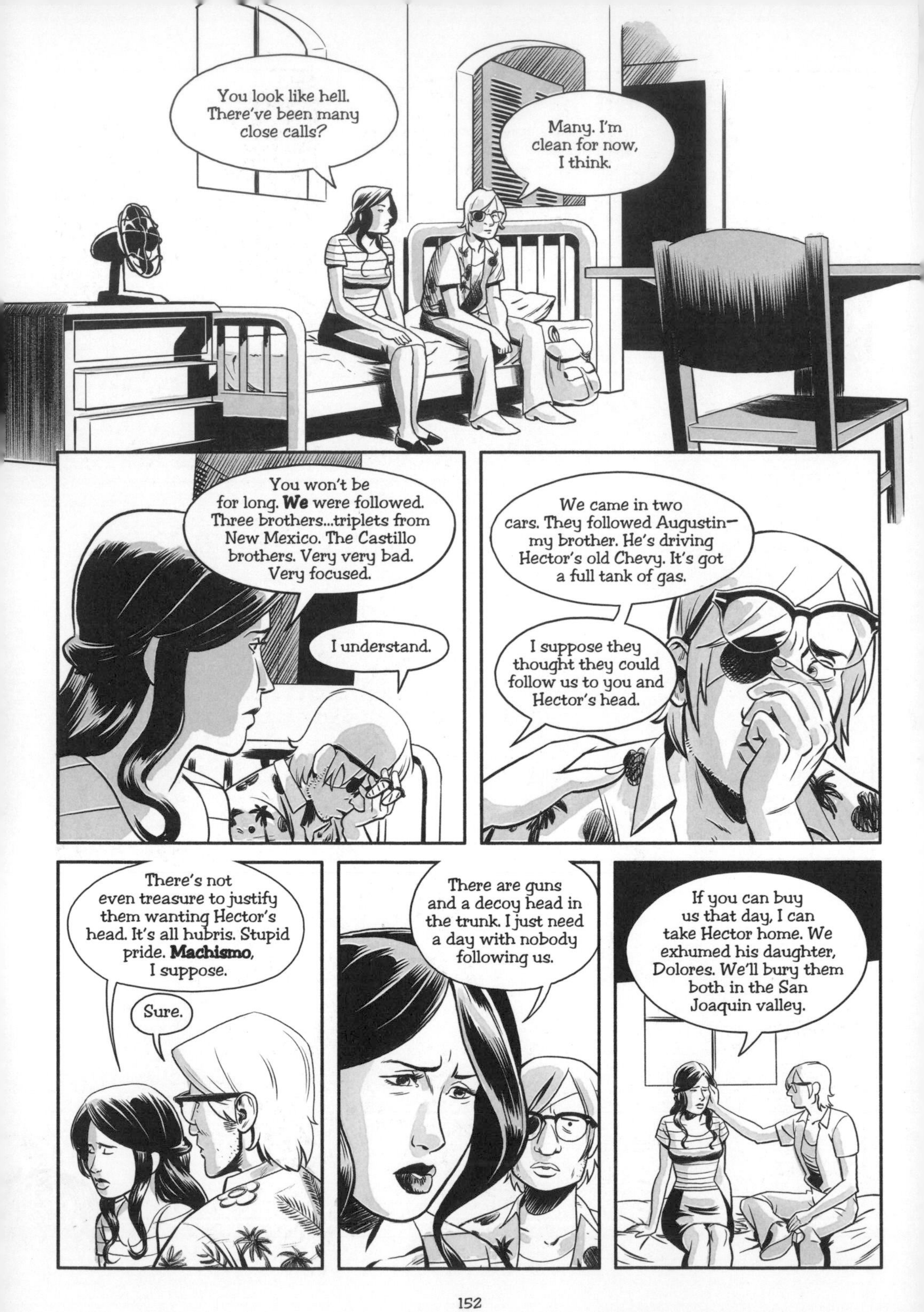

You look like hell. There've been many close calls?
Many. I'm clean for now, I think.
You won't be for long. **We** were followed. Three brothers...triplets from New Mexico. The Castillo brothers. Very very bad. Very focused.
I understand.
We came in two cars. They followed Augustin— my brother. He's driving Hector's old Chevy. It's got a full tank of gas.
I suppose they thought they could follow us to you and Hector's head.
There's not even treasure to justify them wanting Hector's head. It's all hubris. Stupid pride. **Machismo**, I suppose.
Sure.
There are guns and a decoy head in the trunk. I just need a day with nobody following us.
If you can buy us that day, I can take Hector home. We exhumed his daughter, Dolores. We'll bury them both in the San Joaquin valley.

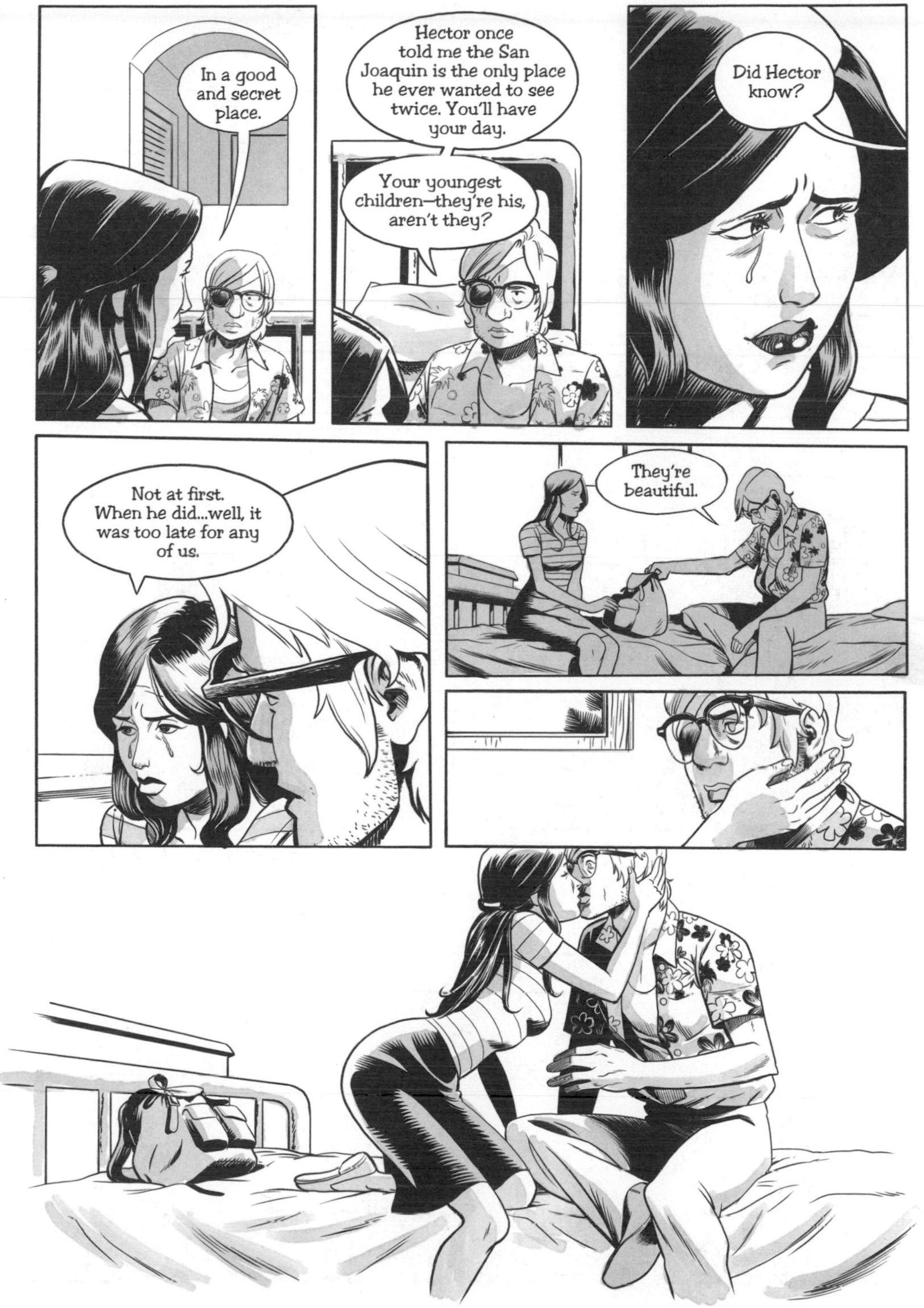
In a good and secret place.
Hector once told me the San Joaquin is the only place he ever wanted to see twice. You'll have your day.
Your youngest children—they're his, aren't they?
Did Hector know?
Not at first. When he did...well, it was too late for any of us.
They're beautiful.

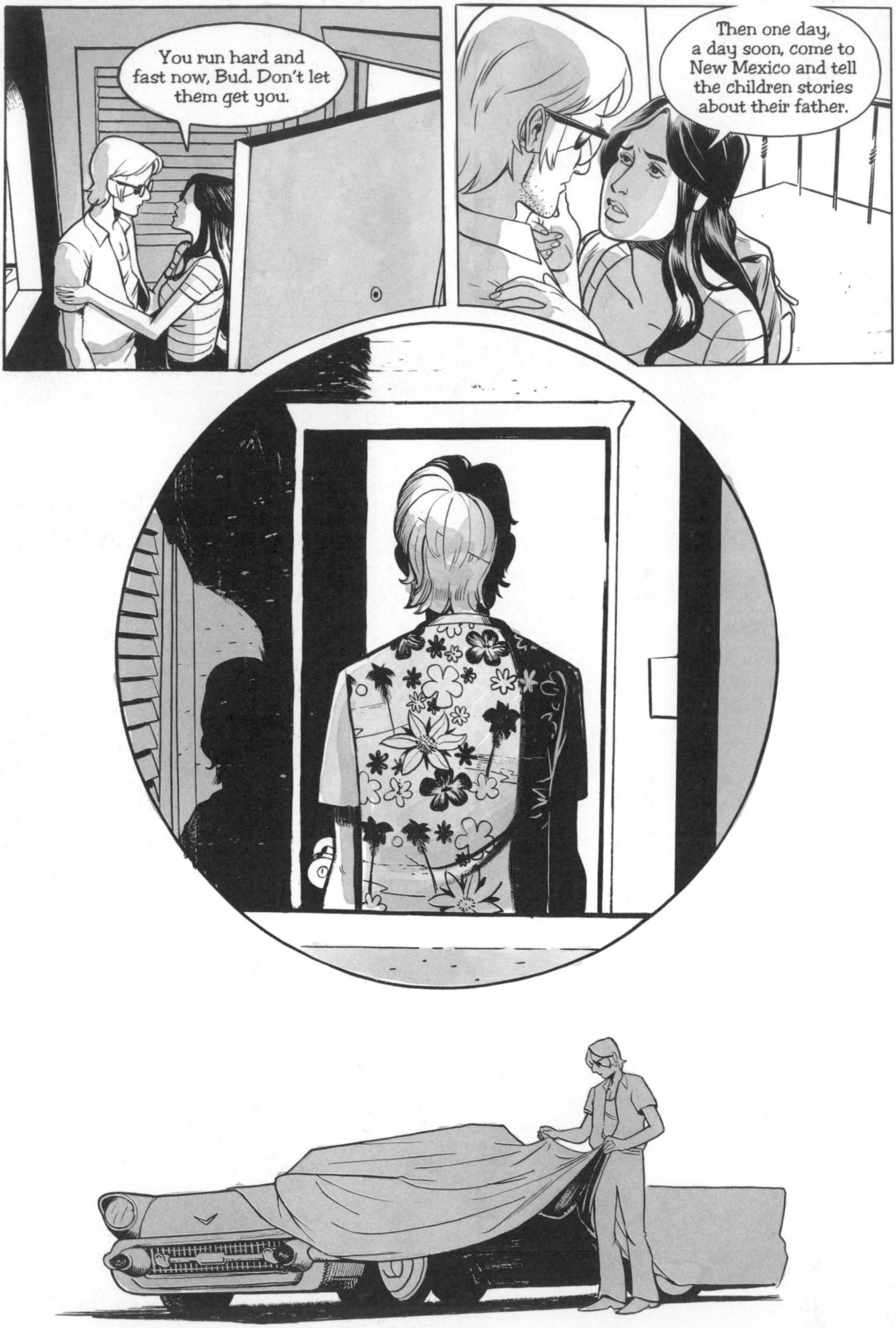
You run hard and fast now, Bud. Don't let them get you.
Then one day, a day soon, come to New Mexico and tell the children stories about their father.

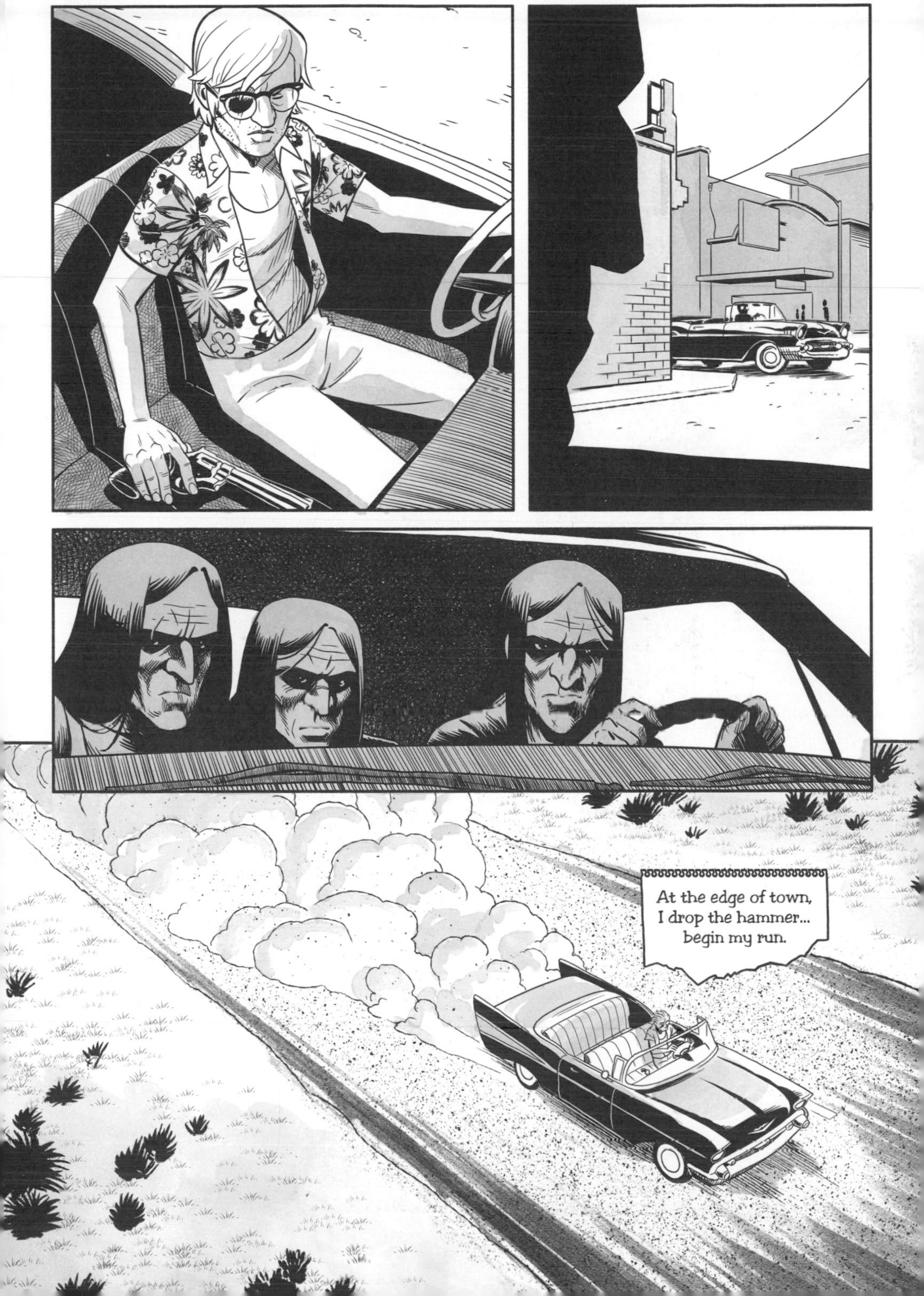
At the edge of town,
I drop the hammer...
begin my run.

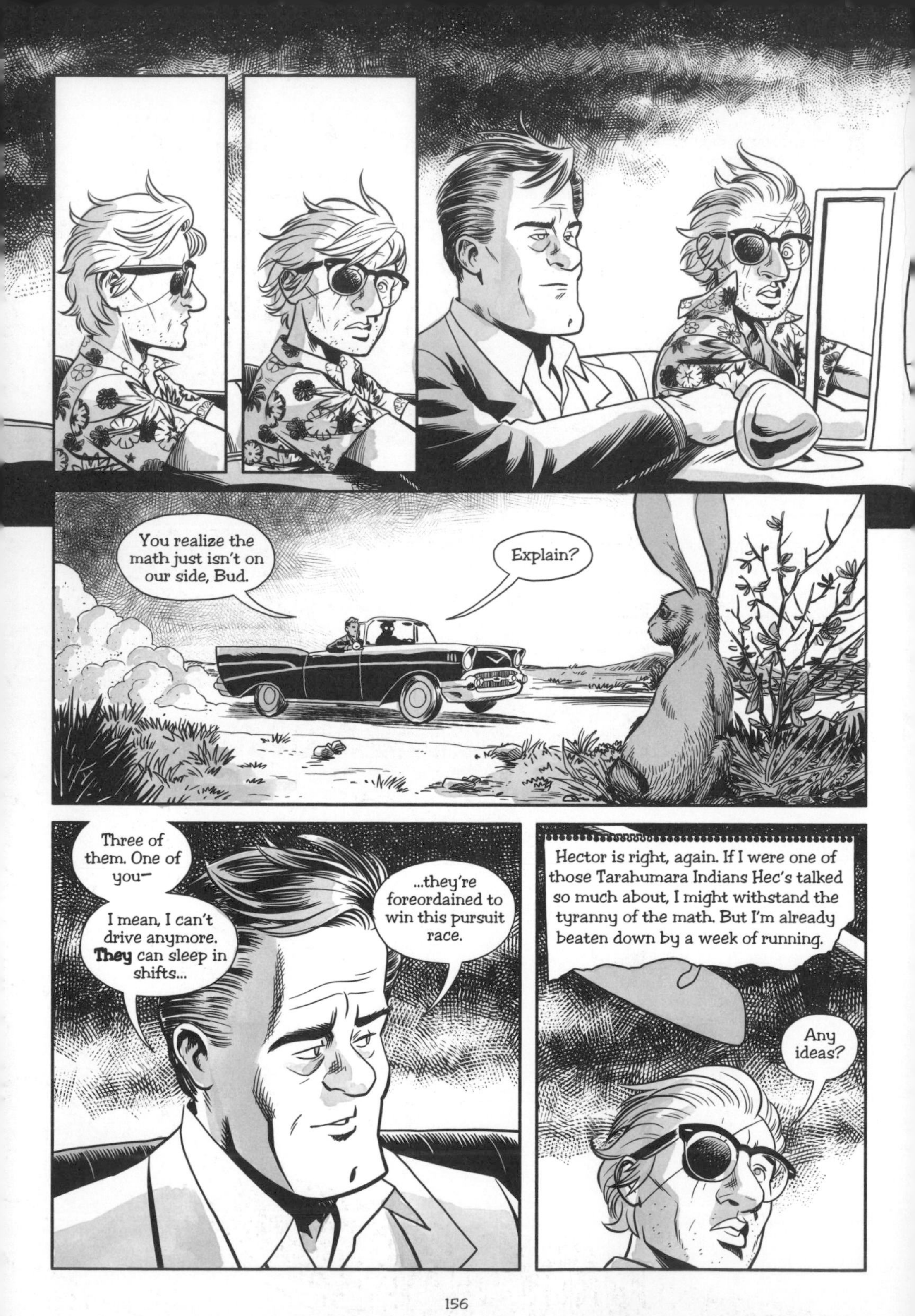

You realize the math just isn't on our side, Bud.
Explain?
Three of them. One of you—
I mean, I can't drive anymore. **They** can sleep in shifts...
...they're foreordained to win this pursuit race.
Hector is right, again. If I were one of those Tarahumara Indians Hec's talked so much about, I might withstand the tyranny of the math. But I'm already beaten down by a week of running.
Any ideas?

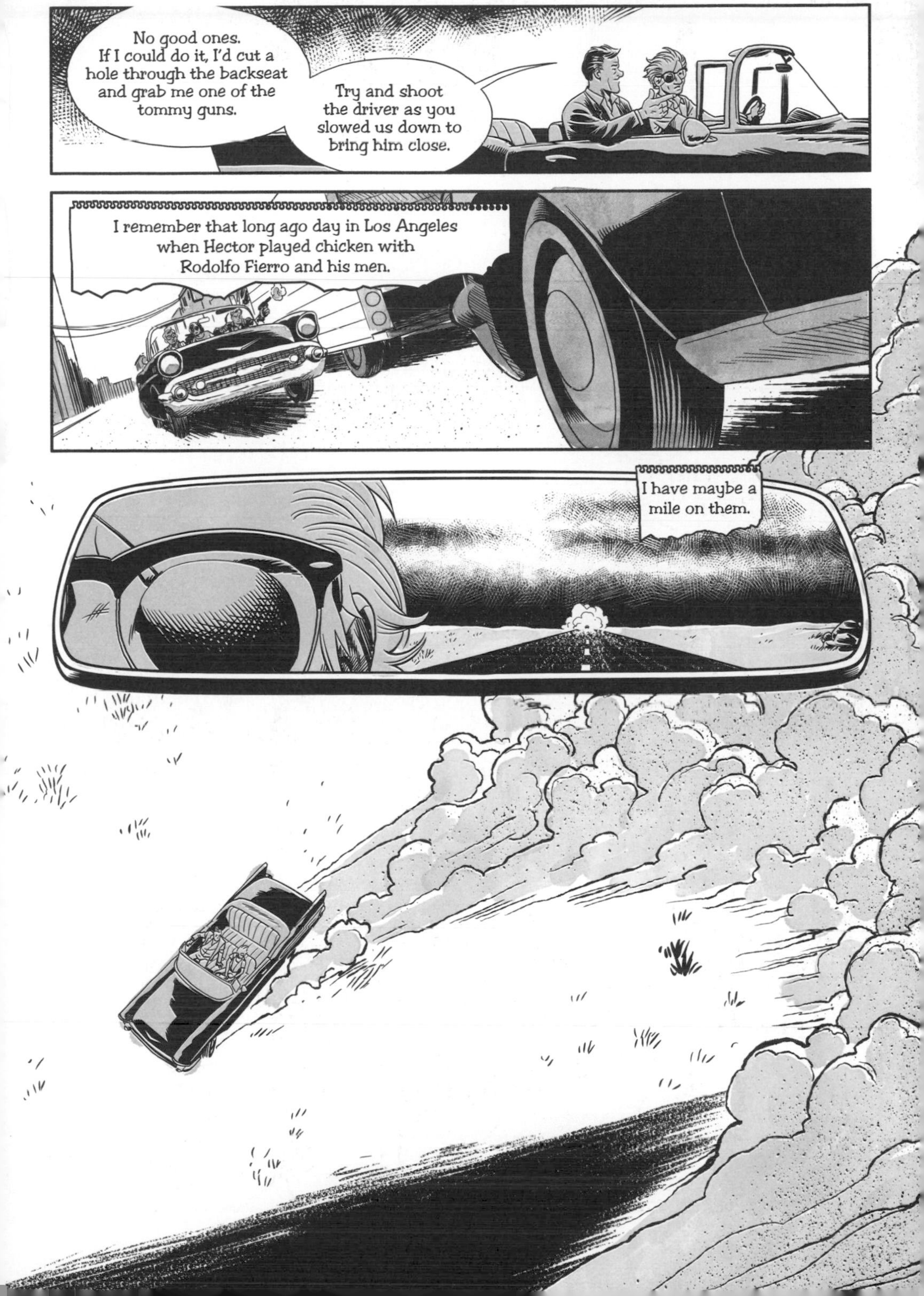
No good ones.
If I could do it, I'd cut a hole through the backseat and grab me one of the tommy guns.
Try and shoot the driver as you slowed us down to bring him close.
I remember that long ago day in Los Angeles when Hector played chicken with Rodolfo Fierro and his men.
I have maybe a mile on them.

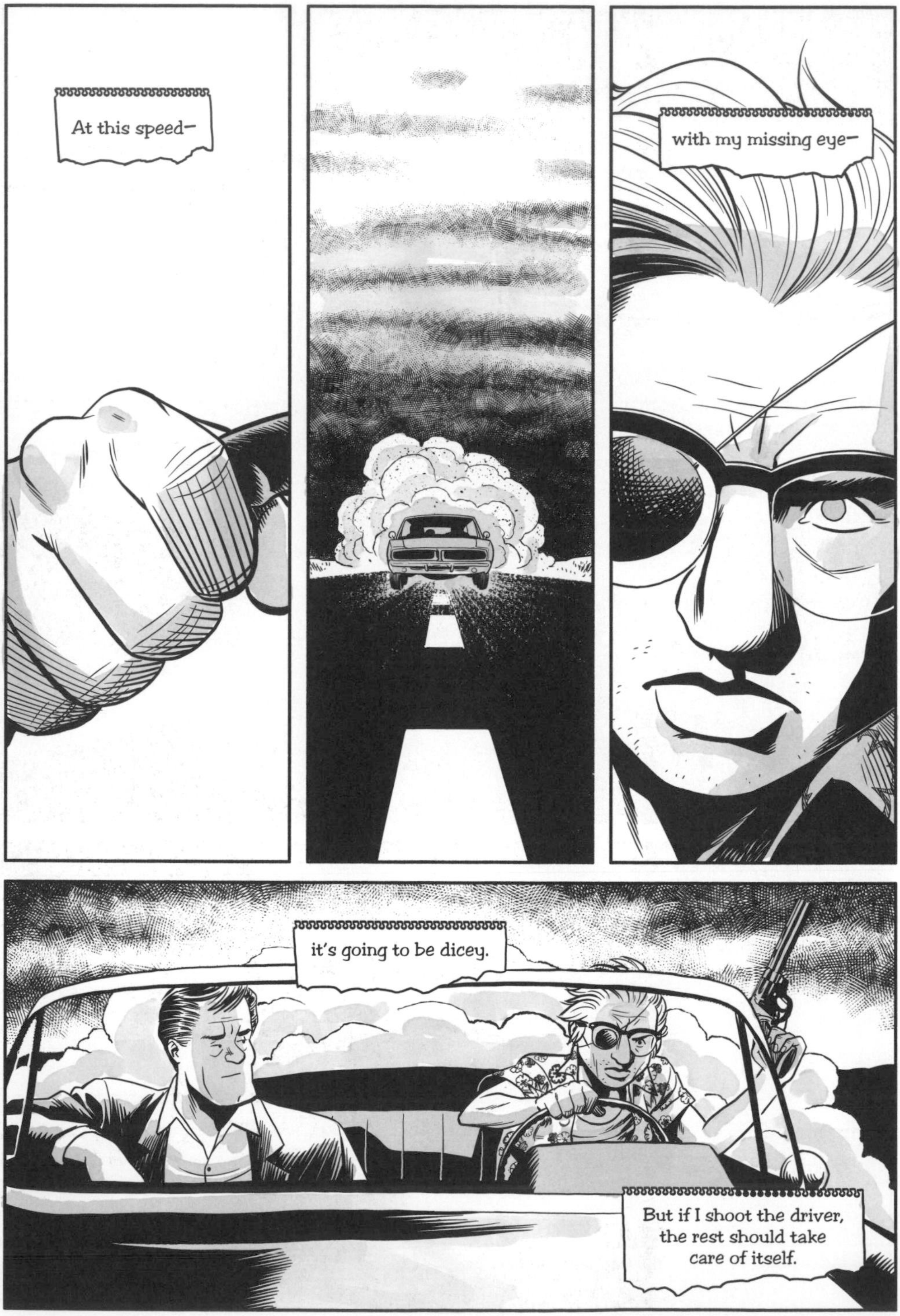
At this speed–
with my missing eye–
it's going to be dicey.
But if I shoot the driver, the rest should take care of itself.

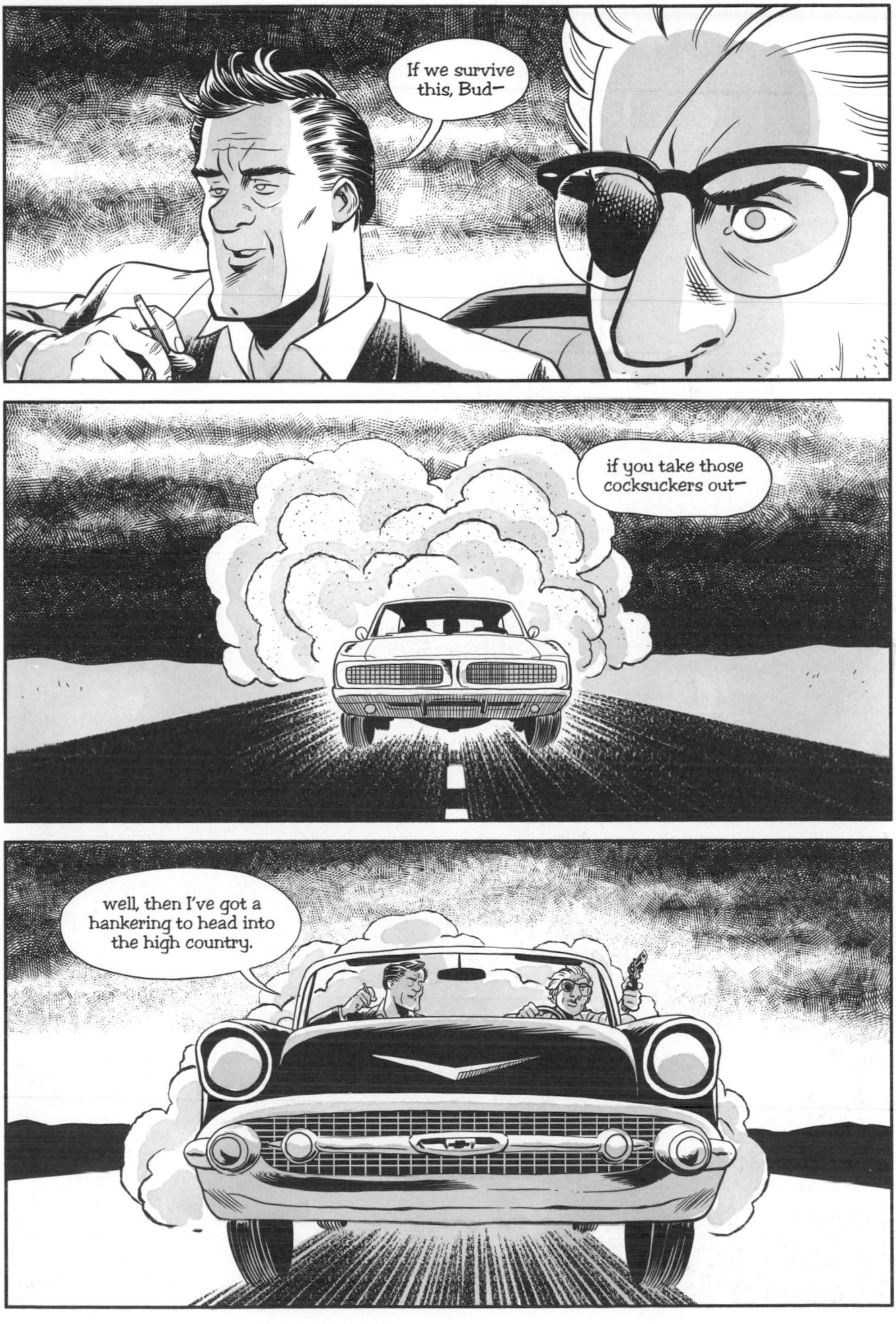
If we survive this, Bud—
if you take those cocksuckers out—
well, then I've got a hankering to head into the high country.

What do you say we go find those Tarahumara Indians?

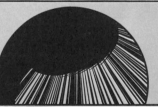

See if we can't figure out what makes those bastards run like they do.

Afterword

"Same vineyard, different grapes"

"First novel" and "debut novel" are often treated as synonyms.

More often than not, they really aren't. Certainly it wasn't so in my case. Like many published novelists, I had my share of manuscripts behind me before my "debut novel" saw the light of day.

Long about 2005, casting around for something that might stick—might finally make some publishing house editor take notice—I hit upon this idea for a novel about the stolen and still missing head of the Mexican revolutionary Francisco "Pancho" Villa.

In summary, *Head Games* seems a quirky and possibly uneasy mix: a caper, a road novel, and a study of a damaged man struggling to shoulder the burden of his own myth-making.

Despite its rather blackly comic, Kerouacian pedigree, *Head Games* was a finalist for several crime fiction awards. It was sold into translation in several countries, and—most cool this—it was picked up by First Second for adaptation.

Those who became aware of and anticipated this graphic novel often asked about the process of adapting my "debut novel" to a visual format.

From my perspective, it didn't seem the long reach others suspected.

At the most elementary level, I think of myself as a very visual writer. Before I realized I ultimately don't have the chops, there was a time I thought I'd be an illustrator. I started down that path before transitioning to writing. Even so, I mostly write to images.

I record the story I see in my head. I tend to think in terms of dialogue. I toggle between the points of view of my characters as they kibitz. I see them in close-ups, wide shots, and I see settings in establishing or tracking shots.

They say a picture's worth a thousand words. Speaking as a writer, I'll grudgingly confess there's too often some piercing truth to that cliché.

And the novel and graphic novel *are* very different beasts, of course.

The great danger in adapting a novel into a graphic format is ending up with a sea of word balloons bracketing talking heads who just yammer on.

So you're always looking for ways to change the camera angle, so to speak. You seek new ways to shorthand matters through visual means. All that prose you spent so much time polishing and honing goes straight out the window. The old writing cliché "murder your darlings" looms large.

On the other hand, you get to do some *other* things. In my case, because the series was largely already completed when I wrote the script for the *Head Games* graphic novel, I took the opportunity to creep in elements from the other novels. I layered in some characters who figured in Hector novels already written but not yet printed when this process of adaptation started. So call the book you hold in your hands now *Head Games*, the "director's cut."

Author James Sallis has a nifty phrase for it: "Same vineyard, different grapes."

Not long after finishing the script for this graphic novel, a certain French filmmaker came knocking, and I found myself producing a third version of the same story for yet another medium. I convinced myself take three would be far easier, that the graphic novel script was a kind of *de facto* film script.

But *uh-uh*: again, concessions and changes were critical to fulfilling a different medium's needs.

Having since adapted a second, non-Lassiter novel into a graphic novel script, I can see real advantages for novelists in attempting to recast their stories through the prism of the graphic novel, particularly.

You learn to pare more closely. You find means to communicate information with an image—or a montage of images—that would never occur to you when you can just put it across by slinging words, particularly dialogue, at all that empty white space.

You maybe learn to paint better and more arresting pictures in readers' minds.

I wrote the story of *Head Games*. The characters are the children of my imagination. But even in the early stages of shaping this version of the story, while looking at Kevin Singles' first sketches of the world I first saw in my mind, I could feel my own firmly embedded take on all that falling into eclipse under Kevin's and later Les' visions of that world.

There were growing pains, of course.

First sketches of Hector came back looking like a circa-1950s Ernest Hemingway with Polo shirts and burly arms, a ragged beard and receding hairline. I had to explain that Hector was more polished, even in this roughest year of his life; a snappy dresser given to sports jackets and being clean-shaven...far more William Holden than debauched Papa.

Alicia, too, took some tweaking up front. (For whatever reason, Bud Fiske landed pretty perfectly formed from the get-go.)

It's been a long and winding road, but overall, it's also been a fascinating process of reinvention.

One of my favorite fellow crime novelists, James Ellroy, has an oft-quoted phrase he offers up when asked about the experience of turning his novels over to filmmakers: "My book, their movie."

I see now *Head Games* is my novel, but as Hector moves into the domain of illustration, it becomes Kevin Singles' and Les McClaine's world. I just get the privilege of living in it and writing a few words there.

—Craig McDonald

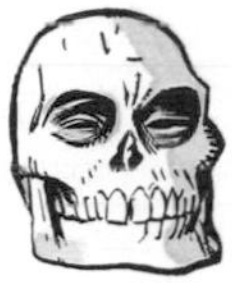

First Second

Text copyright © 2017 by Craig McDonald
Illustrations copyright © 2017 by Kevin Singles

Published by First Second
First Second is an imprint of Roaring Brook Press, a division of Holtzbrinck Publishing
Holdings Limited Partnership
175 Fifth Avenue, New York, New York 10010
All rights reserved

Library of Congress Control Number: 2016961594

ISBN: 978-1-59643-414-1

Our books may be purchased in bulk for promotional, educational, or business use. Please
contact your local bookseller or the Macmillan Corporate and Premium Sales Department
at (800) 221-7945 ext. 5442 or by e-mail at MacmillanSpecialMarkets@macmillan.com.

FIRST

EDITION

First edition 2017
Book design by Angela Boyle
Printed in China

10 9 8 7 6 5 4 3 2 1